IMAGEMAKER:

WILL ROGERS

AND THE

AMERICAN

DREAM

WILLIAM R.

BROWN

UNIVERSITY OF

MISSOURI PRESS

Acknowledgements

I thank Professor Wayne Brockriede, who guided me in my original study of Will Rogers; Robert and Paula Love, of the Will Rogers Memorial, whose work in collecting Rogers material significantly speeded my progress; Bill Rogers who, on behalf of the Rogers Company, gave me permission to quote his father's work; Professor Roger Nebergall, who helped to test my ideas; and my wife, Darlene Newman Brown, whose understanding, encouragement, and secretarial skills made the critical difference in finishing this task.

I am grateful for the help of Mrs. Nan Gamble, former humanities librarian at Oklahoma University; my thanks are due the Faculty Research Committee of the university for support in producing the final manuscript, and Miss Barbara Barnes for her care in typing it.

I thank, too, those scholars whose work enabled me to summarize events and ideas related to the American dream.

W.R.B.
Norman, Oklahoma,
May, 1970

For All

My Family,

in Whom

I See the

American

Dream

Preface

On November 14, 1967, the CBS television network
rebroadcast by popular demand an hour's interview with
Eric Hoffer; it was a restatement of what has come to
be considered "the American dream": the immigrant
workingman, unanointed by formal university training,
speaking wisdom learned on his own, praising this
country as "God's gift to the poor," and holding forth
as general expert on topics that ranged from race to
religion, Marshall Plan to Vietnam, Kennedy as a
European ("Count the number of times he crossed the
Atlantic and the number of times he crossed the Appalachians.") and LBJ as a President whose greatness came
from the American people.

Eric Hoffer, then, has been a success with the
American public not only because he is an intelligent,
articulate, and zestful man, but also because he appealed
to many people by embodying the ideal American looking
hopefully to the future of this country. In these years of
discontent, his is a timely message—believed in because
in a time of national doubt it affirms in large part what
Americans *want* to believe in.

The attraction of the same American dream, in its
main outlines, at least, accounts in my view for the
remarkable believability that Will Rogers, another
workingman philosopher, possessed. Whether the dream
is consistent, paradoxical, naïve, impossible, hypocritical,
or anything else, it is a fact of the culture that predom-
inates in the United States; no one can speak to most
Americans' deepest hopes and highest ambitions without
identifying himself with them and with the American
dream.

In this study, I have let Emerson, Whitman, Thoreau,
Jefferson, and other earlier Americans speak for the
unspeaking masses who have gone on before; their
American dream I define as a set of ideas and actions
that, together, form the character and the world of the
ideal American. In turn, when a communicator exem-
plifies these values in detail, he becomes a mythic

national hero, believable because he is most symbolically one with the national eidolon, the god with four faces: the American Adam, the American democrat, the self-made man, and the American Prometheus.

Perhaps to some scholars it seems unimportant to spend an entire study answering, "What was it that made Will Rogers, this comedian and homespun philosopher, so believable?" But that is what I do; it seemed important to me—in a time of mass media and images, credibility gaps and charisma—to explore the question in more detail than has been done before. This study is, then, rhetorical rather than biographical, literary, or historical. Given the ideals of the audience (the American dream), the context of the times (the anxieties of the twenties and thirties), and the person of the communicator, how do his sayings relate all three? Often I speak of Rogers' *public* biography and his *public* pronouncements in order to underline my reluctance to equate the legend with the individual; at other times, to avoid belaboring the distinction, I simply say that Rogers was the American Adam. I think, of course, that there were correspondences between the private man and the public image; to believe otherwise would be to picture a charlatan, and I do not believe that Will Rogers was a charlatan. The emphasis in the study, however, is always on the public image of the cowboy philosopher, and the reader will do well to keep that emphasis in mind.

Here, then, are the American dreamers—with their spokesmen, Emerson, Whitman, and others; given their dreams and the disturbing times of the twenties and thirties, here is Will Rogers enacting the richest possible elaboration of the American dream for his audience. That symbolic dance made Rogers a mythic hero and a credible source.

Contents

The Man Against the American Sky, 15

Will Rogers, American Adam, 37

Will Rogers, American Democrat, 91

Will Rogers, Self-Made Man, 161

Will Rogers, American Prometheus, 209

Perspectives, 259

Notes to Text, 279

Bibliography, 289

Index, 298

The Man Against the American Sky

In Watts, California, today, in Will Rogers Memorial Park, youngsters played tag while couples walked in the grassy open spaces. Occasionally, a first-time visitor appeared and read this legend at the base of the flagpole, inlaid in stone: "There ain't but one word wrong with every one of us, and that's selfishness." But the bust of the cowboy philosopher that formerly rested in its place of honor has disappeared and, with it, perhaps, some of the presence of Will Rogers.

In Washington today, a guided tour of pilgrims to the nation's shrines saw the bronze statue of Will Rogers and heard the story of how Rogers is placed so that he can keep an eye on Congress; probably, a tourist has noticed the shiny toes of the sculptured shoes, heard that it was good luck to rub them, and reached out in a moment of half-piety and half-superstition to touch them and bring himself good fortune. In this moment, Will Rogers stands as a secular saint, an American talisman, the source of whose sainthood may not be understood.

In Claremore, Oklahoma, today, visitors from several states and perhaps a foreign country came to the rambling, airy Will Rogers Memorial and stood before the display case in which is preserved the gray, pin-striped, double-breasted suit that he was wearing when he died. The clothes seem too small for such a heroic figure. A sculptured suit of the same cut on the statue by Jo Davidson, in the foyer of the memorial, seems more nearly the size to fit Will Rogers, who was a legend in his own lifetime, as testified by the display of scores of letters and telegrams from Americans great and small to "Will of the People." In reading them, visitors sense some of the reasons for naming parks for Will Rogers and for other signs of secular sainthood. What was there about Will Rogers, a humorist, to inspire monuments from Watts to Washington, and from Fort Worth to Point Barrow?

Will Rogers was indeed a humorist—but one whose commentaries received serious attention. As early as 1918, Theodore Roosevelt, talking to Albert D. Lasker, advertising

15

executive, reportedly gave this estimate of the Oklahoma cowpuncher: "This man Rogers has such a keen insight into the American panorama and the American people that I feel he is bound, in the course of time, to be a potent factor in the political life of the nation."*

Some Americans wanted Rogers to exert his political influence directly, by seeking public office. In 1928, a large but uncounted number of voters wanted him to receive the Democratic presidential nomination. One admirer, refusing to accept Rogers' dismissal of the idea and realizing that the Presidency would require "the strength of Hercules and wisdom of Pericles," insisted in a letter to *The New York Times* that Rogers was far more than a comedian, that he showed in his grasp of affairs a wisdom rendered attractive by humor reminiscent of Lincoln. A Baptist minister in Brooklyn renewed the nomination from his pulpit: "It might seem like a joke," he admitted, "but when he got down to business, making speeches over the country, the Republicans would find that Mr. Rogers was no joke." Embryonic presidential booms for Rogers occurred in Texas and California in 1931 and 1932, the former being fostered by a former governor of that state, James E. Ferguson; a National Recovery Administration official suggested his candidacy for the California governorship in 1934; in 1935, a splinter party announced that it would draft Rogers as its presidential choice for 1936. Others wanted him for state level offices. Former Senator Mike Monroney, who as a reporter covered some of Rogers' Oklahoma visits, averred that he could have won any elective office in Oklahoma.†
But Will Rogers never ran for any office.

More important than any influence he might have exerted as an officeholder was that he exercised as commenta-

*L. H. Robbins, *The New York Times,* 3 November 1935, VII, p. 4. The Roman numeral indicates the appropriate section of the Sunday edition and will be used throughout in references to such editions. Future references to the name of the paper will be shortened to *NYT.*

†For these comments relating to Rogers' political potential, see *NYT,* 11 February 1928, p. 16; 13 February 1928, p. 19; 7 February 1931, p. 9; 26 February 1932, p. 22; 20 July 1935, p. 15; 10 January 1934, p. 23. Monroney's remarks occur in Part Two of "Biography in Sound: Will Rogers," produced by NBC News, May 22, 1955. Throughout, when I document several statements in a footnote, the sources will appear in the order of the references in the text.

tor on the American scene. In 1927, the National Press Club recognized his stature as a political force by appointing him "Congressman at Large for the United States of America," his duties being to "roam over the country, pry into the state of the Union, check up on Prohibition enforcement and report at regular intervals to the National Press Club." A few months later, a Nebraska congressman praised him on the House floor during debate on the Nicaraguan intervention as "the only man of any party in the United States who has had the courage to ask a great question: 'Why are we in Nicaragua and what the hell are we doing there?'" *The New York Times* reviewer of Rogers' *Letters of a Self-Made Diplomat to His President* affirmed, "America has never produced anybody quite like him, and there has rarely been an American humorist whose words produced less empty laughter or more sober thought." To the praise of reporters, politicians, and critics was added that of Reinhold Niebuhr in his first sermon as a faculty member of Union Theological Seminary. Making the point that the church is often cowardly, the theologian recalled the tradition that only the king's jester had been able to tell truth, and only then by putting humor into it. "That has also become the technique by which King Demos is approached," Niebuhr pointed out. "Note Will Rogers' facility in puncturing foibles which more pretentious teachers leave untouched."[1] To many Americans, Rogers was social commentator as well as comedian.

Statements immediately following the humorist's death in 1935 further indicate the power of the "court jester" with King Demos. House Speaker Joseph W. Byrns, interrupting regular debate, said, "Will Rogers had the ear of the public as few in this country did." An editorial in the *New Orleans Times-Picayune* announced, "He was, in the true sense of the term, a national figure, wielding a wider and more wholesome influence than many who pose—as he did not—as national leaders and guides." In the West, the *Denver Rocky Mountain News* commented, "The plain people of America lose a spokesman and a beloved friend." And in the East, the *Baltimore Sun* added, "He made his material out of governments, politics, international situations and the secret, simple urges of the generality of men. Thus he became commentator and philosopher, too."[2]

More than a third of a century has passed since such tributes appeared, but during that time evidence of Rogers' influence has continued to accumulate. President Franklin Roosevelt, on the occasion of the launching of a memorial fund drive for Rogers, wrote in a telegram to national headquarters of the Will Rogers Memorial Commission:

> The first time that I fully realized Will Rogers'
> exceptional and deep understanding of political and
> social problems was when he came back from his long
> European trip a good many years ago. While I had
> discussed European matters with many others, both
> American and foreign, Will Rogers's analysis of affairs
> abroad was not only more interesting but proved to be
> more accurate than any other I had heard.

Later, when the Claremore Memorial was dedicated in 1938, Roosevelt, during a nationwide radio broadcast, again assessed Rogers' contribution: "Above all things, in a time grown too solemn and somber, he brought his countrymen back to a sense of proportion." Herbert Hoover, in an earlier network broadcast, had agreed that Rogers' humor had provided a safety valve for public anger and fear and added, "His was a great understanding of the background of public events."[3] In 1939, Will Rogers' statue joined those of other esteemed Americans in the National Hall of Fame in the Capitol. More recently, in 1955, Speaker Sam Rayburn, a long-time acquaintance of Rogers, spoke on network radio from a perspective of over forty years in public life. "Will Rogers," pronounced Mr. Sam, "really served his day and generation as few men have by calling attention, in public, to matters of public interest, upon which he always had fine judgement."[4] While Rogers was alive, people would chuckle or laugh and then turn to one another and say, "By golly, he's *right* about that." After his death, he continued to be truth-teller as well as jester.

That Rogers is on his way to becoming an American tradition is indicated by the continuing flow of biographies and of anthologies of his sayings. Carl Sandburg, appearing with Sam Rayburn on the NBC radio network in 1955, did not hinder such tendencies when he said:

> A fine and great American tradition is that of Will
> Rogers. He ought to be taught in the schools because of
> what he embodied of the best of the Constitution and the
> Declaration of Independence. I could repeat that the
> whole Rogers tradition is homely as a mud fence, and yet
> as beautiful as a sunrise over an Oklahoma field of
> alfalfa.[5]

Will Rogers was a humorist who won recognition as a secular saint. Without ever holding office from which to shape events, he nevertheless got a respectful hearing from his national audience, from presidents to people to poets. The question of his source of influence is interesting not only for what its answer would reveal of the man but also for what it would show of his audience of millions of Americans. And the question becomes all the more absorbing when attentively examining the apparently easy answers.

For instance, what of the idea—already suggested in the comments made in 1928 supporting his presidential candidacy, in the praise from Niebuhr, and in the estimates by Roosevelt, Hoover, and Rayburn—that Rogers' grasp of foreign and domestic problems generated a kind of magic with his listeners and readers?

True, the student of his magic respects the Oklahoman's discerning analyses on such matters as the need for air power and the need for an anti-imperialist foreign policy; but he also discovers that Rogers' insight into other major national and international issues was something less than brilliant. For *The Saturday Evening Post* in 1926, he wrote approvingly of Mussolini, judging the Italian partly by his opposition to communism. At the time of the 1929 stock market crash, the cowboy from Oklahoma apparently heard little more than the cries of those getting their deserved punishment:

> I have been in Washington on Inauguration Day,
> Claremore on the Fourth of July, Dearborn on Edison's
> Day. But to have been in New York on "Wailing day"! . . .
> You know, there is nothing that hollers as quick and as
> loud as a gambler, they even blame it on Hoover's fedora
> hat. Now they know what the farmer has been up
> against for eight years.

Evidently, he did not perceive the connection between extended business profits, stock market speculation, reduced consumer power, and the crippling of the national economy. "You read all this sensational collapse of Wall Street," he wrote later. "What does it mean? Nothing." On a great question of the time, Rogers aligned himself firmly on the side of the isolationists; a nationally syndicated dispatch is typical of Rogers' view that we should stay out of Europe's quarrels: "Mr. Franklin D.," he counseled, "shut your front door to all foreign ambassadors running to you with news. Just send 'em these words: 'Boys, its your cats that's fighting. You pull 'em apart.'"[6] To say that Rogers was no seer is only honest. To one remembering that audiences sometimes require later developments to prove to themselves the discernment of an analyst, the idea that Rogers' impact depended upon other causes occurs naturally. Often right and often wrong, the man from Oklahoma must have gained his influence by means additional to his "fine judgment."

What, in the second place, of the idea perhaps already suggested by Rogers' views on Wall Streeters and European entanglements—namely, that he won the hearts of Americans by saying well what they already thought? Homer Croy, a friend and biographer of Rogers, phrased this view succinctly when he concluded that Rogers' philosophy "was what the average person was thinking but Will stated it in terms of entertainment." Fred Allen, who as a comedian was for years a student of American audiences, expressed in a network broadcast in 1955 much the same view of Rogers' source of influence when he commented, "It seemed to me that the little man in the street accepted Will as a voice that he would like to say the things that Will was saying for him."[7]

However, while I do not deny that Rogers often did reflect popular sentiment in his epigrams, he did not fear opposing that sentiment. To a nation tired of war and complacent about military preparedness, he constantly addressed warnings. In 1930, for example, he wrote, "To reduce your navy in these times is exactly like a man who is not doing so well financially canceling all his life insurance, figuring it's a dead loss because he hasn't died yet." Against an

American public all too prone to hysteria in a Red scare, he consistently stood for an open society. In 1935, for instance, with a world-wide depression apparently aiding Communist efforts at world revolution, he praised English institutions of free speech like soapbox speakers in London's Hyde Park and wished that "we would do a little more of that over here." A few years earlier, when the "America First" organization had sought to define Americanism and to enforce conformity by appeals to superpatriotism, Rogers used his nationally-syndicated columns to make the movement appear ridiculous.* He opposed public opinion often enough and on sufficiently important questions to raise doubts about the hypothesis that his power arose simply from his saying well what the public already thought. If he did state the thoughts of the people, those thoughts were possibly on a different level from that of opinions on specific events.

That level, perhaps, is the symbolic level. The answer, however, raises the further question of what that symbol represented. Was Rogers, as Donald Day suggests, the prototype of "the big honest majority"? Was he, as L. H. Robbins of the *Times* proposes, the "apotheosis of the common man"?[8] To deny that Will Rogers exhibited and thus symbolized many of the qualities of the average man would be useless. In significant ways, however, he did not behave, write, or speak as the embodiment of the man on the street. In spite of his simple tastes, he was a sophisticate, capable of dining and then talking all night with the likes of George Bernard Shaw and J. M. Barrie.

Another cause unacceptable to the man on the street, but supported by Rogers, was that of religious tolerance. Many Americans did not accept it—if events surrounding the Scopes trial and if individual reactions in the election of 1928 were indications of public opinion on such matters. Moreover, at times, Rogers exhibited an almost aristocratic repugnance for the caprices of public opinion. For instance,

*NYT, 28 October 1930, p. 25; text of radio speech in NYT, 12 May 1935, p. 29; on "America First," see NYT, 2 November 1927, p. 29 and magazine of *Tulsa Daily World,* 13 November 1927, p. 4. Future references to the *Tulsa Daily World* will be shortened to *TDW;* unless otherwise noted, all weekly articles come from *TDW;* all daily telegrams come from *NYT.*

his daily wire dated June 19, 1935, had a tinge of Swiftian imagery in its last two sentences:

> At the great San Diego World's Fair yesterday Mr.
> Hoover received a tremendous ovation.
> There is no country in the world where a person changes
> from a hero to a goat, and a goat to a hero, or vice versa,
> as they do with us. And all through no change in them.
> The change is always with us.
> It's not our public men that you can't put your finger on.
> It's our public. We are the only fleas weighing over 100
> pounds. We don't know what we want, but we are ready
> to bite somebody to get it.

Finally, except for fleeting moments, the "little" people do not install in their pantheon one who truly is one of them. Will Rogers once wrote in his daily squib, "There is nothing impresses the 'common folk' like somebody that ain't common."[9] He must have symbolized, for his audience, more than simply the common man.

Among those who have sought to find Rogers' symbolic meaning for America by relating him to the tradition of the crackerbox philosopher, many have necessarily spent most of their effort in showing the continuity of the line of home-spun philosophers from Benjamin Franklin's Poor Richard to Will Rogers. To say that Rogers as crackerbox philosopher was influential with American audiences is not, on the other hand, to explain what made the crackerbox philosopher, himself, so appealing to the American imagination. Constance Rourke, in her pathfinding study of American humor as an index to the national character, showed the symbolic value of the folk-humor tradition. With its comedy, "irreverent wisdom," and "sudden changes and adroit adaptations," this tradition provided, says Rourke, "emblems for a pioneer people who required resilience as a prime trait."[10] Part, then, of what Will Rogers represented to Americans was the adaptiveness of the pioneer.

Others interested in understanding Rogers' meaning for his audience have suggested additional dimensions of his appeal. Carl Sandburg's judgment of Rogers is relevant here if the reader remembers that the poet and biographer felt that Rogers' philosophy should be taught in the schools because of what it embodied of the best of the Constitution and the Declaration of Independence. In her *Will Rogers Book,* Paula McSpadden Love, Rogers' niece and curator of the Rogers Memorial, expressed the belief that he symbolized not so much the common man as the triumph of the common man. Novelist Clarence Budington Kelland, puzzling over Rogers' source of power as he watched the cowboy philosopher in action, experienced the insight that Rogers was really Uncle Sam, minus costume and beard. Scholar Orrin Klapp, writing in the *Journal of American Folklore,* concluded that Rogers was more than simply a clever hero: Rogers was not only homespun philosopher and friend of the common man, but he was also a democratic hero and a national symbol.

All the judgments thus far point to the conclusion that the sources of Rogers' appeal as a hero were rooted more deeply than might appear at first glance. If it be true, as many have hypothesized, that national heroes such as Rogers personify national ideals, those who speak of Rogers' meaning to the American public as representing native resilience, or as expressing the ideals of American democracy, or as denoting the triumph of the common man surely point toward the source of his power. What constellation of values classified Will Rogers as a hero? What were the cultural values by which Rogers' audience could find in him a symbol of their best hopes in a time of need? Possibly, that cluster of ideals was the great American dream, reconstructed by examining ideas of representative spokesmen and studying other American heroes. Possibly, during the period of uncertainty and big change in the twenties and thirties, audiences identified Will Rogers with the dream of the dignity and worth of the individual, of freedom and equality, of success, and of progress. He would, therefore, be one with the dreamers of the dream in his audience—a steady friend who could be trusted, believed, and taken seriously.

The dream, like Rogers himself, had its origins in the past. Much of it grew up with mankind, so that to call it the *American* dream may seem chauvinistic. Yet it is true that the dream grew here with fewer impediments, and as it did, the family of Will Rogers also grew. The beginnings of both are important for this story: The interrelationship of Rogers and the American dream is probably in great part the source of the interrelationship of Rogers and his America.

When Columbus made his landfall in the West Indies and thought he had reached Asia, it seemed to be the fulfillment of Renaissance man's dream of boundlessness. With the passing of four centuries, filled by the traversing and settling of a continent, the American dream developed. The riches of the East were at hand in the West, and the hope of fulfillment was implicit in the gardenlike newness of the land. Out of the dreams of empire, out of the Puritan hope of the millennium, and out of American adaptations of Locke's and Rousseau's personal visions would appear American idealism, the great American dream.

(At the time of the European discovery of the American continent, forefathers of Rogers were already living in present-day Georgia. Rogers traced his ancestry to the Paint, the Wolf, and the Blind Savannah clans of the Cherokee Nation.)

One source of the great vision was the dream of empire that would, as James Truslow Adams in *Epic of America* has phrased it, "singe the beard of the king of Spain and make a shrewd thrust at the Pope." By the middle of the seventeenth century, though, this grand design, while destined to survive as the dream of an independent American empire, formed the common man's own dream of empire: personal advancement and escape from Europe. By the 1640's, writes Adams, "The American dream was beginning to take form in the hearts of men. The economic motive was unquestionably powerful, often dominant . . . but mixed with this was also frequently present the hope of a better and freer life, a life in which a man might think as he would and develop as he willed."[11] By about 1750, as Russel Nye has noted in *This Almost Chosen People,* the mercantilist system of empire, with its strict regulations, no longer satisfied the Colonies with their ready supply of land and a small labor force.The colonists who found themselves disadvantaged along the seaboard settlements drove westward toward the Appalachians, seeking prosperity, social esteem, and self-realization.

In this first real frontier in America, the ideal of equality seemed natural enough to settlers whose poverty leveled them and whose inferior status as "Buckskins" goaded them not only to prosper but to minimize class distinctions. "Here," wrote Crèvecoeur, one picturemaker of American life, "are no aristocratical families, no courts, no kings, no bishops, no ecclesiastical dominion . . . no great refinements of luxury. The rich and the poor are not so far removed from each other as they are in Europe." Thus the common man's dream of empire had with it hopes of equality. With it, also, was a vision of freedom, in the sense of relief from exploitation by superiors. The American, motivated by self-interest, raised exuberant crops, observed Crèvecoeur, "without any part being claimed either by a despotic prince, a rich abbot, or a mighty lord." In such a setting of plenty and novelty, it was natural to see the American as a brother in spirit to the first Adam: "The American is a new man, who acts upon new principles; he must therefore entertain new ideas and new opinions," asserted the man made famous as the "American Farmer." (Will Rogers would be, when his time came, this new man, the American Adam.)

Crèvecoeur's writings, as well as other publications, led to the "myth of the garden" that Henry Nash Smith in his *Virgin Land* found to be a "collective representation, a poetic idea . . . that defined the promise of American life."[12] The frontier offered a paradise-like bountiful haven for those driven by want from Europe or from American cities. Benjamin Franklin showed the old dream of empire changing to the new dream of the common man's empire when he argued that agricultural development of the interior would not only produce bigger outlets for the British mercantile empire but would also provide a refuge for city laborers—an argument that would later be termed the "safety-valve" theory. In 1775, Lewis Evans articulated the American version of the old dream of empire when he foresaw "all the Wealth and Power that will naturally arise from the Culture of so great an extent of good land, in a happy Climate." There was room in this vision of empire for the dream of the common man; and along with his hopes for an economic rise in the "good land in the happy climate," he looked forward to an equality of opportunity in his progress toward that rise and, further, toward resulting self-realization and social equality. He could be a new man.

(By about the middle of the eighteenth century, the mingling of European and Cherokee blood that was to produce Will Rogers had begun. On the paternal side, one great-grandmother was a full-blooded member of the Savannah Clan; she was the wife of an Irishman. The other paternal great-grandmother, half-Cherokee and half-Irish, was also married to a son of Eire.)

Coexisting in time with the dream of empire, the Puritan vision of an approaching millennium provided a second great source for the American dream: Its secularization reinforced the economic dream of success, the social dream of equality, and the political dream of free democracy.

The dream of the millennium was of a new heaven and earth. It was thus an explicit statement of a dream of a new and better way of life, with an implicit belief in progress through the working of Providence, as Nye has shown. Its central hope was the establishment of a "New Jerusalem," a city of God, free of wickedness and full of happy virtue, a beacon of inspiration of all peoples. "Wee must consider," wrote John Winthrop, "that we shall be as a citty upon a Hill, the eies of all people upon us." By 1650, Edward Johnson envisioned the new land as the site "where the Lord would create a new heaven and a new earth, new churches and a new commonwealth together." Later, William Stoughton, in an unmistakable allusion to the "Promised Land," rejoiced that "God had sifted a whole nation that he might send choice grain into the wilderness." Thus, stated Leland Baldwin in his *Meaning of America,* the Calvinists' belief that they were planting a city of God initiated the Utopian view of America.

A typical architect of the city of God was John Eliot, whose *Christian Commonwealth* appeared in 1659. The two assumptions on which his Utopia rested were that Christ is the King of Kings and that all laws should "arise and flow from the Word of God." Thus, the basis of the perfect society lay in a covenant with God to live up to His enumerated purposes, with rewards by Divine Providence to the extent that the Puritans kept the covenant. In Eliot's book, men could voluntarily form an organization to keep the covenant and to elect their rulers who, like them, were to obey the covenant. Though this vision of a New Jerusalem created by means of the covenant was to fade and die after a century or more, parts of the Puritan dream in a secularized form lived on, particularly in the dream of a free, ideal society.[13]

First, the American dream of prosperity and material success received impetus from the covenant idea and from the Puritan dedication to work. Cotton Mather, as witness for orthodox Puritanism, revealed the beliefs that success was a sign of covenantal virtue and that being busy was being godly. "His *Two Brief Discourses,*" says Marshall Fishwick in his study *American Heroes,* "asserted that man must serve Christ, and achieve success in a personal calling."[14] With such views to provide theological foundation, it is little wonder that preachers like John Lathrop could later exult in the immensity of the country and in the increasing population, with a resulting "astonishing commerce with the nations of the world," and could find virtue in such a "great and highly respectable nation," with its "industrious and good people." The dream of economic power had become part of the hope of the millennium. With such legitimizing of the economic motive, the dream of success was destined to become one of the most glittering guides to the hoped-for American return to perfection. (When his time came, Will Rogers would be a self-made man, a hero of success.)

Another beacon to the ideal state was an anticipated equality among men. To this the Puritan vision also added strength, almost inadvertently. Part of this strength came, perhaps, from the Puritans' belief as Christians that infinite value inhered in the individual soul, even in the state of original sin. More specifically, however, as Nye has shown, the Puritans contributed in at least three ways to the American idea of equality, notwithstanding their emphasis on inequality of the elect and nonelect and their distrust of levelers like the Quakers: The Calvinists removed the priest as intermediary between God and believer; they rejected much of the church hierarchy; and they provided for elections in certain parts of their polity.

Finally, although in some instances the Puritan had little or no desire for democracy in government (or for liberty in religion),[15] the tenets of Calvinism as held by the English colonists ultimately lent support to the dream of political democracy. Speaking of "mythus" as a body of beliefs that by its emotional appeal produces loyalty, Baldwin states the relationship succinctly: "Calvinism lent itself to the democratic mythus. It taught Natural Rights, the compact theory, and the right of revolution. Democracy found all of them useful." Moreover, the Puritan belief that one should become prosperous and be responsible could, Baldwin says, "be adjusted to the democratic belief that the benefit of one is the benefit of all and that all are responsible."[16]

That the influences of Calvinism and democracy are mutual seems only probable; but doubtless the one was inextricably entwined with the other by the time of the successful conclusion of the American Revolution. By that day of rejoicing in 1783, when John Rodgers preached his sermon revealing the display of Divine Goodness in the American Revolution, the millennium was to be not only a religious one, but also a secular one of freedom from oppression of any kind:

> What great things has the God of Providence done for
> our race! By the Revolution we this day celebrate, he has
> provided an asylum for the oppressed, in all the nations
> of the earth, whatever may be the nature of the
> oppression. And that, while he is hereby accomplishing
> those great things, that are opening the way for the more
> general spread of the gospel, in its purity and power; and
> in due time, the universal establishment of the Messiah's
> kingdom, in all its benign efficacy on the hearts and lives
> of men.[17]

In the Puritan belief, the recurrent motifs of an approaching millennium, of the godliness of work, of the earthly reward for earthly virtue, and of the value of the individual all found their way into the manifest content of the emerging American dream—in the form of a steadily Utopian secular tradition, in the dream of the self-made man, and in the dream of a government that existed to serve the governed.

(While John Rodgers was active in his ministry, there came and passed the twentieth anniversary of the arrival in present-day northern Alabama of a young Welshman named John Gunter, who was to become a prosperous salt trader with the Cherokees, who was to take to wife a member of the Paint Clan, and who was to be a maternal great-grandfather of Will Rogers.)

A third great source for the American dream was the congeries of political ideas associated with the American Revolution. From 1660 on, the Colonies produced opponents to the British policy that sought to integrate the resources of English North America with those of the mother country, to the disadvantage of the colonists. At first, the emphasis in their arguments lay in seeking their rights as Englishmen—first in relation to the colonial charters and then in relation to the nature of the British Empire and constitution. But in the lull after the crisis created by such revenue-producing laws as the Stamp and the Molasses acts, an important shift in emphasis was occurring in the Americans' arguments for relief, according to Adams (page 86): The more the Americans "pondered the Anglo-American constitutional relation, . . . the more it became apparent that if the question should ever have to be forced to an issue, the only ground to take would be the broad one of the rights of man as man."

Too, as Bernard Bailyn has startlingly shown in his *Ideological Origins of the American Revolution,* the colonists had for a half-century prior to the Revolution been increasingly convinced that a conspiracy of "power" against "liberty" was afoot, aiming at the destruction of the English constitution. This image of conspiracy, believes Bailyn, drove the Americans to revolution, with the "pivotal issue" being the question of sovereignty. The ideas regarding sovereignty and the nature of power versus liberty, Bailyn shows, came partly from Romans who saw their republic threatened, partly from English common law, partly from antiauthoritarian British radicals, and partly from Enlightenment thinkers—chief among whom was Locke, who had synthesized the trends of revolutionary thought. Locke had found the origin of government not in a God-given order to would-be rulers, but rather in the necessity of men's forming a social contract to protect the rights of life, liberty, and property that were theirs in the state of nature in which they had originally found themselves. Government thus found its reason for being in the protection of these rights, its power in the consent of the protected ones, and its death when it no longer filled its purpose in life. On the Continent, Rousseau tellingly reinforced the social contract idea, praised the happiness of man in the natural state, and extended the idea of equality, says Nye (page 311), to require it as a "necessary precondition of a free and just government." Added to these thinkers were coffeehouse radicals and spokesmen for libertarianism, who—in Bailyn's view, as he examined his collection of colonial newspapers and pamphlets—"shaped the mind of the American Revolutionary generation" to a greater degree than any other group through their powers of tying together the "disparate strands of thought" in the emerging revolutionary canon.[18]

Americans had begun naturalizing Locke and the other political philosophers years before the Revolution. James Otis, for one, had combined Locke's natural rights with British constitutional rights in his 1764 justification of the Colonies' claims. Fiery Samuel Adams, however, was to be better remembered for couching the rationalism of Locke in the romantic appeals of Rousseau and the fire of the libertarians, blending each in a heady mixture that could please aristocrat as well as commoner. In a report to a Boston town meeting in 1772, Adams declared that the natural rights of life, liberty, and property were but a branch of the first law of man in nature, that of self-preservation; the report may have served as the model for the Declaration of Rights of the first Congress in 1774, for the Declaration of Independence, and for the Virginia Bill of Rights.[19] In addition to this influence, Adams had the common men, whose hopes and aspirations he harnessed, urging such Lockean, Rousseauan, and libertarian pronouncements of his as "the natural liberty of man is to be free from any superior power on earth, and not to be under the will or legislative authority of man, but only to have the law of nature for his rule."

Another major figure in the naturalization of European thinkers was Thomas Paine, whose *Common Sense,* as Perry Miller has pointed out, was immensely successful, not so much because the idea of independence from England really was common sense as because of the appeal of Paine's Rousseauistic contention: Only in America existed a people close enough to nature to be sufficiently simple and uncorrupted to make possible the operation of common sense in the first place. The Lockean flavor is unmistakable also in Paine's explanation of the origin and purpose of government:

> Government, like dress, is the badge of lost innocence:
> the palaces of kings are built on the ruins of the bowers
> of paradise. For, were the impulses of conscience clear,
> uniform, and irresistibly obeyed, man would need no
> other lawgiver; but that not being the case, he finds it
> necessary to surrender up a part of his property to
> furnish means for the protection of the rest.[20]

Thus, it would follow that man had a right to choose from time to time whatever form of government would most likely ensure security, which was "the true design and end of government."

Perhaps in Thomas Jefferson, spokesman for the American mind, was the completion of the process of making Locke at home. Lockean in his belief in a state of nature, in human equality, and in a government by the consent of the governed, Jefferson modified significantly the Englishman's enumeration of natural rights and thus gave the Declaration of Independence its flavor of American idealism. Man was, indeed, naturally endowed with permanent rights of life and liberty; Locke's "property," however, became Jefferson's "pursuit of happiness." This substitution recognized the aspirations for a return to an ideal state that characterized the colonial aristocrat as well as the roughest Buckskin out on the frontier. By eliminating "property" from the list of man's rights, Jefferson made sure that the ideal state would give no preference to the rich or well-born; at the same time, his "pursuit of happiness" left the way open for myriad definitions: American aristocrats could dream of freedom from injustices under the sovereignty of Parliament; members of the lower classes could dream of freedom from injustice by their own governing classes. It is small wonder that many colonists regarded the Declaration as though it were promulgated in heaven.*

The successful conclusion of the war for independence

---

*See Craven, *The Colonies in Transition,* 285 and 320, for explanation of the growth of the power of colonial legislatures for reasons sometimes unrelated to any desire for independence from the crown.

did much to legalize the claims of the Declaration. Legal scholars like James Wilson were to find the justification not only of the Revolution but of the new government itself, in the concept of the sovereignty of the people; the new Constitution, reserving to sovereign states all powers not expressly delegated to a federal government, represented an attempt to give substance to the ideologies of natural rights and sovereignty of the people. It completed the transformation Bailyn has shown of European ideas of representation, nature of constitutions, and sovereign power; the result was the emergence of an American democrat. (When his time came, Will Rogers would be such a democrat.)

Throughout the struggle for independence, the revolutionary's dream of freedom reinforced tendencies traced earlier in the economic and Puritan backgrounds of the dream. Its "pursuit of happiness" often was equated with the pursuit of wealth; the ideal of equality flourished explicitly on the frontier and implicitly in the Puritan strongholds; the love of freedom shown in the pioneer desire to be let alone to pursue success and preserve liberty reached a crescendo in the agitation preceding the Declaration. The progress, in turn, of the Colonies from aggregations of disadvantaged Englishmen to sovereign states in a new, more perfect union certainly lent validity to the common man's dream of his own progressive economic rise and to the secularized version of the Puritan millennium, a new heaven on this earth.

Americans praised the new era. James Wilson, in his oration of July 4, 1788, in Philadelphia, urged continued progress toward the perfect existence promised by the American dream when he said, "A PROGRESSIVE STATE is necessary to the happiness and perfection of man. Whatever attainments are already reached, attainments still higher should be pursued." With the dream of progress thus placed in the nexus of American idealism, Wilson exhorted, "Let us, with fervent zeal, press forward and make *unceasing advances* in everything that can SUPPORT, IMPROVE, REFINE OR EMBELLISH SOCIETY." (In his time, Will Rogers would be an American hero of progress.)

Out of the common man's dream of a rewarding economic rise, out of the Puritan covenanter's vision of a New

Jerusalem, and out of the common-sense revolutionary's thrust for natural rights emerged the major categories of the great American dream: the belief in the dignity and worth of the individual, the anticipation of enjoying freedom and equality in a democracy, the hoped-for opportunity for success, and the vision of progress. It was, in short, the dream of Paradise to be regained.*

Washington himself voiced the sense of destiny attaching to the growth and progress of the great dream when, in his first inaugural address, he proclaimed that "the preservation of the sacred fire of liberty and the destiny of the republican model of government are . . . *finally,* staked on the experiment intrusted to the hands of the American people."

(And as the American nationality and dream began to take form during the years of quiet that Washington's diplomats tried to buy with the Jay Treaty, the family lines of the still-to-be-born "ambassador of good will" grew clearer. The daughter of John Gunter and his Cherokee wife was born and named Elizabeth; in that same year of 1806 was born her husband-to-be, Martin Matthew Schrimsher, of German descent. They would be the maternal grandparents of Will Rogers. On the paternal side, the one-eighth Cherokee great-granddaughter of that first European ancestor of Will Rogers, Major Downing, was born and named Sallie Vann; her husband-to-be, Robert Rogers II, was born in 1803 and was himself one-fourth Cherokee.)

Damon Runyon once wrote, "Will Rogers was undoubtedly America's most complete human document."[21] It is time to read the document and the man, the better to relate him to the concept of the American dream. In each of the chapters to follow, therefore, will appear the levels of the American dream as the cultural background by which Americans could assess the worth of Will Rogers; the means

*To Frederic I. Carpenter, "The American Myth: Paradise (to be) Regained," *Publications of the Modern Language Association of America* (hereafter cited as *PMLA*), 74 (December, 1959), 599-606, I am indebted for this superordinate category of the dream; however, I use it more inclusively than does Carpenter. To Miller, *New England Quarterly,* 28 (December, 1955), 435-54, I am indebted for the terms "puritan covenanter" and "common sense revolutionary." See also Delmage, *Proceedings of the American Philosophical Society,* 91 (December, 1947), 307-14, for interrelation of aspects of the dream.

by which Rogers may have been influenced to identify with each category of the dream; the nature of the times in which such identification became effective; the publicity and his own words that achieved identification. From these chapters will emerge the reason for Will Rogers' influence: He embodied the American dream in a time when Americans needed such a symbol.

Will Rogers, American Adam

During all the years when millions of Americans enjoyed —over their breakfast coffee—a daily visit with Will Rogers in the local newspaper, there gradually emerged from the rambling discourse a picture of Rogers as a believer in the worth and goodness of people, in the rights of all men and in respect for those rights, and in the better future that lay ahead for people who looked forward to it instead of to the past. His posture was that of a man who cast a welcoming eye toward the fellow who could turn a dollar, and he approved of the rise from low to high estate.

These images, combined with a potpourri of humor and comment, come through in a montage of Rogers' "one-or-two liners," arranged chronologically:

It is getting so that a Republican promise is not much more to be depended on than a Democratic one. And that has always been considered the lowest form of collateral in the world.

We will never have true civilization until we have learned to recognize the rights of others.

The American people are a very generous people and will forgive almost any weakness, with the possible exception of stupidity.

[In the old days,] your looks meant nothing to them. It was what you did that counted.

The South is dry and will vote dry. That is, everybody that is sober enough to stagger to the polls will.

Box score for today: Died by gunshot and other natural Chicago causes, 13; wounded, 23. Bad weather kept outdoor shooting down to a minimum.

The Supreme Court of Tennessee down here has just ruled that you other States can come from whoever or whatever you want to, but they want it on record that they come from mud only.

Happiness and contentment is progress. In fact that's all progress is.

37

Will Rogers

By Golly I am living now. I am eating real biscuits and real ham and cream gravy. Oklahoma will show the world how to live yet.

I have heard so much at this [national] convention about "getting back to the old Jeffersonian principles" that being an amateur, I am in doubt as to why they left them in the first place.

If we diden't have to stop and play politics any administration could almost make a Garden of Eden out of us.

Everybody is a-picking on that poor boy out there in California that run the wrong way with that football . . . . All I want is . . . to get this boy a medal for at least doing something different from one million other college boys. Even if it was wrong, his mind wasn't standardized.

If every history or books on old things was thrown in the river and if everybody had nothing to study but the future, we would be about 200 years ahead of what we are now.

I believe the Lord split knowledge up among his subjects about equal after all. The so-called ignorant is happy. Maybe he is happy because he knows enough to be happy. The smart one knows he knows a lot and that makes him unhappy. . . . The more you know the more you realize you don't know.

You got to sorter give and take in this old world. We can get mighty rich, but if we haven't got any friends, we will find we are poorer than anybody.

Us middle class over here never have to worry about having old furniture to point out to our friends. We buy it on payments and before it's paid for it's plenty antique.

Yesterday a true democrat, not politically, but religiously, died. A New York priest, Father Duffy, by long odds the most beloved man in New York City. I am of his faith. You are of his faith, for his faith was humanity.

The world is with the fellow coming up. Let the fellow that's already up look after himself. Every crowd wants to see a new champion crowned.

The old dollar might be filthy lucre, but there is quite a
bit of energy and spirit yet in earning one.

*There is no finer and more satisfying business in the
world than the cow business when you get half a
chance, but when the elements are agin' you, you are
just like a candidate that runs second.*

Was you ever driving around in a car and not knowing or
caring where you went? Well, that's what Wiley and I are
doing. We are sure having a great time. If we hear of
whales or polar bears in the Arctic, or a big herd of
caribou or reindeer we fly over and see it. . . . Maybe
Point Barrow today.[1]

Rogers never saw Point Barrow, but he had already established himself during his years of conversation with his
American audience as an icon of its dream of the dignity
and worth of the individual. For even in those comments
not obviously relevant to such a vision, there was the breath
of exhilaration with life and the sense of new beginnings
appropriate to an American like the "new man" whom
Crèvecoeur had described many years before. That Will
Rogers was like a new Adam will be apparent in a better
perspective after examining in more detail the ideal of the
new Adam's dream.* It was a dream expressed on several
levels: those of ideas, ideal behavior to embody or achieve
the ideas, and heroes who exemplified the behavior and the
ideas.

IF, AS Washington had said, the American experiment in
freedom to achieve ideals was indeed entrusted to the
hands of the American people, a deducible antecedent idea
was belief in the powers and value of the common man. Not
only was the common man thus capable, but he was also

*I am indebted to R. W. B. Lewis, whose *The American Adam:
Innocence, Tragedy and Tradition in the Nineteenth Century* sets
forth in detail the image emerging from American literature of the
ideal American as a new Adam. Frederic I. Carpenter, in *PMLA*, 74
(December, 1959), 599-606, holds that Lewis and other critics mistakenly
believe that the newness of Adam was that before the fall, living
innocently in a state of noble primitivism. Carpenter asserts that the
truly American mythical character seeks the "primitive" life not as a
savage existence but as the "ideal" existence.

innately good. If the powers and virtue of the common man be granted, it follows that one of the greatest goods in the American dream would be the highest possible self-fulfill-ment of every individual. Given these ideas surrounding the dream, its American supporters provided a strategy for the achievement of the dream, a strategy that itself seemed a part of the hopeful vision. From this cluster of ideas and normative behavior emerges the heroic image of the new Adam, who found his place in the myth of the garden that had gradually been developing since colonial days.

The common man was, in the great American dream, an untapped reservoir of talent, wisdom, and leadership. This is understandable in part, at least, points out James Trus-low Adams, because the common man kept the great dream alive through his uprisings in the causes of Jefferson, Jack-son, Lincoln, and Bryan. For, holds Adams, the unique idea for which America has stood has been a commitment to the belief in the powers of the common man. Henry Bamford Parkes, in his *American Experience,* sees in the trust of the common man "the animating principle of American na-tionality."[2] Malcolm Cowley, exploring the literary myth-ologies of America for the *Saturday Review,* found that one of the primary messages transmitted by the heroes of one American mythology was faith in the individual.

The high priests of the dream of the dignity and worth of the individual were Emerson, Whitman, and Thoreau, whose optimistic hopes for the common man were so confirmed that they believed in a *laissez faire* of the spirit —to the extent that the individual could grow to his fullest possibilities.

In *Nature,* "Self-Reliance," and "The American Scholar," Emerson expressed indelibly his trust in the capacity of the common man. "In all my lectures," he summed up, "I have taught one doctrine, namely, the infinitude of the private man." Greatness lay within the reach of the common man: "In every work of genius we recognize our own rejected thoughts." Not only did the private man thus have the ca-pacity to be great, but he faced issues that demanded that greatness. Did great consequences depend upon the actions of great men of the past? Then "as great a stake depends on your private act to-day as followed their public and renowned steps." Because of his confidence in the common man, Emerson looked forward to a new epoch in the history of the world; he praised "the elevation of what was called the lowest class in the state," and he anticipated the celebration of the ordinary. "I explore and sit at the feet of the familiar, the low," he wrote. The quality that made Emerson's idealism typically American, believes Frederic I. Carpenter, is "its close relation to the common experience of his own time, and its appeal to the American experience of the future."[3] Thus, Emerson too was drawn to the concept of American idealism.

Whitman also believed that from the common man would come something uncommon in achievement. The common folk of generous nature expressed for him the real spirit of the country:

> Other states indicate themselves in their deputies . . . but the genius of the United States is not best or most in its executives or legislatures, nor in its ambassadors or authors, or colleges or churches or parlors, nor even in its newspapers or inventors . . . but always most in the common people, south, north, west, east, in all its States, through all its mighty amplitude.

More specifically, Whitman believed that the common man used his powers to control events: "He, in these States, remains immortal owner and boss, deriving good uses somehow, out of any sort of servant in office, even the basest."[4] The power to bring good out of evil had previously been assigned to God; Whitman gave a generous portion to the common man.

Another attribute of God in older philosophies had been His infinitude; this, too, Whitman claimed for the common man—as had Emerson. In the 1856 edition of *Leaves of Grass,* he had penned this line in answer to his self-posed question on the nature of man: "I pass death with the dying, and birth with the new-washed babe, and am not contained between my hat and boots." This ideal self created by Whitman thus has the infinite ability to empathize with and pervade everything. So, thus, infinite are the ideal American folk symbolized by Whitman's ideal self. The common man's powers were not only great, but potentially unlimited.

The exaltation of the common man, the belief in his value and powers, may actually have begun centuries before when noble knights on crusades against the Turks had to sell some of their privileges to good burghers in order to raise traveling cash; it had remained for the dreamers of the American dream, however, to elevate average humanity almost to deity.

As God is good, man-become-God must also be good. Another article of faith in the common man was that he was the repository of innate virtue. Though he disapproves of such a dream and sees it as hallucination, Leslie Fiedler testifies that up to recent times "America had been unremittingly dreamed from East to West as a testament to the original goodness of man."[5] A journal article in 1839 proclaimed the goodness of an America with "a clear conscience unsullied by the past." The new country was sprung, it seemed, full-grown from the soil of the new world—a new creation unblemished by the tainted breath of Europe. In addition, the essence of a belief in man's original virtue that would have delighted Rousseau clung about the Emersonian party of hope delineated by R. W. B. Lewis.

"Men in all ways are better than they seem" wrote Emerson in an essay dealing with reformers. "Nothing shall warp me from the belief that every man is a lover of truth." Behind such statements, perhaps, lay Emerson's doctrine of self-reliance. God, as moral law, was everywhere, and the world was an emanation from God. Man, subject to moral law and living in a world that was derived from God, was himself divine, and the self to which Emerson referred in "Self-Reliance" was the spark of divinity in every man. Because God was good and God was everywhere, evil was an illusion—or else existed only in the negative sense that good was absent. Man, having God within him, was naturally good. "The league between virtue and nature," wrote the Sage of Concord, "engages all things to assume a hostile front to vice." Thus, the "natural" man to Emerson was good because he was in harmony with nature, and nature—going beyond mountains, valleys, trees, and flowers—was the operation of moral law. Emerson's idea of the naturally good man was, perhaps, more commodious than a conception of the "noble savage."

Whitman seems somehow more Rousseauan in his belief in natural goodness. The picture of the ideal self that emerges from "Song of Myself" shows a being who has thrown off every possible influence of corrupting civilization:

> Trippers and askers surround me,
> People I meet, the effect upon me of my early life
>   or the ward and city I live in, or the nation.
> . . . .
> The sickness of one of my folks or of myself, or the
>   ill-doing or loss or lack of money, or depressions or
>   exaltations,
> Battles, the horror of fratricidal wars, the fever of
>   doubtful news, the fitful events,
> These come to me days and nights and go from me again,
> But they are not the Me myself.
> Apart from the pulling and hauling stands what I am,
> Stands amused, complacent, compassionating, idle, unitary,
> Looks down, is erect, or bends an arm on an impalpable
>   certain rest,
> Looking with side-curved head curious what will come
>   next,
> Both in and out of the game and watching and wondering
>   at it.

Ridding himself of influence, the ideal self achieves both the detachment and wonder of innocence and a kind of primeval goodness. The goodness is more potential than present and, like the tough outer coverings of unpolished pearl, the layers of outworn convention must be peeled off. The common man can then commence his grand experience of development.

Emerson philosophized about the natural goodness of man; Whitman dreamed of it and created an eidolon of natural goodness; Thoreau engrossed himself in an experiment to recover that goodness by becoming that natural man. R.W.B. Lewis has said that Thoreau sought to cleanse the traditional, conventional man precisely so that the natural man could be brought into being. Thus, *Walden* can be read as having a structure similar to Thoreau's own purification rite. At first, Thoreau is in Concord with its conventions; then there is the shearing off of convention by removal to the forest and pond, with the rhythm of nature in the passing seasons; finally, spring arrives—and what Lewis (page 25) calls "a representative anecdote about the sudden bursting into life of a winged insect long buried in an old table of apple-tree wood." Man's natural goodness, like the life of the long-dormant insect, can assert itself when the dead wood of convention is touched by life.

The common man himself probably made verbal short-hand of all this simply by uttering something like, "There's good in everyone." Certainly, he was less articulate than Thoreau on the purifying effects of a return to wilderness; but he may have been convinced, nevertheless. The American dream of the goodness of the common man lived through his belief in the virtue possessed by the yeoman farmer living in the nature of his own freehold. To the American devotee of the great dream, the common man had within him the potential of being uncommonly good.

With such dazzling possibilities of talent and virtue in the "average fallows" of humanity, a natural consequence in the great dream was the hope of highest possible development. This, perhaps, is another dimension of the famous "pursuit of happiness" in the Declaration of Independence. It is certain that the hope of self-fulfillment was a magnet for the imagination of believers in the dream. True, material prosperity was often the motive for the pursuit but, as James Truslow Adams has eloquently pointed out, the American dream "has been a dream of being able to grow to fullest development as man and woman, unhampered by the barriers which had slowly been erected in older civilizations, unrepressed by social orders which had developed for the benefit of classes rather than for the simple human being of any and every class."[6]

Everything that has been said so far about the dream of the dignity and the worth of the individual can be construed as the dream of self-fulfillment; if the common man can realize his infinitude and his own value, and achieve in himself the consciousness of a good self, he will be well established in his growth toward "fullest development as man." In addition, however, Whitman could envision traits in his ideal folk that signaled the fullest development of the individual. The ideal American would be possessed of robust health and of the hearty good spirits that would accompany it. He would have developed an abiding sense of hospitality that would open him to brotherhood with man; he would love children, women, and comrades. Yet he would be prudent in all that he felt; in balance, perhaps, to the gregariousness of his personality, he would be self-reliant* in the sense of being able to be "both in and out of the game, and watching and wondering at it."

Along with the theorems of the dream just discussed, the dreamers offered corollaries, in the form of recommended actions, that together constituted a strategy for realizing the vision of the dignity and worth of the individual. The action corollaries were more, however, than simply a means to an end: Their observance offered tangible evidence that the common man was developing his boundless possibilities, that he was claiming virtue for his own, and that he was growing to his fullest possible self-realization. In this light, the action corollaries seemed a substantive part of the dream.

The American experiment was a new one, calling for new answers to new problems. Accordingly, the grand, over-all strategy of Emerson, Whitman, and Thoreau for the realization of the ideal self was, suggests Carpenter, threefold: First, the American would reject the conventions of the past; second, he would quest for the ideal American life; finally, he would partially realize that life. The key to the rejection, the quest, and the partial realization was experience. Emerson defined it inclusively, including the mystical as well as the sensual, and Whitman's ideal self sought this key in order to make the world a part of himself. Through experience, the American would at once develop his powers, reinforce his natural goodness, and reach to his highest self-fulfillment.

From the transcendentalists' doctrine that wisdom is not

*These categories of fullest development of the individual are drawn from the comments of John Robert Willingham, "The Whitman Tradition in Recent American Literature" (Ph.D. diss., University of Oklahoma, 1953), 14.

acquired but, rather, is innate and waiting to flower, Emerson deduced advice that would result in self-reliance and personal growth for the new American Adam. "Trust thyself," he wrote, "every heart vibrates to that iron string." Such self-reliance would lead to greatness:

> Do that which is assigned you, and you cannot hope too much or dare too much. There is at this moment for you an utterance brave and grand as that of the colossal chisel of Phidias, or trowel of the Egyptians, or the pen of Moses or Dante, but different from all these.

And yet, this self-reliance was not an introspective sort. "Do not craze yourself with thinking," Emerson counseled, "but go about your business anywhere. Life is not intellectual or critical, but sturdy." As a result, the ideal American whom Emerson celebrated was the "sturdy lad from New Hampshire or Vermont, who in turn tries all the professions, who *teams it, farms it, peddles,* keeps a school, preaches, edits a newspaper . . . and so forth . . . and always like a cat falls on his feet."[7] All of this was appropriate to the strategy for the new man that was the American, believed Emerson. "He emphasized," says Carpenter (page 29) in his full-length study of the dream, "the need of intuition and self-reliance for modern men because the new laws and 'traditions' of the new world had not yet been formulated."

Besides relying upon intuition and practicing self-reliance, the new American would develop his powers and virtue, Emerson believed, by attuning himself to the time in which he lived. In "Self-Reliance," he advised, "Accept the place the divine providence has found for you, the society of your contemporaries, the connection of events. Great men have always done so, and confided themselves childlike to the genius of their age." In "The American Scholar," the prime influence upon character was nature, in both the mystical and sensual aspects: "Every day, the sun; and, after sunset, Night and her stars. . . . Every day, men and women, conversing—beholding and beholden." In summary, the American would develop his fullest stature by balance of all his experience: The highest possibilities of man become reality when he attunes himself with the universe, develops his talent as a call to vocation, and is himself—fearless and independent.

46

Whitman, for his part, had faith in impulses. His program of action, accordingly, was untethered experimenting of the soul in varied situations. The perfect image of this strategy appears in "There Was a Child Went Forth," for whom "the first object he look'd upon, that object he became." The early lilacs, the horizon's edge, the salt-marsh and shore-mud fragrance became, says Whitman, "part of that child who went forth every day, who now goes, and will always go forth every day." More specifically, the program of behavior for the new American was as follows:

> This is what you shall do: Love the earth and sun and the
> animals, despise riches, give alms to everyone that asks,
> stand up for the stupid and crazy, devote your income
> and labor to others, hate tyrants, argue not concerning
> God, have patience and indulgence toward the people,
> take off your hat to nothing known or unknown or to any
> man or number of men, go freely with powerful
> uneducated persons and with the young and with the
> mothers of families . . . reexamine all you have been told
> at school or church or in any book, [and] dismiss
> whatever insults your own soul.[8]

If by such a strategy of rejection of convention and acceptance of direct experience the dream of the individual's worth could materialize, a richer and fuller life for Americans would follow; a paradise would be within reach. American writers, either inspired or disillusioned with the hope of the dignity and worth of the individual, began to shape in literature the form of an American Adam. They placed him in a new garden and the result, even for doubters, was another level of the American dream—the heroic level.

By 1855, believes R. W. B. Lewis (page 1), "the image contrived to embody the most fruitful contemporary ideas was that of the authentic American as a figure of heroic innocence and vast potentialities, poised at the start of a new history." Emerson, Whitman, Thoreau, and others who shared such optimism created a vision of the real American as being emancipated from the past, unblemished by inheritance of taint, and thus new and innocent. They saw him as being filled with vast power or potentiality in his aloneness, his self-reliance, his detachment not from life but from the past,* and as moving in measureless space. Through their heroes, American novelists, tellers of folk tales, and biographers either affirmed, denied, or modified the Adamic vision.

James Fenimore Cooper vivified the American Adam in his Leatherstocking series.† His central character, moving backward in time through the series, was the gallant hero of the sentimental novel transferred to the garden of the forest and there transformed into a noble primitive with such control of nature that the powers of the natural man seemed unlimited. By the time of his appearance in *The Last of the Mohicans,* Natty Bumppo has become Hawkeye, whose intuitive self-reliance and ready inference enable him to solve the problems of a new being in new circumstances. Significantly, he was thus able to save those men and women representing conventional society who are entrusted to his care. And Hawkeye is innately good, although this goodness or innocence is not of a sort that makes him prey for the unscrupulous; his is a wise innocence.

The result of Cooper's art was that Bumppo, placed in a primeval environment, kept only the highest principles and not the trappings of civilization; he embodied the moral ideal of America. Bumppo-become-Hawkeye became a genuine folk hero of the people: As Perry Miller has pointed out, "For years Cooper more than any single figure held up the mirror in which several generations saw the image of

---

*I think this should not be read as meaning that Americans have had no interest in the past; as Daniel Boorstin, *The Americans: The National Experience,* 362-90, has shown, Americans have ardently examined their past in search of national symbols. At the same time, however, the relatively small interest Americans have shown in their genealogical backgrounds seems to me to justify this aspect of Adamism: "As the frequent tendency of the genealogists to defend their efforts suggests, many persons seem to have regarded the whole business as contrary to the true spirit of democracy and most of them, as since, remained indifferent," Wesley Frank Craven, *The Legend of the Founding Fathers,* 99.

†David W. Noble, in *The Eternal Adam and the New World Garden: The Central Myth in the American Novel Since 1830,* 3-24, argues cogently that Cooper meant to indict the notion of an American Adam living in isolation and innocence; throughout his book, Noble distinguishes this Adam from the Eternal Adam, inheritor of the sin of the father of the race. I believe, however, that whatever Cooper's intentions, his hero has been admired as an American Adam.

themselves they most wished to see—a free-ranging individualist."[9] As has been pointed out, the dream of the individual's worth and dignity involved belief in the unlimited powers of average humanity, together with a belief in his virtue. Bumppo-become-Hawkeye was the personification of will over nature; he was not only master of forest, beast, and foe, but he was also unstained by the touch of woman or by the sordid savagery of mercenary whites or depraved red men.

Another new American Adam is Huckleberry Finn, the boy who has engaged the fancy of American businessmen and T. S. Eliot alike. If his prowess in overcoming evildoers lies more in his cunning than in the omnipotence of a Hawkeye, it is perhaps a stronger testament to the powers of the common man. Like the American Adam, Huck seems sprung from nowhere: His mother is never mentioned, and his father appears for only brief moments, never as a shaper of his son but only as another tester of his powers. Likewise, Huck moves in measureless space with the great river his haven of isolation to which he returns for spiritual renewal. He is self-reliant, making his own way in life with only an occasional half-welcome gesture of support from a widow more in need of him than he of her. His innate goodness reveals itself in his reflex-like brotherhood with Jim, the escaped slave. His innocence is more complex, and perhaps more satisfying, than that of Hawkeye. His embrace of evil (as defined by society) in resolving to aid Jim in escaping is, on the one hand, profoundly naïve; on the other hand, his constant pose of naïveté as a defense against the encroachments of a do-gooder guardian, the wiles of a drunken father, or the fraud of a pair of river rapscallions is the epitome of the same durable innocence of Hawkeye. Finally, like the American Adam, Huck keeps the values, without the trappings, of civilization. He can be an altruistic social being, gallant in the best sense of the word, but he cannot stand shoes. The reader's last sight of him is when he leaves civilization for Indian territory.

During the nineteenth century, as Constance Rourke has shown, tellers of folk tales and purveyors of folk humor created a composite figure resulting from the shrewd Yankee, the tall-tale telling frontiersman, and the Negro minstrel. He was a figure whose Adamic power emerged in comic triumph over Old-World culture, or a cruel nature, or evil men. The sense of starting anew was present in this figure's return to first principles. Surrounding him, whether sharp-tongued Yankee or roaring backwoodsman, was the aura of wise innocence, "with a blank mask in common and a similar habit of sporting in public the faults with which they were charged," says Rourke. Finally, in the composite figure was the detachment from time, space, and tradition, typical of the American Adam. Americans were drawn to him because he had been a wanderer and had severed ties. This composite, says Rourke, "embodied a deep-lying mood of disseverances carrying the popular fancy further and further from any fixed or traditional heritage."[10]

Adam in his innocence, power, newness, and detachment was a magnet for the American imagination. He was fascinating because he represented one kind of synthesis of the ideas in the dream of the dignity and worth of the individual. When American writers have magnified one trait of the American Adam, they have, justifiably, denied the warping of the dream.

Robert Montgomery Bird, amplifying the trait of naïve innocence, exposed a gentle Quaker to the brutality of an American jungle and produced a psychopathic avenger aptly named Nathan Slaughter, who thus doomed any dream of naïve innocence for the American Adam. Hawthorne's Dimmesdale is witness to the ravages wrought by a community-wide, repressive innocence. The earlier Melville amplified Adam's hopeful expectancy and sent hero after hero to destruction because of it, until reaching his artistic height in *Moby Dick* where, says Lewis (page 146), he gave "narrative birth to the conflict with evil: that evil against which a spurious and illusory innocence must shatter itself." Present-day deniers of the dream aim their criticism at an hallucinatory hope of a naïve innocence.

American writers have also modified the American Adam's innocence before affirming it. Melville's Billy Budd embodies the Adamic power of innocence and goodness at the cost of his own life; in steady acceptance of his unjust sentence, Billy gradually assumes a Christ-like character. Henry James, writing generally later than Melville, showed his American innocents colliding with evil and developing a new wisdom by adopting a conscious innocence. Christopher Newman, Isabel Archer, and Lambert Strether all went to Europe for their naïve assault upon fastnesses of an older society. Usually, James' characters, bruised but uncrushed, come through the ordeal with considerably more worldly knowledge and a commitment to the course of wise innocence: Newman holds the power to ruin his tormentors and declines to use it; Strether, duped by Chad and his mistress, chooses to lend his honor in support of the compromised woman.

As many Americans were drawn to the Hawkeyes, the Hucks, or the mythical Yankee or frontiersman, others found a representation of the dream in such heroes as those of James—a dream of Adamism not to which one is born, but rather to which one can only be reborn after an experience of evil.

Other Adamic heroes emerged from legends surrounding real people. The Daniel Boone drawn by biographers added a new motif to the dream of the dignity and worth of the individual. True to the Adamic tradition, the Boone drawn by John Filson and John James Audubon is innately good as a powerful and larger-than-life apotheosis of the common man—gigantic (actually, Boone was five feet, eight inches tall) and incapable of uttering untruth. But, in the biographies, Boone is not only Adam but Moses; given his real capacity for leadership, notes Fishwick, "the component parts of the myth were recognizable: . . . a Promised Land beyond the mountains; land-hungry families who considered it an Eden; someone leading the people westward; a lone wanderer guiding his generation on a God-sanctioned mission."[11]

Like the great dream, itself, the nature of a new American Adam was ambiguous. Good, but also aware of the "main chance," his return to innocence could range from naïveté to a conscious choice of the innocent stance, to the use of that stance to win his encounters with an alien tribe. As a figure synthesizing the dream of the individual, however, he fascinated Americans on all levels of society. The wise, reborn Adam of Henry James might find his paradise within himself, but the Adam who embodied the hopes of the masses found his habitat in the new garden of the West, which formed another synthesis of the dream.

The vision of a vast agricultural society, as we have seen, had begun as the common man's dream of his own empire and had found its earliest American expression in words of spokesmen like Crèvecoeur and Lewis Evans. The connection of ideas in the garden dream that grew throughout the nineteenth century included at least three key concepts: the land as a safety valve, the soil as a paradise, and the forests and prairies as givers of virtue.

Adam and Eve had been driven out of the garden. At least as early as the time of Franklin, the American West had promised a haven for their sons and daughters, economic exiles. Hamlin Garland, in his preface to *Jason Edwards,* explained why the associations of the word "West" were "fabulous, mythic, and hopeful": "Whenever the conditions of his native place pressed too hard upon him, the artisan or the farmer turned his face toward the prairies and forests of the West. . . . Thus long before the days of '49, the West had become the Golden West, the land of wealth and Freedom and happiness." The primal pair, driven out of the eastern gate, had come almost full circle to knock at the American western gate of a new paradise.

James Lanman, writing in a September, 1841, issue of *Hunt's Merchants' Magazine,* echoed Crèvecoeur: "The exhilarating atmosphere of a rural life, the invigorating exercise offered by its various occupations, the pure water, the abundance of all the necessaries of subsistence, leading to early and virtuous marriages, all point to this pursuit as best adapted to the comfort of the individual man." That Hamlin Garland would later expose the dream of a pastoral paradise as a cruel nightmare attests only to the power of the vision.

More than all this, the West had the power to imbue its people with unique virtue. It was in the sturdy western yeoman, free of the "pernicious influences" of cities, that Lanman found the defender and promoter of the virtue of the state. In "Farming," Emerson placed the new Adam in his new garden, though not limiting it to the West. The farmer, wrote Emerson,

> stands well on the world—as Adam did, as an Indian
> does, as Homer's heroes, Agamemnon or Achilles, do. He
> is a person whom a poet of any clime—Milton, Firdusi, or
> Cervantes—would appreciate as being a piece of the old
> Nature, comparable to sun and moon, rainbow and flood;
> because he is, as all natural persons are, representative
> of Nature as much as these.
>   That uncorrupted behavior which we admire in
> animals and in young children belongs to him . . . the
> man who lives in the presence of Nature.

In 1903, Frederick Jackson Turner rehearsed anew the theme of a beneficent influence emanating from the West to produce not only a paradise but also supremely virtuous common men: "This great American West took them to her bosom, taught them a new way of looking upon the destiny of the common man, trained them in adaptation to the conditions of the New World, to the creation of new institutions to meet new needs." The mother West, continued Turner, dowered these new institutions not only with "material treasures" but also with the "ennobling influence that the fierce love of freedom, the strength that came from hewing out a home, making a school and a church, and creating a higher future for his family, furnished to the pioneer."[12]

The frontier thus became the Eden where the common man as the American Adam could develop his talent, nourish his virtue, and fulfill himself. The grand goal of the dream, a return to an ideal state, was explicit. Henry Nash Smith believes that the picture of the West as a paradise was so strongly a part of the American imagination that to the end of the nineteenth century it represented the core of the nation and "long survived as a force in American thought and politics."[13]

(In 1839 were born the parents of Will Rogers: Mary America Schrimsher was one-fourth Cherokee, the daughter of Martin Schrimsher and Elizabeth Hunt Gunter, whose mother had been a member of the Paint Clan; Clem Vann Rogers was three-sixteenths Cherokee, the son of Robert Rogers II and of Sallie Vann, great-granddaughter of Major Downing, who had immigrated from Ireland over a century before. In that year of 1839, Emerson was establishing himself solidly as an essayist and lecturer; Thoreau had finished Harvard only two years before and had begun his stint as a school teacher, in the best tradition of the "sturdy lad from Vermont"; Herman Melville, too, was teaching, his trip to the South Seas still two years away; Walt Whitman, in his twentieth year, was writing for newspapers in New York; four-year-old Mark Twain moved to Hannibal, Missouri; and Cooper was but two years away from finishing the portrait of his American Adam in the last of the Leatherstocking series.)

JUST AS the family line of Will Rogers experienced its growth during the genesis of the dream, much in his actual surroundings was suitable to effect in him the character of the new Adam. The land to which his people had been driven for refuge itself seemed to be a Paradise regained. At the time of Cherokee settlement, what is now northeastern Oklahoma was reminiscent of Eden, with plentiful rain, sweet air, and gold-suffused light. Flocks of parakeets spread their plumage over the bottom lands as they fed on sycamore balls; quail and prairie chickens swarmed in the tall grass; wild turkeys gave their distinctive calls. And, like Adam, the children of Sequoyah named the land with melodic syllables: Tahlequah, Tahlonteeskee, and Cooweescoowee—the last being the district of Rogers' birth. He assuredly did not look upon the nearly virgin scene that spread itself before the Cherokee exiles around 1838. But enough of it remained to give him a sense of a new country and new beginnings, especially in contrast to the population centers of Kansas City, St. Louis, and Chicago, where he was to visit. The Indian Territory of the Cherokee Nation was a good place for testing the myth of the garden. "The past," wrote Collings in his study of the Rogers ranch, "had no part in the Cooweescoowee country."[14]

Perhaps more important to the development of Rogers' stance as the new American Adam was his exposure to the customs and manner of living coming from the mixture of Indian and white cultures in his family. Descending from white men who had put behind them the society of the Old World, and being born of Indian great-grandmothers,

Rogers could be expected to catch what well may have been accompanying attitudes of detachment from the past, facing to the future, and living in readiness to front anything that might present itself. In Will Rogers' family were influences that would produce an Adamic sense of ironic detachment strong enough to enable its possessor to see the humor in something happening "in all seriousness." When, years later, the time would come that a burglar was to make off with Rogers' savings, he would try to comfort his young wife by illustrating his family's Adamism. His wife, Betty Blake Rogers, told the story in her biography of Rogers:

> I was brokenhearted. Will wanted to laugh it off and tried
> to console me with the story of what a good sport his
> sister Maude had been when her house burned. They had
> been curing meat in the smokehouse that day and a
> spark had blown to the roof of the main house, which
> was being painted. The fresh paint caught fire and in a
> moment the whole place was in flames, with the painters
> rolling and jumping from the roof. Though Maude had
> lost everything, the antics of the painters were so
> ludicrous that she saw the funny side of it and laughed.
> And she always laughed afterward whenever the fire was
> mentioned. I listened to the story and admired Maude's
> fortitude, but still I couldn't laugh.[15]

Whether this saving grace of humor was a gift of the Cherokees to the new man that Will Rogers was can never be ascertained, but the objectivity and detachment that it provided in his character were appropriate to the character of a forward-looking Adam.

Besides the Edenic landscape and the family Adamism, boyhood odysseys may have contributed to the natural man in Will Rogers. There were all-day fishing trips to the perch-filled Four-Mile Creek on lazy, sun-and-shade-filled days when time slowed down; there were joyous Frostian ridings of "buckin' " sapling trees; there were days of swimming in the Verdigris River, nights of sleeping out under the Coo-weescoowee sky, mornings and afternoons of pony racing across the prairie country. The world of Rogers' roamings had all the appeal of Tom Sawyer's Jackson Island. "To young Will Rogers," one biographer has written, "growing up on his father's range, that frontier was the garden spot of the world."[16]

Out of all this came Rogers' ability to live a complex life simply, the epitome of Thoreau's dreamed-of return to the state of natural man. In her book, Rogers' observing wife, who was to watch him live for more than a quarter of a century, has reported on his never-ending zest for life:

> Will had superb health, great physical energy and mental vitality; and along with this, an inner serenity that was seldom ruffled. Through his whole life, including those years when his activities multiplied and every minute was crowded with action, he was unhurried, and worry was unknown to him. If things went wrong they just went wrong and were forgotten with a new day. . . .
> That was Will's secret. He either worked at something or he rested. There was no spending of nervous energy in worry or the futile threshing of a problem. When he had a job to do, he did it. But when the job was done he was able to turn off a faucet of energy or to turn it in a different direction (pages 23, 25-26).

Will Rogers was always to retain the quality of Adamic boyishness. As an adult, he would return to his California ranch from long journeys with all the interest of a boy with an ever-new toy; he rode, roped, and played polo not as a devotee of physical fitness but rather as a young spirit reveling in the strength of the body.

Living in a new land, coming from a new people, possessing a strong forward thrust born in turn of a basic good humor and an undying sense of the newness of life, Will Rogers was the new American Adam. Concomitantly, the man from Oologah had a trust in the goodness of people. One revealing anecdote, related by his wife, tells how the young couple had wanted to raise cash by selling a valuable diamond ring; Rogers entrusted it for sale to a man to whom he had barely been introduced by another acquaintance, a fellow by the name of Brady. Rogers did not even know the name of the prospective buyer. Mrs. Rogers was amazed at her husband's naïveté:

"Don't worry," he told me, "he's all right; Brady knows a
friend of his." More weeks passed and I decided that Will
might at least get some much-needed worldly wisdom in
exchange for his big yellow diamond. As more weeks
went by, even Will had begun to wonder. But one day an
envelope arrived and we learned the name of the racing
man. It was written on the bottom of a check for $1,000.
That was all the envelope contained. Will was not
surprised. He took for granted that every man was
honest, until he proved himself otherwise (pages 99-100).

Later in this study, Rogers' belief in the goodness of people
and his trust in the powers of the common man will be
revealed through his own words. Too, a later examination
of the conditions that may have contributed to Rogers' belief in the dream of freedom and equality will demonstrate
how they would have likewise contributed to his adherence
to the dream of the dignity and worth of the individual.

Gradually, then, a constellation of ideas on the worth and
dignity of the individual had grown in America; in American families, including that of Will Rogers, were members
suited by temperament and shaped by circumstances to live
up, to some degree, to the traits of the culture hero, the
American Adam. What of the status of the dream of Adam
in the period of the twenties and thirties, when Rogers'
influence reached nationwide?

IN GENERAL, it was a time requiring an affirmation of the
dream of the dignity and worth of the individual. During
the decade after the war, the dream of the sturdy yeoman
farmer seemed illusory: The farm was no Eden.

Between 1920 and late 1921, wheat in Minneapolis
dropped from $2.94 a bushel to $.92; good beef steers went
from nearly 15¢ a pound to only 7¢; cotton and corn suffered
similar declines. The value of all agricultural products
plunged by a full third between 1920 and 1921, and this price
drop, coupled with high costs of production, was catastrophic. Foreclosures increased. The spiritual descendants
of that famous American farmer, who had seen in the yeo-

man of the New World a new man, knew that something was wrong and deluged the Secretary of Agriculture with letters from sharecropper and big commercial farmer alike. They wrote their bankers, too, often mixing pathos and humor, as did a Montana farmer to his banker:

> I got your letter about what I owe you. Now be patient. I
> ain't forgot you. Please wait. . . . If this was judgment
> and you were no more prepared to meet your Maker than
> I am to meet your account, you sure would have to go to
> Hell. Trusting you will do this, I remain, sincerely
> yours.[17]

True, by the middle of the decade, farm prices had recovered to a higher level than in the period of good farm times prior to 1914; more tractors, trucks, stationary engines, and electricity were in use. Yet the farmer suffered by comparison to the purchasing power of other groups in the economy. Because of continuing rises in taxes and declining land values, price rises were actually not so great as they appeared. "Now they [the financiers suffering in the crash of 1929] know what the farmer has been up against for eight years," Will Rogers would say, and farmers would recognize a kindred spirit in his saying it. Somehow the powers of the individual on the farm seemed limited by shadowy figures manipulating prices on the futures market—figures that denied the dream of goodness of man by interposing themselves between the common man (as farmer) and his hopes of self-fulfillment.

The twenties were uneasy times in other American places, too. In Washington, events between 1920 and 1924 challenged both the dream of the goodness of man and that of the common man's powers to derive good uses out of the worst servants. The Harding Administration was scandal-ridden and corrupt; heading the list was the Sinclair-Doheny scheme that would have taken a $200,000,000 profit from the government. One agrees with John Hicks, who in his *Republican Ascendancy* infers that "similar but undisclosed transactions were probably a commonplace of big business."[18] Was it, as Hicks suggests, that people among the average fallows took this sort of thing for granted as another aspect of normalcy? Or was it that Americans turned aside to avoid the pain of looking deeply into what might have appeared to be the grave of hopes for that "more perfect union" so optimistically anticipated at the birth of the country? Perhaps Americans felt they simply had no way to control such events. To answer such questions would be to test the factual working out of the dream of the powers and goodness of the individual in America.

There were, at any rate, writers greatly disturbed by the realities of postwar America. Growing up during a prewar time when a general world movement toward peace and goodness among mankind was taken for granted, they had sallied forth to set affairs right during the great war, only to suffer cultural shock in peacetime by rediscovering an America in which a sense of self-righteousness was coupled with a great appetite for war profits. At this point, writes Spiller, "they took up, with all the enthusiasm they had put into the military crusade, a battle for literary and moral integrity both in America and in themselves."[19] Thus, dreamers of dreams at heart, they produced (in their efforts to confront America with what they understood to be her own shortcomings) the myths of "bitter America" and of "the lost generation." Their messages were to challenge most of the categories of the American dream. Appropriate to the vision of the power and dignity of the individual is the appearance in 1922 of T. S. Eliot's *Wasteland,* picturing not the new garden, but a desert, not the new Adam in his power and goodness, but modern man caught in death-in-life, acting out his share of meaninglessness. Where were the powers and goodness of the individual visible?

If individuals read such writers (and, probably, the majority of Americans did not) the dream of the individual may have seemed challenged. Americans did, however, read the chain newspapers of the time, in which any belief in the innate goodness of people seemed refuted. Sensational murders and kidnappings, together with robberies and sex crimes, received headline attention. In this enterprise of heralding the violence of American life, new tabloids provided assistance for those who could not read by printing grisly illustrations of man's inhumanity. "The newspapers have dug up another sensational murder trial

—man and woman and dead husband," Will Rogers wrote, late in 1927. "Watch the sales double."[20]

Somehow, too, Americans got the idea that the younger generation was engaged in actively redefining natural goodness—if Freud's doctrines on sex made it natural and if anything natural was good. To Americans who could not so view what was considered a part of a revolution in morals, "the fact remained that many young adults not only talked about sex with an abandon that shocked their elders, but indulged their desires freely without benefit of clergy," remarks Hicks (page 181).

Nevertheless, notwithstanding governmental corruption, financial greed, crime, and a revolution in morals, most Americans probably derived their enjoyment from mahjongg, crossword puzzles, radio, movies, and automobile trips—leading the life of the "big Normal Majority," as Will Rogers would phrase it. By 1929, somewhat fewer than 12,000,000 families had radios; 95,000,000 Americans a week were movie-goers and saw on the screen the affirmation of the worth and dignity of the individual that the papers and radio news broadcasts often seemed to deny. For there in the magic of the darkened theatres appeared Douglas Fairbanks and Mickey Mouse, each in his own way affirming the power of the individual over events by, as Fishwick (page 229) has pointed out, means of "activism, pluck, and ingenuity."

Other heroes moving on the stage of real events appeared before the people. There was Coolidge, Adamic in what was perceived as being his simple manner of living, his rugged honesty, and his detachment and silence. "The average American had heard that his fathers had these virtues," Gamaliel Bradford has said, "and had made a great nation by means of them."[21] There was, thus, something reassuring about Coolidge. In Lindbergh, hero-worshippers in America found embodiment of many aspects of the American dream, but relevant to the dream of the individual's worth and dignity was "Lindy's" celebration as the American Adam. "By singling out the fact that Lindbergh rode alone, and by naming him a pioneer of the frontier, the public projected its sense that the source of America's strength lay somewhere in the past and that Lindbergh somehow meant that America must look backward in time to rediscover some lost virtue," wrote a student of American culture.[22]

For not only had events of the decade possibly caused Americans to look to the movies and public figures as icons of ideals from the young American past, but also an anti-Adam had gradually begun to emerge as rival to the great culture hero. His artistic beginnings, perhaps, lie in the appearance, before the war, of Mark Twain's Satan, central figure of *The Mysterious Stranger.* The average man, in Satan's eyes, is a tiny, inconsequential, wriggling mass of protoplasm, worse than beasts in his cruelty to other men precisely because at the same time he claims possession of a conscience, supposedly placing him above beasts. This worm not only is not good, but he has no power whatsoever to order the events of his own life; he is, like the universe, simply an illusion. The amoral Satan, by comparison, is much more admirable than man. Then, during the twenties, through newspaper columns, gradually emerged a real-life anti-Adam. Defying federal enforcement of an unpopular prohibition law, escaping plots against his life on the part of rival crime syndicates, he seemed alone, invincible, admirable: He was Al Capone. "What's the matter with an age," Will Rogers would ask, "when our biggest gangster is our greatest national interest?"[23]

Thus, during the twenties, the times called for an embodiment of the dream of the worth and dignity of the individual. During the thirties, when the great famine came, citizens cried out for such affirmation. Where were the dignity and worth as the hungry in the cities stood in line for bread or soup; as lonely men left families and walked or rode forth on the quest not for holy grail but for gainful employment—only to be lost or followed later by wives and children with nowhere to go except to look for the father; as farmer and factory worker looked with hate at the occupants of the big Packards roaring by on highway or city street; as professional men, still wearing dress suits for lack of work clothes, lined up for any kind of work, including ditchdigging; as there seemed no end to the suffering in winters and no way of counting human misery? Moreover, above the streets and garbage heaps, from the theology of the emerging Protestant Neo-orthodoxy came the reinterpretation of man's original sin, with a consequent lessening of the powers of the individual; here was the fallen Adam, the shorn Samson.

Not until 1936 would Carl Sandburg affirm the dream in his creation of Paul Bunyan in *The People, Yes* as a symbol of recovery of the ideal of human dignity from all the ravages of want and hopelessness; not until 1939 would John Steinbeck express his faith in the powers of average humanity in *Grapes of Wrath*.[24] Thus, such reaffirmations of faith in the dream were yet to appear when Will Rogers was talking with and writing for his Americans.

IN HIM, through the twenties and thirties, Rogers' public found alive the common man's dream of the dignity and worth of the individual. One way they saw the dream alive in him was in reading his publicity in news stories, printed interviews, and magazine features, as well as by hearing anecdotes circulated by word of mouth. More importantly, they found a voice of the American dream when they heard him speak or read his columns.

The publicity that Rogers received (and virtually all of it came without the aid of press agent) enabled him to appear to his public as an American Adam. The public's picture of him was of the eternal boy; he was the natural man, the optimistic Adam, the wise innocent, the true friend to comrades, and a self-reliant, Emersonian Jack-of-all-trades. Public knowledge of his character was refreshing and reassuring in the twenties and thirties.

From what people read and heard about Will Rogers, he appeared to keep the joyous exuberance of boyhood. A 1930 article in the mass circulation *American Magazine* made the statement directly. "Will is only a child himself. He would rather play with kids than sit around and talk with grownups. He never has become an adult—and in that lies much of his charm."[25] Stories of his joyous boyishness circulated freely. On one movie lot the incident was told of his roping a great Dane, with which he was on the best of terms by virtue of their having worked together on a motion picture. The only trouble was that the dog learned to take cover from the lasso by hiding under a clothesline. "Here was a problem," reported Charles Dwyer, who told the story, "and Rogers worked toward its solution. After many trials he found that he could cast his rope over the line in such a manner that the loop swung down underneath and lassoed the dog. The dog was crestfallen but Rogers was jubilant."[26]

No roping problem could deter him. On a windy day, according to the story, Rogers spent three quarters of an hour trying to lasso, with a too-light rope in a high wind, a movie lot statue of a horse. When he finally got the wind-wafted line around the target, he jumped with delight into his car parked on the lot, drove around the area several times, and happily honked the horn to help him announce his success to the whole company. Stories of his eternal boyishness probably circulated wherever he went. Moreover, the breath of zest and enthusiasm he gave to all his pursuits would have been apparent to all who read or heard of them and would have added depth to the image of the eternal boy.

If the public picture had stopped here, of course, Will Rogers would have simply seemed an example of arrested development, but adding to his Adamism was his role as the natural man. Rogers dropped into many newspaper offices and cafes across the country to meet the "real bird" and get the local slant on current events. On such occasions, his appeal lay in his natural Adamism. "It wasn't so much a matter of wise-cracking or cracker-box humor, although Rogers' remarks were full of amusing and pat allusions, as it was the perfect naturalness, simplicity and above all the genuine human kindliness of the man," wrote an observer of one such occasion.[27] Wherever Rogers went, he projected the impression of a man who simply did as he pleased, pleasing others by what he did. "He's an old oak, meant to grow in its own way, and any attempt to train it would spoil it," said the article in *American Magazine* (page 62). "His entire success lies in the fact that he is just himself." The ways in which Rogers manifested this selfness lay chiefly in his personal habits (about which the public was and is apparently insatiably curious). He liked to wear old clothes; he generally needed a haircut; he "snorted" at conventions. "Clothes mean nothing to him," Betty Rogers told readers in the interview. "If he heard that the Prince of Wales was across the street, even though Will might be in pajamas and slippers, he would jump up and run across the street and say, 'Hello, Prince. How are you?' " (page 113). In doing as he pleased, however, Rogers kept to the simple pleasures, in line not only with the rural part of his constituency, but also with the spirit of Thoreau. He rode, roped, and talked with folks. When George M. Cohan spoke of Rogers' naturalness on a 1935 national broadcast to honor the memory of the Oklahoman he was only echoing a picture that his public already had of him:

> Rogers was a natural. I think that Will Rogers was the
> most natural man I ever met. He was a natural humorist,
> a natural actor, he was a natural success. I heard a great
> man of the theatre at a dinner one night—a dinner
> tendered to Will Rogers—say that he considered Will
> Rogers the most successful success he had ever known,
> and he qualified that statement by adding, that he had
> never met a member of the theatrical profession who
> envied Will Rogers' success.[28]

Interfused with the boyishness and the naturalness was Will Rogers' public stance as the forward-looking, optimistic Adam (a representation as appropriate to the believer in progress as was the natural man appropriate to the American Adam). The mass American audience of *The Literary Digest* had access to an English review that was quoted in the American publication. There, Rogers' forward-looking optimism showed in his energy and confidence. To the English critic, Rogers was "an incarnation of the artful, absurd, bubbling energy of the Middle West, quite sure of itself." Another English writer, quoted by Donald Day, had seen the forward-looking Adam. In Rogers was "the whole American pose," consisting of "the experimental zest which will not accept tradition, or what other people have done, the approachableness masquerading as antipathy to race or joy of mongrelism, that Frankness which only the stupid will mistake for bad manners, the charm which seeks to disguise itself under a show of impudence, the obvious sincerity of the belief in world salvation through 'boost' and 'pep'. . . ." In 1935, a writer for *The New Republic* judged that Rogers' persona had been one "moving toward a final triumph over everything that was new or fancy or politically not right."[29] How many Americans were also aware of this Adamic sense of triumph surrounding the public figure of Rogers? They had, at least, magazine writers who perceived it and wanted them to see it.

As can be seen, Will Rogers had in his public status the appearance of the hopeful, innocent Adam. Those who presented his picture to the public made it clear that this was a wise innocence, however. "He gives the impression of being the crossroads general merchandise store talkers of a continent rolled into one," wrote an American critic in 1925. Actually, he concluded, Rogers was "an expert satirist masquerading as a helpless, inoffensive zany."[30] Many of the press releases for his lecture tour of 1926-1927 contained a paragraph making essentially the same point:

> Tall, gaunt, rather awkward in his movements, to see
> Will Rogers for the first time one might imagine him to
> be a farmer taking in the sights. Yet Rogers has seen life
> from all angles. He has known princes and paupers, he
> has been sought after by politicians with all sorts of
> offers to lend his wit to their cause. Rogers, however,
> prefers to stand on his own platform for truth as he sees
> it. Few Americans have caught the faith of the American
> people as he has.[31]

The posture projected by Rogers of the wise innocent was enough to convince the American people of his identification as the wisely-innocent Adam.

He appeared so to his public in another way: A seasoning of goodnaturedness, together with his mask of ignorance, allowed him to be appealing in spite of the satiric barbs he cast. "He did lots of good by speaking the truth," Fred Stone, a fellow performer, would remember, "and it didn't offend because no matter how the truth struck home, it was always said in such a humorous way that you laughed with him."[32] In this sense, perhaps, Rogers' wise foolishness was in the strain of many court jesters.

About his public biography clung the essence of an earthy goodness that added to the impression of a living American Adam. He was clearly a gentleman, found an editorial writer for *Commonweal,* in 1935. In 1928, the single act of cancelling his own more lucrative lecture contracts to substitute for the plane-injured Fred Stone, and make possible the opening of a Stone Broadway musical, showed his goodness and love of comrades. Newspaper writers did not skimp in their praise. One wrote:

> No, it isn't money that means anything in this sacrifice. It is the prompting of one man's affection for another that is the big thing. It is the urge of Will Rogers' friendship for his injured pal that counts. It is his willingness to give up something he'd rather do to save the Stone show that makes it an unusual event on Broadway. And so Rogers emerges again as a big man in show business and in fact, an impulsive, generous, clean-souled sentimentalist.[33]

Thus, Americans had knowledge through the press and through word of mouth of Will Rogers' devotion to friends; it was the quality that lent warmth to the larger benefactions that would identify him to the public as both the free individual meeting his responsibilities and as the steward of success.

Finally, the public knew him as an emblem of Emerson's sturdy lad who tried all professions and always, like a cat, landed right-side-up. From the time of the first feature article on Rogers, which had appeared in 1915, nearly every sizeable story included the outlines of his versatility: his ranching days, his travels, wild West shows, vaudeville, and the rest. No neater picture of the new Adam as Jack-of-all-trades was given, however, than that in the widely-read *Scientific American* in 1929:

> During his amazing career from cowboy to diplomat, Will Rogers has garnered many distinctive titles. He has been billed as a broncho-buster, lariat-twirler, circus rider, vaudeville actor, musical-comedy comedian, monolog artist, film star, journalist, lecturer, writer of advertisements, after-dinner speaker, mayor, presidential candidate, congressman-at-large, and unofficial ambassador.[34]

Will Rogers was, in his publicity, the American Adam. His public picture as free cowboy, hero of the dream of freedom, was simply the amplification of the American Adam's liberation; when he embodied the benefactor, hero of the dream of success, he transposed the individual's concern for others to the success dream; when he emerged from newsprint as a hero of progress, he modulated the theme of the new Adam's forward-looking to a major key.

Will Rogers also was known to live in a way that further identified him with the dream of the dignity and worth of the individual. He showed that he believed in the value and powers of the common man by the nature of his personal encounters on his many journeys. Governor Frank F. Merriam of California would in 1935 recall many such meetings in which he had watched Rogers and "the folks." "He was always happiest," the Governor recalled, "while exchanging cordial courtesies with the common people whom he enjoyed so much and served so well." One possible reason for that enjoyment appeared when the Governor added, "He constantly saw evidences of culture in people with whom he associated in work or play even though they might be far removed from the metropolitan centers of social refinement."[35]

By such behavior among people whom he met, Rogers not only showed them that he thought they were worthy of respect, but also symbolized the dream of equality, as will be seen later.

Given the outlets of mass communication, and being disposed to be at one with the great American dream, Rogers could and did receive publicity that pictured him as the dream personified. Most importantly, his own messages, amplified by the mass media until they were potentially available to almost every American ear or eye, merged him with the American dream. Part of the time, he identified with the dream by speaking directly to its values; part of the time, he became one with the dream by telling of personal incidents that accorded with the action corollaries of the vision. In both cases, his identification was on the material level—in the former, it was *directly* material to the dream and in the latter, *indirectly* material to it. At the same time, in the way Rogers talked or wrote, the form of his presentation provided an identification with the great dream.[36] Thus, by means of formal identification, Rogers at times could actually look like the personification of the American dream. Coupled with what the public knew of his life through publicity, his own words provided the second great means for making Will Rogers a representation of the hopeful vision for his national audience. Over the years from

1922 until 1935, his discursive conversation with his public on the American dream gave him a high degree of source credibility. For purposes of exposition, it is time to render that rambling discourse into a systematic analysis.

WILL ROGERS was dedicated to the vision of man as being intrinsically worthy. Growing up as he had in a new country in which there was no overcrowding to cheapen human life, living as the king of creatures in that new country, and being himself the unique product of the mixing of New and Old World cultures, he could reasonably be expected to value the unique individual. If such a dedication to the worth of the individual might be called American innocence, Rogers often combined with it a sidelong, wise glance that made him the wise innocent. Comments resulted such as that expressing belief in the generosity and goodness of the American people, whom he believed would forgive anything except stupidity. If he was innocent in not understanding the hullabaloo over a football player's running the wrong way, he was wise in seeing that what counted was the fact that the boy's mind wasn't standardized. The over-all effect, therefore, was that the saw of Rogers' words had teeth all the sharper because they were "cross-set" in their wise innocence.

At times, he stated head on a commitment to the powers and virtue of the common man. "No man wants to admit that he is average," Rogers once wrote, perhaps aware that Americans dreamed of their limitless potentiality. "Did you see the picture and specifications of the average man they located last year? That took all the joy out of wanting to be average," he added. It is clear in such a comment that being average meant being homogeneous; Rogers had little ever to say in praise of such a concept of the common man. "I never did go in much for this typical American stuff," he wrote in a daily squib.[37] He preferred, rather, to talk about what he liked to call the "big Normal Majority"—the generality of "little" people who could not be categorized except by their powers of common sense, of balanced reason.

> This American Animal that I thought I had roped here
> is nothing but the big honest Majority, that you might
> find in any Country. He is not a Politician. He is not a
> 100 percent American. He is not any organization, either
> uplift or downfall. . . . He hasn't denounced anything. . . .
> He don't seem to be simple enough minded to believe
> that EVERYTHING is right and he don't appear Cuckoo
> enough to think that EVERYTHING is wrong. He don't
> seem to be a Prodigy, and he don't seem to be a Simp. In
> fact, all I can find out about him is that he is just
> NORMAL.[38]

In these people, whether small town residents, farmers, ranchers, or, later, members of the nation's army of unemployed, Rogers apparently found great strength and powers. "We got some great people in this country," he wrote, "and they aint all on Wall Street, or at Luncheon Clubs, or in the Movies or in the Senate."[39] Many of these great, little people were small city, small town, or rural folk. In the fall of 1925, Rogers began the first of a series of annual solo tours that took him from one end of America to the other. Later, he seemed impressed on two relevant levels by the little people's powers.

First, he expressed admiration for their acuity of judgment. "Read? Say, the audiences in the smaller towns make a monkey out of the big cities for knowing what is going on in the world. They know and read everything." Further, these Americans retained their powers of independent thought, Rogers said. "You can kid about the old rubes that sat around the cracker barrel, spit in the stove, and fixed the nation, but they were all doing their own thinking. They didn't have their minds made up by some propagandist speaker at the 'Get Nowhere' Luncheon Club."[40] Such sentiment accorded well with the dream of the garden, with its sturdy yeoman as its hero, and therefore would harmonize with the agrarian dream of freedom.

Second, Rogers expressed a belief in the little people because of their powers of stamina. During the years of the locust,[41] during the times of twenty-five cent wheat and nickel beef, of choking dust that drifted like snow along fence lines and on the lee side of barns and homes, during those times that in lusher farm areas would lead to futile farm holidays, he kept in touch with the little people. "When you ever have any doubt as to what might happen in these United States," he wrote, "go to the country and talk with the people and you will come back reassured." During the time of scourging in the cities, when those who were worst-off scavenged for garbaged vegetables and salvageable meat, Rogers stated his perception of their powers of stamina. "Many, many people out of work, some even in actual want, yet carrying on in confidence, and in hope. When the little fellow, that is actually in want, can have faith in his government, by golly the big ones should certainly carry on, for they have never missed a meal so far." And again: "Fear has never come from the fellow with no job or no food. He has stood it wonderful. I doubt if a parallell [sic] will be found where millions hung on with such continued hope and patience as in this country."[42] Rogers had seen these qualities of judgment and stamina in the big normal majority years before, in the time of abundance; he had seen that a time would come when crisis years would summon all the greatness of the common man:

> No element, no Party, not even Congress or the Senate can hurt this Country now; it's too big. There are too many men just like those Dog Team drivers and too many Women like that Nurse up in Nome [who by combined efforts prevented a diphtheria epidemic] for anything to ever stampede this old Continent of ours. . . .
> Even when our next War comes we will through our shortsightedness not be prepared, but that won't be anything fatal. The real energy and minds of the normal majority will step in and handle it and fight it through to a successful conclusion. A War didn't change it before. It's just the same as it was, and always will be, because it is founded on right and even if everybody in Public life tried to ruin it they couldn't. This Country is not where it is today on account of any man. It is here on account of the real Common Sense of the big Normal Majority.[43]

Besides reflecting optimism for the future and thus being relevant to a dream of progress, such a statement is reminiscent of Whitman's belief that the powers of the common man enabled him to derive "good uses, somehow, out of any sort of servant in office." To be able to bring good out of evil is to be touched, at least, by deific power. Rogers spoke of the potential of the common man in America, appearing to be consubstantial with those who dreamed of the inherent greatness of the private citizen.

He did not speak of the infinite powers of man in the abstract. According to him, for instance, the big normal majority was keeping its sense of balance amid the partisan uproar over the effects of prohibition. He said he wanted the viewpoint of unemployed men on some of the government depression commissions, and he voiced approval of the levelheadedness of San Franciscans under the stress of the general strike of 1934. Rogers' words, in the context of events calling for affirmation of the dream of the dignity and worth of the individual, increased his authority, and he gained power by proving the potentialities of the common man. His words helped establish his emerging image as the dream-alive and made his imaged smile seem admiring and approving. They also helped identify him with the vision of the goodness of the common man in the dream of individual dignity.

Rogers gained the reputation of being one who attacked foibles, whether possessors of those frailities were congressmen, senators, big businessmen, preachers, celebrities, or the general public. Yet he never consistently vented Swiftian savagery toward the Yahoos; he was never so blackly pessimistic regarding the nobility and goodness of man as had been Mark Twain. Instead, without being a pollyanna, he concentrated on the better side of humanity. In his writings and talks, he expressed a belief in the goodness of the common man in two chief ways, through the concept of innate goodness and through his attention to instances of virtue.

First, in the tradition of Rousseau and his American followers, Rogers said that the man freed from the deteriorating influences of corrupt modern society is unspoiled, naturally good and happy. And if such a view would seem to contradict the dream of progress, it simply mirrors similar tensions within the constellation of ideas in the great dream itself.

Will Rogers

> I doubt very much if Civilization (so called) helped
> generosity. I bet the old cave man would divide his raw
> meat with you as quick as one of us will ask a down and
> out to go in have a meal with us. Those old boys or girls
> would rip off a wolf skin breech clout and give you half
> of it quicker than a Ph.D. would slip you his umbrella.
> Civilization hasent done much but make you wash your
> teeth, and in those days eating and gnawing on bones and
> meat made tooth paste unnecessary.[44]

The noble savage was also happy, not merely engaged in the pursuit of happiness. On the occasion of being asked by Will Durant for a statement of his "philosophy of living," Rogers typed his reply in open letter style to Durant. "There aint nothing to life but satisfaction," he began. "If you want to ship off fat beef cattle at the end of their existence, you got to have em satisfied on the range. Indians and primitive races were the highest civilized, because they were more satisfied, and they depended less on each other, and took less from each other." How did the present compare? "We couldn't live a day without depending on everybody. So our civilization has given us no liberty or independence."[45]

Such statements on the goodness and happiness of the natural man could appeal to the ambivalence with which Americans regarded their spiraling technology. Perhaps every American who had longed to take a Huck Finn trip down the Mississippi in those depression days agreed with Rogers when he wrote in his daily wire in February, 1930, "The more you see of civilization, the more you feel that those old cavemen about had the right dope."[46]

Rogers strongly implied the presence of decadence from the primitive ideal in "so-called civilized" members of society when compared to "primitive" individuals. On the other hand, he portrayed the goodness of his cultural contemporaries.

The second way in which Rogers identified materially with the dream of the virtue of the common man was his publication of instances of Americans' concern for their fellow men, a goodness of the highest sort. Many times in his career Rogers was to speak or write like the following, uttered in support of a Community Chest drive, as people all over the United States gathered to hear him and Herbert

Hoover on an all-network radio broadcast. "I'll bet you that every town and city comes through," Americans heard Rogers say, and perhaps imagined him before the microphone—hat on and cud of chewing gum rolling in his jaws. "I have seen lots of audiences and heard lots of appeals, but I have yet to see one where the people knew the need, and the cause was there, that they didn't come through—even Europe who hates us and thinks we are arrogant, bad mannered and everything else, but they will tell you that we are liberal, dog-gone it, our folks are liberal."[47]

Dispatches for his string of newspapers often attested to the virtue of the "big Normal Majority."

> Right here in Memphis today over twenty-five policemen went to a hospital and volunteered to give blood transfusions to a kid that was near death. I know that I am out of order in speaking of the good things that cops do, but I am one of the old-fashioned people who believes if somebody pounced on me I could holler for one and he would come and help me out without me having to pay him anything.
>
> The poor fellows can't catch many criminals as our towns have them too busy marking cars that have been parked too long.[48]

On occasion, Rogers would blend other categories of the great dream with that of the worth of the individual. In a daily column showing the goodness of some of the former delinquents whom police had once managed to catch, he stirred in a strong flavor of the success dream:

> The most human thing I read in the papers today, or this month. The reform school in New Jersey gave a home coming and alumni meeting where over two hundred men who had been there as boys, lots of them now prominent, came back and told what they were doing. Some brought their wives and families with 'em. One told that he served five years there for larceny, and was now a big contractor installing burglar alarms in banks, and was bonded for $150,000.
>
> It didn't give their names, but it ought to, for I believe it would endear every one of their standing in their home communities. It would at least be a change from that old success formula, "I started as a newsboy."[49]

Rogers was identifying with heroes of progress, as well as with those who trusted the basic virtue of the common man, when he told of the big-heartedness of the "boys" on the Western Air Express who bought toys and clothes and air-dropped them for Christmas to an isolated western ranch family that had lost the father.

Will Rogers did not use the language of transcendentalism to state the dream of individual goodness; he wrote as though he had never heard of Rousseau or Whitman, and his own flights to the wildernesses of Mexico or to friendly ranches were probably only coincidences with, and not echoes of, Thoreau's sacramental idylls. Nevertheless, he wrote and said much in the general tenor of those dreamers of the dream; his words on the goodness of the common man had about them the breath of experience with nature. His faith, like that of Father Duffy's, seemed to be in humanity. If Rogers satirized foibles of humankind, he apparently did not do so in despair of the basic worth and virtue of people. If the common man had powers of judgment and stamina and possessed an innate goodness then, according to the dream, his self-fulfillment should follow if given the opportunity.

In performing the action corollaries of the dream, the ideal American should also reject whatever of the past stifled the individual, should seek and trust experience on all its levels, and then realize to a degree his highest development as a man as one who possessed the wisdom born of wise innocence, who kept a sense of irrepressible life for himself and who could also feel regard and devotion for others. Rogers used words that depicted a commitment to this program of action. In writing about his actions, he identified with the indirect level of the dream of the individual, and at the same time emerged as a hero of that vision.

"If every history or books on old things was thrown in the river. . . ." The word-twirling cowboy from Oklahoma seemed to his readers to turn away from the past in the best manner of the American Adam seeking his own fulfillment.

The past, for many Americans from Samuel Clemens to Henry James to Will Rogers, was bound up chiefly with Europe, with its layers and levels of custom, tradition, hierarchy, and achievement. On a trip to the Continent in 1926,

Rogers visited France, Germany, Italy, and Switzerland, besides spending a good bit of time in England and Ireland. His reactions to the past as present in Europe were reminiscent of those of other "innocents abroad." Works of art, for instance, were too often thought to be great simply because they were old. "In the first place, I don't care anything about Oil Paintings. Ever since I struck a dry hole near the old home ranch in Rogers County, Oklahoma I have hated oil, in the raw, and all its subsiduaries [sic]," he wrote to the readers of *The Saturday Evening Post*. "This thinking that everything was good just because it was old is the Apple Sauce." Those venerable structures recalling past glories won little admiration from the touring cowboy philosopher, although other Americans avidly haunted them: "They get up early in the morning to start out to see more old Churches. Now a Church is all right, and they are the greatest things we have in our lives, but not for a steady diet." The only alternative to church-visiting was ruin-looking, but a "ruin don't just exactly spellbind me; I don't care how long it has been in the process of ruination. I kept trying to get 'em to show me something that hadent started to rue yet."[50]

With the works of Michelangelo, the ruins of the Forum, and the birthplace of Columbus, it was the same reaction. Columbus' feat, after all, would have been more remarkable had North and South America been as small as Switzerland. With other figures from the European past, Rogers was equally irreverent. The Tudors, for instance, received cavalier treatment in a 1929 weekly newspaper article: "This old Henry was just an old fat big-footed . . . Baby," at the head of a country that "stood just about like the Red Sox in the American League." Henry as "a younger brother was just a Democrat, he had to take what was left," but as survivor of Crown Prince Arthur he "not only inherited the direct line to the King, but he took over all Prince Arthur's estate, including wife," Catherine of Spain, whose nation was "the General Motors in those days."[51]

In view of such reactions, Rogers' general evaluation of Europe was inevitable. "I say there is nothing new there; we got everything over home, only bigger and better," he told his *Post* readers. As a matter of fact, Europe had almost nothing to offer the Eden-seeking American Adam liberated from the desert of the past, "You take the Guides and the Grapes out of Europe and she is just a Sahara. It's great for you to see, if somebody is paying for it, or paying you to do it. But just as a pure educational proposition or pastime, it ain't there."[52]

To the American audience, such a rejection of the past as embodied in Europe was possibly more than simple chauvinism. Had the monarchy and the hierarchy welcomed the aspirations to self-fulfillment of the common man? Had not the great art works been patronized by a class of idle aristocrats? Was it not satisfying to be able to declare cultural independence by a casual dismissal of the European past? Whether justifiable or possible in any real sense, the act stood as a token of the worth of the man who could so dismiss the Old World.

Further, the rejected past need not be limited to European shores. "If a foreign Fiddler comes here, as soon as he is fumigated they throw him down and get a musician's dress suit on him, and put him in Carnegie Hall for a 'Recital,'" Rogers asserted in a 1926 weekly article. He was still at it in 1935. During a network broadcast revealing his own long-awaited "plan" for national recovery—a national lottery, based upon "sound" historical precedent at Yale and Harvard—he admitted that Harvard had been so disgusted with the football players paid for by lottery that "they never held any more lotteries and became so disgusted they took up the English language instead of the American language—and today . . . it's the only college that is carried on in a foreign tongue." Paul Revere's ride, the stories of houses where Revolutionary heroes reputedly slept, the history of Philadelphia, and other chapters in American history received a light touch that was free with details and accorded with the character of this new Adam who would be made uncomfortable, if not stifled, by the past-worshipping Daughters of the American Revolution.[53]

Will Rogers as the American Adam seeking self-fulfillment projected an image of gay insouciance toward the past—his true identity was not to be found there. To the extent that books also represented that past and to the extent that a rejection of the past called for intuition in dealing with the present, Rogers expressed a trust in the broadest possible direct experience with the present. Life, itself —not books—was the textbook for the new man, the American, at the second stage of his search for self-fulfillment.

America's "natural" philosopher made the point strongest, perhaps, in a weekly article discussing letters he had recently received: "An educated man just teaches the things that he has been taught, and its the same that everyone else has been taught that has read and studied the same books that he has. But if these old fellows [like cattlemen] know anything, it come direct to them by experience, and not by way of somebody else." The knowledge gained from such direct experience provided "a lesson of every day life in every little animal or Bird we have"; it would create confidence in those to whom it came secondhand, for "they would know that it come from a prairie and not from under a lamp." Its possessor was the "old broad minded man of the world of experience," with whom the "Educated Guy" felt lost, "FOR THERE IS NOTHING AS STUPID AS AN EDUCATED MAN IF YOU GET HIM OFF THE THING HE WAS EDUCATED IN."[54]

If the method of attaining knowledge and self-fulfillment was thus empiricism in its broad sense, the American Adam would be also an intuitive searcher. In the context of the hastily-devised measures for relief and recovery from the depression in the first Roosevelt years, Rogers spoke to his radio audience on the importance of intuition. "Now—my plan—my plan is: don't plan. Whatever you do, don't do it purposely—you know—live haphazardly—just kinda go through life haphazardly—well, even more than we are now." Even when Will Rogers wrote about his use of language to convey the results of his own experience and intuition, he added to his image as the American Adam, the natural man. Words, like men, animals, and events, required firsthand experience: "Course, the Greeks have a word for it, and the dictionary has a word for it, but I believe in using your very own for it," Rogers wrote, pointing out that unfamiliar words were detour signs to readers, who would cuss and take a different "route" next time. "I love words," he concluded, "but dont like strange ones. You dont understand them, and they dont understand you, old words is like old friends, you know em the minute you see em."[55]

Will Rogers

Thus, relying upon experience and his own intuitive ability to assimilate it meaningfully, Rogers went forth each day (in the eyes of his public) as had Whitman's eidolon— to meet men and creatures, and to know the earth and the sun in order to have the widest experience possible. The daily datelines told of places seen, people met, food eaten, and of sights, sounds, and affairs both ugly and beautiful. The dateline might read Pittsburgh, Wilkes-Barre, Utica, or New York City, in what Wolfe would later call the "good, green East." "New England," Rogers wrote, "the most beautiful place in the summer time, and for those that like their snow, its fine all the year round. Up state New York is great." Word came, too, from places like Chicago, Cleveland, and Kalamazoo: "All the Middle West, with its rolling prairies and big grain farms," he found to be great. From places like Denver, Butte, and Los Angeles, might come something like the following: "The Northwest, just anything in the way of scenery you want, any crops, any view. The whole Pacific Coast and its adjoining mountainous States. California, the Chamber of Commerce will take that up with you. . . . Nevada has a freedom and independent spirit that is slowly reaching out all over our land. Utah is a great state. . . . Colorado is our grand stand seat to see our world from." Or from the Southwest and places like Tulsa, Dallas, and San Antonio, might come observations like: "Texas? . . . Texas has got everything that any other State has and then 'Ma' and 'Jim' besides. Oklahoma? A lack of vocabulary is all that stops me. I should have stayed in Oxford another year to really have done justice to Oklahoma." With joyous hyperbole, he might add a note on disappointment of Republican hopes on election day there: "Why there is Republicans who live so high up in them skyscrapers in Tulsa and Oklahoma City that they aint been down to the ground since November eight [sic]." From the South, from Nashville, Birmingham, and Atlanta might come comments on sights seen earlier or yet to be seen. "Arkansas? Scenery, vacation land, fertility, beautiful women." Or he might mix in politics: "Was you ever down in Long Valley? There is a wonderful, beautiful poetical valley along the length of our great Mississippi River. Cities, beautiful, prosperous ones, hanging moss from century old trees. Charming and delightful people in this valley. Its not called Long Valley on any of your maps, its labelled Louisiana."[56]

This is the kind of untethered experimenting that Whitman had dreamed of. From "Manahatta" to California, from the land of the live oak to "Kanada," the part-Cherokee son of the Mississippi Valley went in the company of all kinds of people, Whitman's "en masse," absorbing and reporting what he saw.

Along with all this, he typed out messages to his public that showed that in the course of such experiential grazing he was achieving a degree of self-fulfillment, his highest possible development as a man. In such a national role, he was the emblem of the dream of self-fulfillment. In at least three ways, Rogers showed that he was developing to their highest his powers and goodness. First, he was the wise innocent in his humor and his commentary. Second, he was the eternal boy in the sense that he seemingly retained a deep joy in life. Finally, he was the good friend of all, considerate of creatures and of his fellow man.

His posture as the wise innocent appeared to follow from a clear-eyed look at the past and from a breadth of experience. The result was a mixture of the sophisticated and the naïve, of the sly and the open, of the worldly and the visionary.

He may have understood the necessity of a consciously-practiced wise innocence. With his role as humorist, for instance, his strategy was to seem artfully unaware of the incongruity he was presenting. "You see," he told readers of a weekly newspaper article, "the subtle thing about a joke is to make it look like it was not a joke."[57] His persona throughout his career was that of the country boy who only seemed to be taken in by the sights and wiles of the big town. Here is, for instance, the magazine article version of a joke that found its way into at least one movie and possibly into dozens of personal appearances. Rogers was trying to get a passport to Europe without being able to present legal evidence of his birth:

> "Well," I told her "Lady I have no birth certificate; and as for someone here in New York that was present at my birth and can swear to it, I am afraid that will be rather difficult." "Havent you somebody here that was there?"

she asked. You know the old-time Lady's of which I am a
direct descendant. They were of a rather modest and
retiring nature, and being born was rather a private
affair, and not a public function.

I have no one here in New York that witnessed that
historical event, and I doubt very much if even in
Oklahoma I could produce any great amount of
witnesses. My Parents are dead, Our old Family Doctor,
bless his old heart, is no more. So what would you advise
that I do? Will it be necessary for me to be born again,
and just what proceedure [*sic*] would you advise for me
doing so? . . . You see, in the early days of the Indian
Territory where I was born there was no such things as
birth certificates. You being there was enough. We
generally took it for granted if you were there you must
have at some time been born.[58]

This is the same straight-faced pose of an innocence
wiser than it seems as practiced by the sharp Yankee; it has
the exuberance of the tall-story backwoodsman subdued
but not repressed; it bespeaks a gay and poised spirit that is
finding fulfillment.

Rogers practiced the art, too, when speaking on topical
matters. In a time when Florida and California Chambers
of Commerce jousted ceaselessly over comparative advantages of their topography and climates, Rogers—as a California mayor—seemingly innocently and good-naturedly
strafed Floridian publicists in a daily telegram. He had, he
said, rushed down to the pressroom of a Miami paper to get
the details on an earthquake in California (for his family
was there) but couldn't find any; he had found, though, details of a quake that was happening at the moment, "so I am
not going to get excited till next Friday's earthquake. That's
when they report a big one," he concluded, behind his mask
of innocence.[59] At times the mask would slip and loosen
restraint on the exuberance; but in the fun Rogers had with
blue-nosed prohibition, with puffy senators, with disarma-
ment conferences, and all the rest, he consistently followed
his dictum that the subtle thing about a joke was to make
it look like it was not a joke. "There ain't nothing to life but
satisfaction," he had said. He seemed in his humor to be
getting satisfaction from what he experienced as he grazed

all over the new Eden. In humor, his strategy was the wise *innocence.*

When he came to straightforward news commentary, his manner was that of the *wise* innocence. Rogers pretended to be more "dumb" than he was by prefacing many of his comments with expressions such as "All I know is what I read in the papers," "I'm just a dumb comedian," "Now, this is just a rough idea of mine," and variants of each. For Rogers' audience, perhaps, the effect of such disclaimers was at least twofold: They produced the effect of modesty of judgment appropriate to the wise practice of the golden mean and they magnified the words of wisdom that followed by decreasing audience expectations relative to that wisdom.

When Rogers combined with this posture of the American innocent the application of everyday principles to complex affairs, he did seem wise. To make the complicated National Recovery Administration work, "the whole NRA plan should be written on a postcard." For in these few words the NRA could be expressed: "Nobody can work a man over a certain number of hours (without extra pay) and nobody can pay anyone under a certain sum (no matter what line of business it was), nobody can hire children." How to stop war? The wise American innocent would apply the everyday principle of outlawed debts: If loot and reparations were limited, countries would be slow to start wars. Meantime, how to meet crises? With the everyday American principle of unsurprise: "Poor old 'Brink'. I dont know of anything we been on more of than we have it. We have tottered on the Brink so long and so much that I think the old Brink has got hand holts on it. I am beginning to believe we wouldent go over it on a bet," Rogers told his readers of a weekly article in 1934.[60] Such words, tied closely to the experience of the intuitive American Adam, seemed wise to their readers who were themselves dedicated to the proposition that through "the school of hard knocks" comes wisdom and, therefore, the highest possible development of the individual's possibilities.

Speaking wisely-innocent words in his humor and commentary, Rogers gradually etched his own public portrait as the American Adam, a new man starting from new beginnings and developing his own powers to their fullest. Rogers showed himself to be the eternal boy in that he seemed always to have a dog or horse handy, and he wrote lovingly of them. One dog was "Sealingham," a gift of Lord Dewar in 1926. Five years later, the dog had met his death, and Rogers told readers, "We have petted him, complained at him, called him a nuisance, but when we buried him yesterday we couldn't think of a wrong thing he had ever done." On another occasion, a favorite family pony died, a pet of many years' standing. "I first saw him at a town in Connecticut, I think it was Westport," Rogers recalled, almost as if he were talking about a human acquaintance. "I liked him, and he come home with me, and I think he liked me." "Dopey," the safe pony on which all the children had learned trick riding, had been intimately connected with the Rogers family. "He never hurt one in his life. He did everything right. Thats a reputation that no human can die with."[61]

In a final way, Rogers' messages pictured a man who was finding self-fulfillment. His words, revealing a continuing zest for life and the consideration for others that was part of the American dream's program for self-fulfillment of the individual, had the ability to say, "By Golly I am living now," in many ways. As already suggested, the joy of his humor, by itself, testified to his enjoyment of life. In addition, however, many times he wrote of the delights partaken of as the eternal boy. One delight was the navy beans cooked "Kinder soupy" with plenty of home-smoked ham and real corn pone at his sister Sallie's. With April came crocuses and the national pastime: "With the baseball season opened and Washington headed for another pennant, boy, Congress better be good from now on!" At the conclusion of the 1932 Olympics, he told those who had not attended, "You have missed the greatest show from every angle that was ever held in America." At Christmastime, readers might find that Rogers was busy replacing presents he had worn out by playing with them himself. A daily wire on what was to be his last birthday testified to Rogers' continuing joy in living and spirit of boyhood. "I am pretty sore today," he began. "Am looking for the ones that reminded me that 55 years ago today at Oolagah [*sic*], Indian Territory, on Nov. 4, 1879, a boy baby was born. Well, anyhow, I played a game of polo and roped calves all day, so there is life in the old nag yet."[62] The same essence of boyishness clung to dispatches from trips around the world and to travels around this country. Any reader could conclude that he was getting satisfaction from living.

Though in his public portrait Rogers was the eternal boy, he was not an egocentric one, thoughtless of all but himself. In his dispatches, the cowboy philosopher expressed a love for comrades from both humble and high stations in life. Many times would appear a daily squib such as the following (which mixed in the dream of equality):

"Mexico, Mo.—Tom Bass, well-known Negro horseman, aged 75, died here today."

Don't mean much to you does it? You have all seen society folks perform on a beautiful three or five gaited saddle horse, and said, "My, what skill and patience they must have had to train that animal."

Well, all they did was ride him in. All this Negro, Tom Bass, did was to train him. For over fifty years America's premier trainer, he trained thousands others were applauded on. . . .

If old St. Peter is as wise as we give him credit for being, Tom, he will let you go in horseback and give those folks up there a great show, and you will get the blue ribbon yourself.[63]

Whether the friend was mail plane pilot, governor of a state, or Speaker of the House, Rogers evidenced in his words the same degree of warm feelings. "If we haven't got any friends," he had written, "we will find that we are poorer than anybody." Rogers apparently was rich. "I am proud of the fact there is not a human being that I have got it in for. I never met a man I dident like," he professed—aware, of course, that liking (as does loving) admits of many degrees.[64] For such a man, happiness seemed to be a possession rather than a pursuit.

In his public pronouncements, Rogers also showed consideration for the religions of others, perhaps the most personal of all matters. In a weekly article in 1933 he answered an inquiry from a Protestant minister and seemed almost to be Whitman's ideal American. "I was raised predominately [*sic*] a Methodist, but I have traveled so much, mixed with so many people in all parts of the world, I dont know now just what I am," he wrote. "I know I have never been a nonbeliever. But I can honestly tell you that I dont think that any one religion is the religion." If the Protestant minister were hoping for endorsement of his own sect, he was probably disappointed in the reply. Whitman, though, urging the ideal American not to argue about religion, would not have been disappointed, for Rogers consistently upheld an ecumenical attitude toward religion. As early as 1923, he told his newspaper audience, "Every man's religion is good. There is none of it bad."[65]

In such messages, Rogers appeared to be considerate of others. Such an impression, paired with that of a man who is eagerly enjoying life itself, spoke relevantly of the dream of the common man's self-fulfillment.

In sum, Will Rogers identified himself materially with the dream of the dignity and worth of the individual by admiring the judgment and stamina of all the unique individuals who comprised "the big Normal Majority," and by expressing a belief in the natural goodness of man and the altruism of his cultural contemporaries. He also merged himself on a second level of the dream by projecting his own individual powers and goodness into the role of the new American Adam who first rejects the stifling past, then seeks broad firsthand experience, and, finally, finds a degree of self-fulfillment in wisdom, joy in life, and consideration for others.

Rogers also identified formally with the dream of individualism in his use of simple gesture and word. The vision of the dignity and worth of the individual held a sense of new beginnings—at its center was the new Adam, personification of the dream in his newness and wise innocence.

Rogers habitually used a gesture that gave him the appearance of the wise American innocent. As he would say words such as, "Course, that's just a rough idea of mine," or "Course, I'm just a dumb comedian," he would lower his head as though to look at the floor, but, instead, would raise his eyebrows and quickly and repeatedly alternate his glance between the audience and the floor. Used constantly in the context of uttered words, the gesture could well have taken on a conventionalized significance (renderable in word symbols) of "wiser-than-I-look." With such a symbolic function abstracted from the total stimulus, audiences could possibly associate meaning and gesture so strongly that the expression could be said to look like the wise innocent (instead of, for example, a groveling Uriah Heep). To the extent that the gesture suggested the wise innocence of the American Adam, it was an iconic symbol and a formal identification with the dream of the individual.

When Rogers used either written or spoken language, the form or appearance of the new Adam was only metaphorically such. But he did utilize the properties of written or spoken language to convey the sense of newness that was so much a part of the American Adam. That sense of newness came chiefly through bending words toward new significations—first, by artistically misapplying a word so that it was made to bear a new sense, and, second, by using slang.

The artful misapplication of a word is a figure of speech and, therefore, distinctly dependent upon the verbal language, itself. As Rogers applied the technique, the impression on his audiences may simply have been one of pleasing newness and of fresh use of language. In the guise of the past-rejecting Adam, he could remark that New England "is mangy with History"; in Genoa, he was going "church prowling," and the cardinal in Rogers' version of English history made possible Henry VIII's marriage to Catherine when he "thought of the bright idea of saying that Prince Arthur and Catherine were never married, that it was two other fellows." When he addressed himself to political matters as the *wise* innocent, he could report that Kansas had "sentenced" Charles Curtis to the Senate; he could hope, after the common man realized his own potential more fully, to see us "extinguish our office seekers every two years"; if the NRA were resubmitted to Congress after being declared unconstitutional, he would be sure that it went there under an "assumed name." Republicans, apparently, were not human beings counted in numbers: "You'd be surprised at the amount of 'em that's showin' up, you know"; on the other hand, senators who earlier had baited President Hoover had demanded unfairly that the President give them the whole "Menu" of a visit between the President and the English Prime Minister. Commenting upon other international events, Rogers took note of the knee breeches worn by diplomats received by the English King and took satisfaction from the fact that America's "Charley [Dawes] was the only one that didn't wear rompers." A few years before, he had professed astonishment over Mexican reaction to an earlier punitive expedition: "They dident appreciate the fact that they had been shot in the most cordial manner possible." By means of such word bending, Will Rogers achieved an effect of freshness in his language. Too, he suggested the new Adam in his use of slang.

One source of slang for him was the transfer of professional or occupational terms from their special vocabularies to a more general one, with an effect much like that of artful misapplication. From bookkeeping came the expression to describe the Ferguson couple in Texas, both of whom became chief executives of that state: "America's only Double Entry Governors." From Rogers' ranching experience came "round up" and "corralling beef" that he applied to corset making; a governor from Maryland had every "earmark" of a future President. From show business he drew many expressions and applied them outside the field: Nations had to "book" wars ahead; Moses' Biblical followers had been his "troupe"; our intervention in Nicaragua had been wrong because citizens of that nation had wanted to use only "home talent" in their civil war; present-day Nevada miners were "descendants of the original casts." This was slang at its best—fresh, vivid, and Adamic.

Another source for Rogers' slang lay in his naturalization of foreign words: From the Spanish *remuda,* he arrived at "remuther" as the name for a ready group of saddle horses; the front feet of cattle were "mongano"; the Spanish *frijole* kept its pronunciation but not its spelling when, as the eternal boy, he loved to eat "free holey" beans out on the range.

Besides using special terms in a more general sense and adapting foreign words, Rogers used shortened forms of words, onomatopoetic words, and coined words to achieve a fresh language.

A division into shares was a "divvy"; a reputation was a "rep"; diplomats wouldn't "dip," and the preferable ruins were those that hadn't yet started to "rue." His Ford car had gone "flooey"; talk about brinks was all "hooey"; talking was also "yowling" and "yapping"; a risqué foreign film was admittedly "snorty" in spots. A back belonging to a coward was a "Spine-a-Marino," and Oklahoma—with its frequent troubles with governors—was "IMPEACHerino." The Old Testament Adam "gave names to all cattle, and to the fowl of the air, and to every beast of the field." Will Rogers, as a new Adam, used new names for old ones.

BY SPEAKING directly of the principles of the dream of the dignity and worth of the individual, by using words to reveal his practice of the action corollaries of that dream, and by using the resources of language, itself, to suggest further the character of the new Adam, Will Rogers gained identification with one great category of the American dream. Of Americans who dreamed of the powers of the common man, Dixon Wecter observed in 1941, "Mother-wit and resourcefulness we love." Of Adam-worshipping Americans, he added this description of their affections:

> Manliness, forthright manners, and salty speech are
> approved. Love of the soil, of dogs and horses and
> manual hobbies and fishing, is better understood than
> absorption in art, literature, and music. . . . Also the
> touch of versatility and homely skill is applauded in a
> hero.[66]

Thus, one face that Americans of the twenties and thirties may well have seen on Will Rogers was that of the new Adam. With that face alone he would have been attractive. With the addition of others—including that of the American democrat—he was a potential folk-hero.

Will Rogers, American Democrat

The ideals of freedom and equality in the American dream received energy from the hopes regarding the worth and goodness of the common man and from the vision of his self-fulfillment. The dream of the garden had included a portrayal of gifts from the soil to democracy. The dream of a society of freedom and equality was in turn intimately related to the dream of the dignity and worth of the individual. As Walter Lippmann has pointed out in his pathfinding study, *Public Opinion,* expression of each man's will in a democracy would be a political good since "the instinct to express one's self in a good life was innate."[1] Thus, the innately good common man found self-expression and self-fulfillment partly through political democracy, by having a share in the day-to-day shaping of his society.

Those who dreamed of the American Adam were also, in a sense, dreamers of freedom. Adam in his new garden was not only unfettered in his attempt to develop his powers and his ideal self, but also his very boundlessness and liberation from the past and evil represented freedom. Indeed, so confluent are the ideas of the dignity and worth of the individual and the implementation of them in a democratic system that Henry Bamford Parkes finds the core of the American tradition in the American dream of freedom and equality.

More specifically, to myth-making Americans like George Bancroft, the dream of freedom took on apocalyptic dimensions. History had been the struggle between freedom and slavery. The contest had covered four epochs: from creation to the time of Socrates; from the time of Athens' greatness to the Coming of Christ; from that Coming to the American Revolution; and from that Revolution on to the millennium. The first three were obviously formative of the fourth. To more humble visionaries, the dream of freedom could seem only a little less revelational. A New England farmer, at the time of adoption of the federal Constitution, wrote, "We do not need any Goviner but the Guviner of the univarse and him a States Gineral to Consult with the wrest of the united states for the good of the whole."[2] Bizarre as it might sound, according to Adams such a proposal contained two of the crucial ideas in the American dream of freedom: limitation of a central government's power and government for the good of the whole.

Other widely-held opinions helped to define the nature of the idealized freedom. One such definition is implicit in the Bill of Rights, which public opinion demanded and has sustained: Negatively defined, freedom is absence of restraint on "basic rights" such as those to assemble, to worship according to conscience, to speak, to publish, and to bear arms. Another attribute of this sort of freedom was the American dream of freedom from special privilege: From the time of a Crèvecoeur who rejoiced in liberation from the bondage of "aristocratical families, . . . courts, . . . kings, . . . bishops . . . [and] ecclesiastical dominion" to the cry of the Populist against "the interests," America epitomized a place where the individual was free from domination by aristocracy, oligarchy, or plutocracy. Lest, however, the dreamed-of state of liberty be generally construed as violent anarchy, the bounds of freedom were qualified to permit freedom of action and expression only so long as they did not injure others. In brief, the political dream was one of free institutions; from what has been said, however, it is also clear that the dreamed-of democracy was likewise an ideal social order.

As was the case with the dream of the dignity and worth of the individual, Emerson, Whitman, and Thoreau were voices of the vision of freedom in America. To each of them, as to many Americans, freedom was more than political liberty. Thoreau virtually equated freedom with his own highly-ethical anarchy. Emerson and Whitman, differing only in degree, advocated a kind of *laissez faire* of the spirit.

Thoreau's own life was his definition of freedom. He was, believes Parkes in his *American Experience*, "the almost complete embodiment of the ideal American of the Virginians, cherishing his own moral and economic independence and refusing to exploit others."[3] His view of the role of government in providing freedom, therefore, turned upon his view of the sanctity of the individual. "There will never be a really free and enlightened State," he urged in "Civil Disobedience," "until the State comes to recognize the individual as a higher and independent power, from which all its own power and authority are derived, and treats him accordingly." The free, morally responsible individual would respect laws in the proportion to which they were good and just. If the transgression of unjust laws (in order to change them) appeared as a remedy to be worse than the evil of the unjust law itself, then what? "It is the fault of the government itself that the remedy *is* worse than the evil. *It* makes it worse." Thoreau had gone to jail rather than pay a poll tax he believed financed government policies of which he disapproved.

Anarchical as it may sound, Thoreau's dream of freedom was based on comprehensive philosophical grounds that ennobled it. His words in "Life Without Principle" pictured a broad freedom. If America was to be the field where the battle of freedom was to be fought, then "surely it cannot be freedom in a merely political sense that is meant." The American may have found political freedom, but not economic and moral freedom.

> Do we call this the land of the free? What is it to be free
> from King George and continue the slaves of King
> Prejudice? What is it to be born free and not to live free?
> What is the value of any political freedom, but as a
> means to moral freedom? Is it a freedom to be slaves, or
> a freedom to be free, of which we boast?

Even if the American people were not inclined to imitate Thoreau—ideal American that he might have been—his dream of freedom differed in degree and not in kind from that of the many.

Emerson, on the other hand, may have tried to express the feelings of all democratic dreamers. Whereas Thoreau's ideal of freedom went to the extreme of philosophical anarchism, Emerson's ideal was only akin to that position. An illustration of the difference is the perhaps apocryphal anecdote related to Thoreau's poll tax experience. Thoreau was morally free and responsible enough to go to jail as was Emerson to visit him there. Instead of advising out-and-out civil disobedience, Emerson, in "Politics," simply said, "Good men must not obey the laws too well."

As already noted, Emerson consistently preached the infinitude of the private man. Besides thus expressing his confidence in the dignity and worth of the individual, he also revealed his dedication to other categories of the dream of Paradise to be regained. Since infinite personalities cannot be limited, they must be free; therefore, Emerson's dream of freedom was like a heavenly city with the free individual in a free democracy. He detailed a wise, just, and free society in which the individual could develop his innate wisdom and justice. In his words, "To educate the wise man the State exists, and with the appearance of the wise man the State expires." The appearance of wisdom in the private character was the remedy for abuse of government.

> The wise man is the State. He needs no army, fort, or
> navy—he loves men too well; no bribe, or feast, or palace,
> to draw friends to him; no vantage ground, no favorable
> circumstance. He needs no library, for he has not done
> thinking; no church, for he is a prophet; no statute-book,
> for he has the lawgiver; no money, for he is value; no
> road, for he is at home where he is. . . . His relation to
> men is angelic; his memory is myrrh to them; his
> presence, frankincense and flowers.[4]

For Emerson, freedom was both a prerequisite and a result of character formation; it was not only political freedom but social and moral as well. His dream may have been of the time when government disappeared, but he recognized a reality when he asserted that the state existed to educate the wise man.

Whitman, too, dreamed of a liberty in which the individual would be a law unto himself. In his "Democratic Vistas," he wrote, "The purpose of democracy . . . is, through many transmigrations and amid endless ridicules . . . to illustrate, at all hazards, this doctrine or theory that man, properly train'd in sanest, highest freedom, may and must become a law, and series of laws, unto himself."[5] The statement of Whitman's dream also contains his qualification of it: Only the man "train'd in sanest, highest freedom" could become a law unto himself. Further, Whitman articulated the balance that has to exist between state and individual: "The problem . . . presented to the New World, is, under permanent law and order, and after preserving cohesion, (ensemble-Individuality), at all hazards, to vitalize man's free play of special Personalism" (page 489). A man who sees that the cohesion of the state must be preserved at all hazards stops short of equating freedom with anarchy, however libertarian his dreams.

Like Emerson and Thoreau, Whitman envisioned a freedom beyond mere political liberty. "Did you, too, O friend, suppose a democracy was only for elections, for politics, and for a party name?" Freedom for Whitman would extend to the social, moral, religious, and intellectual spheres of life: "I say democracy is only of use there [in elections] that it may pass on and come to its flower and fruits in manners, in the highest forms of interaction between men, and their beliefs—in religion, literature, colleges, and schools—democracy in all public and private life" (page 483). Implicit in all this was Whitman's doctrine of what was perhaps a more basic freedom. As says Canby in his full-length study of Whitman, "What literature claims for the heroes and the great lovers, Whitman demands as an ideal for the common man. There can be no enduring democracy without emotional freedom."[6] The liberty to express a comradely love was a unique dream among the great prophets. Thoreau loved humanity, but hated Tom, Dick, and Harry; the Sage of Concord generally managed to keep his distance from such comradely ventures as those at Brook Farm. In Whitman's bold vision of emotional freedom was a frank sensuousness that expressed a consummatory attitude toward American living: Manly love for comrades, passioned love for body—these were to be consumed and glorified, the release of emotion at once freedom and self-fulfillment.

The words of Thoreau, Emerson, and Whitman on freedom were not slogans for the masses; but the writers' grand vistas of the free spirit were nevertheless celestial cities of a sort to the thousands (or millions) who sympathized with or labored for abolition, women's rights, and labor's rights, and who observed with at least a modicum of toleration the liberated attempts of such free spirits as John Humphrey Noyes to realize in a model community the ideal, free society. To the inarticulate American, the dream of freedom might be expressed simply as the desire for elbow room, for air to breathe, for room to graze; it was no less real for lack of fine words.

Will Rogers

Henry Bamford Parkes, after examining the ideals of freedom held by Jefferson, Thoreau, Emerson, Whitman, and others, concluded that "the foundation of an American order can only be a respect for the freedom of every individual, in the confidence that by the fullest development of his own personality he can contribute most fully to the welfare of society and that (since man is a social being) a true individualism prefers to express itself in co-operation rather than in conflict" (page 342).

The vision of equality, like a wheel within a wheel, balanced the dream of freedom. Keenly aware of the balance and paradox was Walt Whitman, whom Canby calls the symbolic voice of the nineteenth century. On the one hand, democracy to the "good gray poet" meant freedom, "individuality, the pride and centripetal isolation of a human being by himself," but on the other hand, democracy also meant to him equality, "the leveler, the unyielding principle of the average" (page 341). These two conceptions, believed Whitman, were ever confronting each other and modifying one another's nature, each making the other of the highest avail. What is the nature of the dream of equality?

The Declaration of Independence states as a "self-evident" truth that all men are created equal. Defining the nature of the dream of equality has plagued visionaries of the American dream ever since. The writer of the Declaration believed in the rise of a natural aristocracy, those with superior talents and virtue. Obviously, men are not created equal in talent, intellect, or physical endowment.

In general, justification of such a dream is twofold: First, men actually are equal spiritually (In his *The Promise of America,* John Morton Blum interprets part of the Jeffersonian concept of equality as being equal claim by all to dignity; Russel Nye holds that Jacksonians believed men to be equal in having their natural rights.); second, the ideal society will provide equal opportunity and minimize the surface inequalities, producing an appropriate degree of outward equality.

Emerson and Whitman envisioned spiritual equality. To Emerson, in "Compensation," it followed necessarily from his emphasis on the infinitude of the private man, for unlimited personalities are equal. "In the nature of the soul is the compensation for the inequalities of condition. . . .See the facts nearly and these mountainous inequalities vanish." And again, in "New England Reformers," "The disparities of power in men are superficial; and all frank and searching conversation, in which a man lays himself open to his brother, apprises each of their radical unity." Whitman, however, is the one who vivified the hope of spiritual equality, in his editions of *Leaves of Grass.* First, personality is unlimited:

> Have you thought there could be but one supreme?
> There can be any number of Supremes—one does not
>   countervail another any more than one eyesight
>   countervails another, or one life countervails
>   another.

Next, there is spiritual equality:

> I celebrate myself,
> And what I assume you shall assume;
> For every atom belonging to me as good belongs to you.

And again,

> In all people I see myself—none more, and not one a
>   barleycorn less,
> And the good or bad I say of myself, I say to them.

The "self" of *Leaves* is not only Whitman's dream of the ideal self for all the American people but is also the unlimited being that sees all other unlimited selves as equals.[7]

Starting from this transcendental view of human equality, Whitman elaborated it almost to the point of an overt social equality. He believed that the masses of people possessed qualities which, because of their commonality, were most universal and therefore closest to the universal will. This is the sense of his phrase, "the divine average." Yet, to avoid having to exclude the superior talent, he said, "Produce great persons and the rest follows." Thus, for Whitman, the spirit of social equality, which was the bedrock of modern society, was nevertheless not incompatible with individuality.

The social dream of equality was, then, to project man's inner equality, to mitigate the differences that kept men graded in their interrelationships, to prevent the erection of marked class variations. Mere absence of noble titles was not enough, although it constituted a hopeful sign. A man was to be accepted or rejected for what he was, for what he had made himself. Russel Nye has summarized some reformers' strategies for realization of this dream:

> Equal rights for women, equal entry to public education, freedom for the slave, the right of labor to organize, the regulation of the conditions of labor, utopian communitarian experiments, and the rest of the reformist ferment of the times were all part of the Jacksonian's demands for complete equality of the conditions of advancement, for the final erasure of privileged inequalities from American society.[8]

Many years after the Jacksonians and Whitman, James Truslow Adams was to recall incidents that would serve as types of the dream of social equality. "I once had an intelligent young Frenchman as a guest in New York, and after a few days I asked him what struck him most in his new impressions," Adams recalled. Quickly the visitor replied, " 'The way that everyone of every sort looks you right in the eye, without a thought of inequality.' " Or, again, Adams would tell of the words of a foreign national who worked for the historian and who sometimes also enjoyed a chat in the study with him. In his homeland, he told Adams once, " 'I would do my work and might get a pleasant word, but I could never sit and talk like this. There is a difference there between social grades which cannot be got over' " (pages 404-5). Such an easy gradation of men would have delighted the Buckskins of the first frontier, smarting under real or imagined social slights from the better-off seaboard dwellers. American women, Negroes, Jews, and other oppressed minorities have dreamed of social equality and have become sisters and brothers in spirit to those Buckskins.

No small part of social equality was to result from political equality. One means for political equality was nearly-universal manhood suffrage. Prior to 1787, a majority of states held property qualifications for voting; by 1820, most of these had changed to taxpaying qualifications. In all but

Tennessee, states later admitted to the Union left out property qualifications, substituting taxpaying ones; in the West, even the latter did not pass into law. When in older states the struggle to widen suffrage occurred, the advocates often drew upon the categories of the American dream to undergird their appeals. In the Virginia Convention of 1829-1830, while John Randolph sought to bracket the desire for elimination of freehold requirements with the scourge of paternalistic government, the nonfreeholders appealed to the great dream embodied in the Declaration. "A harsh appellation would he deserve, who, on the plea of expediency, should take from another his property: what, then, should be said of him who, on that plea, takes from another his rights, upon which the security, not of his property only, but of his life and liberty depends?"

At other times, as in the convention in New York almost a decade earlier, skillful defenders of the status quo could fall back upon the dream of the garden itself, with its vision of the self-sufficient, independent yeoman and its nightmare of festering cities. In that convention, James Kent defended a property-chosen senate in the name of the "free and independent lords of the soil," whose control of their freeholds (and of one house in a legislature) could "find safety through all the vicissitudes which the state may be destined . . . to experience." One of those vicissitudes he detailed: "One seventh of the population of Paris at this day subsists on charity, and one third of the inhabitants of that city die in the hospitals; what would become of such a city with universal suffrage?"[9] The defenders of the dream of political equality invoked the superordinate dream in the Declaration when one delegate added that "the great fundamental principle, that all men were equal in their rights" was already decided and had been decided for all time in this country; moreover, those state constitutions having freehold requirements for voting "were adopted at an early period of the revolutionary war, when the rights of man were little understood and the blessings of a free government had not been realized." Perhaps the ideal of the yeoman in his garden, strong as the dream was, was not equal in attractiveness to the superordinate vision of the rights of man in the Declaration. At any rate, prophets of the political dream of equality succeeded in significantly widening the bounds of suffrage.

Political equality was to arise by means other than conferring the vote. The Bill of Rights promised all citizens equal protection under the laws, with trial by jury of their peers. Majority rule, the explicit principle behind universal suffrage, did not mean a tyranny of the majority; rather, the rights of the minorities could find shelter in a diversity of ways—from rules of legislative debate to the stabilizing power residing in the system of checks and balances. Further, Jackson, the second "people's President," sought in his first annual message to Congress to establish as a democratic principle the notion of rotation in office. "In a country where offices are created solely for the benefit of the people no one man has any more intrinsic right to official station than another," he urged. "He who is removed has the same means of obtaining a living that are enjoyed by the millions who never held offices." Thus Jackson justified his spoils system not only on the basis of sovereignty of the people, but also on that of equal rights of all to office and of equality of economic opportunity with all other nonofficial Americans.[10]

Americans dreamed of a measure of economic equality, for upon it, to a large extent, depended the hope of social equality and, to some extent, that of political equality. Ordinarily, Americans dreamed not of equal sharing of wealth, for that jarred with their belief in their own unlimited possibilities. Instead, what they asked and hoped for was simply the opportunity for an economic rise. Adams, studying the epic of America, has asserted, "If America has stood for anything unique in the history of the world, it has been for the American dream, the belief in the common man and the insistence upon his having, so far as possible, equal opportunity in every way with the rich one" (page 135). When the opportunity for economic rise appeared to lead the way to a place where men could realize their potential and be accepted for what they had become rather than what they had been born, such opportunity was relevant to the twin dreams of freedom and equality. When the opportunity for economic rise became an aim to be sought for itself, the American dream became simply the dream of success.

So powerful, in the meantime, was the prospect of equality in all its aspects that although Darwinism had redefined or negated equality for some Americans, the late nineteenth century historian John B. Crozier could see its actual working out in American society. In America, he wrote, there existed "a natural equality of sentiment, springing out of and resting on a broad equality of material and social conditions." Yet this equality had "just sufficient inequality mixed with it" as manifested in differences of degree in ability, "culture," and property, "to keep it sweet and human." Yet, "no gap was anywhere to be discovered on which to found an order of privilege or caste." This equality was the raising of an entire population: "It is the first successful attempt in recorded history to get a healthy, natural equality which should reach down to the foundations of the state and to the great masses of men." The results corresponded to what in other nations "had been attained only by the few."[11] Crozier's summary of the status of equality in America was itself an assertion not only of the great hope of an equalitarian society, but also of its native American attributes.

The endurance of the dream of the perfect democracy, believed Whitman, depended upon something more than material benefits. In his "Democratic Vistas," unless democracy got "as firm and as warm a hold in men's hearts, emotions and belief as, in their days, feudalism or ecclesiasticism," and unless it developed "its own perennial sources, welling from the centre forever," its strength would "be defective, its growth doubtful, and its main charm wanting."

The dreams of responsible freedom and of an equality without sameness balanced each other in the glimpsed-of ideal democracy. Intimately connected with the hopes for the dignity and worth of the individual, they seemed a pathway to the Paradise to be regained.

As with the vision of the common man's powers, goodness, and self-fulfillment, the dream of the ideal democracy had its action corollaries that seemed almost a part of its content and provided another plateau for the vision of freedom and equality. Some comments appearing earlier provide the starting point for a strategy to achieve freedom and equality. To cherish one's own independence, to exercise freedom of thought and action—without at the same time exploiting or injuring others—to stand up for the stupid and foolish, to bow to no man but to be tolerant of all, to accept people for *what* they are rather than for *who* they are, to express a comradely love, to seek to keep government at its minimum, and to support a system of checks and balances: All of these would go far, thought the American idealists, in producing the great people from which the rest of the ideal democracy would follow.

The essence of the strategy for freedom was cultivation of a free spirit. Dreamers of freedom advocated everything from outright disobedience to strong mistrust of authority, thus continuing a tradition begun in colonial times when opinion leaders felt morally justified in personally nullifying the king's laws. Moreover, the really free spirit had to be willing to live with insecurity, from whatever source it may have come. Rejoicing in his independence, the American Adam as American democrat was to enjoy and preserve that freedom by an isolation from the schemes and intrigues of the wise old serpent, Europe. Destiny had led him away from that continent. In sum, the free-behaving American—given the continent for the grazing of his soul —was to concentrate on that pasture and upon feeding his spiritual sense of elbowroom, being somewhat a law unto himself.

In tension, however, with this ideal was the notion that the free American who was worthy of being a law unto himself would freely choose to meet his responsibility in sharing community efforts. Whitman explicitly made such duties a part of his own portrait of the free American democrat. "To practically enter into politics is an important part of American personalism," he wrote. More hotly, he urged, "It is the fashion among dillettants [*sic*] and fops (perhaps I myself am not guiltless) to decry the whole formulation of the active politics in America, as beyond redemption, and to be carefully kept away from. See that you do not fall into this error." But the freedom-loving American was to remain aloof from parties and, by so doing, the individual in splendid isolation would fuse with the responsibly-free democrat. To Whitman, parties had been and to some extent remained useful, but "the floating, uncommitted electors, farmers, clerks, mechanics, the masters of parties—watching aloof, inclining victory this side or that side—such are the ones most needed, present and future." To all of his free but socially-responsible acts, the American "personalist" and democrat was to apply the gauge of his innate morality: "I mean the simple, unsophisticated Conscience, the primary moral element. . . .I should demand the invariable application to individuality, this day and any day, of that old, ever-true plumb-rule of persons, eras, nations."[12] The moral stature of the free and equal American was erect. In spirit he was independent; yet he met his responsibilities to the community with energy and initiative.

He also had normative behavior in the achievement of equality, which would result from the ideal American's showing his freedom from prejudice. Whitman vivified the idea of such behavior in one of his anonymously-written "biographical" sketches of himself in a review of *Leaves of Grass.* There the poetic Whitman (and the ideal self) is a "rude child of the people—likes the ungenteel ways of laborers—is not prejudiced one mite against the Irish—talks readily with them—talks readily with niggers—does not make a stand on being a gentleman, nor on learning or manners." So much for behavior towards persons who in worlds east of Eden might be considered inferiors; what of the stance of the American Adam as democrat in the presence of those who would by some be considered superior? Given maturity, the superb animal that was the ideal American would be "brave, perceptive, under control, neither too talkative nor too reticent, neither flippant nor sombre." Moreover, his movements would be easy, indicating "a general presence that holds its own in the company of the highest." For, added Whitman, "It is native personality, and that alone, that endows a man to stand before presidents or generals . . . with *aplomb*—and *not* culture, or any knowledge or intellect whatever." [13] Thus, by his behavior toward all sorts and degrees of people, the American democrat was a leveler of class distinctions.

He was a leveler, too, in that he would practice fair play and uphold the cause of the underdog. With his dedication to this fairness passed down from Anglo-Saxon institutions and strengthened by the great American dream, the American democrat, though unawed by governmental authority, defined fair play as obeying rules that prevented people from taking advantage of others. The idea of supporting the underdog was implicit in the nature of fair play, and the American democrat would respond to the plight of oppressed minority or national groups. In so doing, he would be acting in a way that identified him as a champion of equality; it would also be an outward sign of an inward reality, the achievement of part of the great American dream.

As the dreams of freedom and equality balanced in tension, so did their action corollaries. The ideal American democrat would, on the one hand, assert his freedom from governmental power and, on the other, remain the master of the major political parties. He would live in the splendid isolation of his free, individualistic self, but he would also feel greatly responsible for all the members of society. He would make no show of manners or learning, but his behavior in high company would be that of the eminently civilized person. Perhaps the tensions were only seemingly contradictory, as the ideal American would be so jealous of his own rights and freedom that he stood ever-ready to defend them for others as his own best defense; he would understand that manners are the end and not the means of cultivation. He would be, in short, a culture-hero, an organic synthesis, and a third level of the dream of freedom.

Because of the interfused nature of the ideas of the great American dream, the Adamic hero in the vision of the dignity and worth of the individual symbolized American hopes for freedom, as well. A "hero of space" and boundlessness, he was deliciously free, whether a Leatherstocking or roaring backwoodsman or Yankee peddler. In fact, Constance Rourke saw freedom explicitly symbolized in Charles Farrar Browne's literary role as the crackerbox philosopher, Artemus Ward: "He caught the strolling life . . . almost habitual to the Yankee. His role of showman was a symbol—'ime erflote, ime erflote/ On the Swift rollin tied/ An the Rovir is free.' "[14] Huck Finn, the wisely-innocent Adamic hero, is also the icon of freedom and equality in the emotional zenith of the novel. When Huck decides not only to defy society's conventions but also to risk what he thinks will be eternal damnation by committing himself to winning freedom for the fugitive slave, the boy hero perfectly embodies the responsibly-free individual who levels society by accepting Jim for the man he is and by defending the underdog.

It remains, however, to examine briefly the hero supreme among the American pantheon as the symbol of freedom. He has ties, it is true, with heroes of the Leatherstocking type. As Marshall Fishwick has pointed out, Leatherstocking was the free, natural man of Rousseau set down in the American forest; in turn, the supreme American hero of freedom was Leatherstocking in a new setting: "Somewhere between the Alleghenies and the Rockies the followers of Daniel Boone traded coonskins for sombreros, long rifles for six-shooters, and moccasins for spurs—without losing their fascination for the hero-loving American public."[15] Perhaps the basis of that fascination is that the cowboy symbolized freedom above all else. No less a hero-worshipper than Theodore Roosevelt saw the cowboy as being doomed by the civilization of which he was the harbinger; precisely for this reason, perhaps, Roosevelt admired "his bold, free spirit." No historical person became, through legend-making, a real cowboy hero. Perhaps William F. Cody, a frontiersman on horseback who lived on the plains at approximately the same time as did the cowboy, comes closest. Taken from his habitat and metamorphosed into a legendary figure by astute press agents, Buffalo Bill entranced audiences. In his wild West show he was an image of opulence and triumph, but also—says Fishwick—when the westerner galloped forward into the arena, "Cody looked as free as the air" (pages 209, 99).

The cowboy's freedom went beyond space mobility to include psychological liberation. He was free to take direct action to set conditions aright; he retained humanity by making moral choices, but they were simple ones. Whether he had ever heard of Emerson or not, he did not "craze himself with thinking." Thus, says one student of public opinion, the cowboy represented in its purest form "psychological free enterprise."[16] As such a symbol, the cowboy was destined not to die with the passing of the open range, but rather to occupy the American imagination and in turn provide an escape outlet for those people caught in the gears of urban life. In addition, this free spirit was no mean symbol of equalitarianism, considered as fair play. The legendary cowboy had the code of the West, to which he remained faithful: to fight injustice (unless it happened to be directed against sheepherders who with their flocks were destroying nature's beauty and, incidentally, cattle pasture); to ignore a man's past or origins, judging him instead by his present actions; never to shoot a man in the back, draw first, or shoot an unarmed man; and to ride off into the sunset, still the free isolated roamer after having fulfilled his responsibility to the community by restoring law and order. Every American who was a reader of dime novels or of the pulps knew the code.

As the cowboy was the supreme symbol of freedom, Andrew Jackson was the ultimate hero of equalitarianism. It mattered not that "Old Hickory" had been a practicing attorney and a member of the Tennessee Supreme Court, besides having been elected to national office. To his supporters, the men of the West and the city laborers and small farmers of the East, he may well have seemed to be truly one of themselves. Jackson was the American Adam as democrat in the picture drawn of him by James Truslow Adams: "At once a born frontiersman, an Indian fighter, duelist, equalitarian, and strong individualist, the conqueror of the British at New Orleans, . . . a man of almost superhuman strength of will, of sterling honesty, uneducated, but with often uncanny good judgment and happy intuition, Jackson provided just the figure the ignorant but hero-loving and idealistic masses could cling to" (page 173).

In addition to this kind of hero appeal, the story of his rise and success in varied spheres of activity seemed proof of the good fruits of the dream of equality of opportunity. The common man in America had believed that the unique gift of America had been equal opportunity for all, based on the rights of men created equal, and not merely on property rights. The reaffirmation of that dream by Jackson's rise to the Presidency held reassuring significance.

Perhaps because he was born an aristocrat in Virginia, Thomas Jefferson did not as effectively symbolize the dream of freedom and equality. But he was the source of the agrarian synthesis, which presented the political edifice that was the counterpart to the dream of the garden in the dream of the individual. The man who had written that all men are created equal was zealously dedicated to freedom as well, and often remarked that "the last hope of human liberty in this world rests on us." So complete was Jefferson's expression of the American popular mind that by 1825 Tocqueville reported that even Federalists applauded Republican institutions when in public. Jefferson supplied, said Walter Lippmann, the stereotypes, images, and ideas that Americans still used in 1920 to describe politics to each other. Although Jefferson's dream of democracy went beyond a simple set of political institutions, he saw them as means necessary to the ends of the social dream of freedom and equality.

From Jefferson's ideas of individual liberty and the rise of the talented if given opportunity emerges the picture of the society of freedom and equality. It was a decentralized one, with primary governmental responsibility vested in the local government, although the national government stood by to guarantee majority rule, election rights of the people, equal justice, and civil liberties. Besides the state and county, the local unit of government was the "hundred," an area of only five or six miles square, small enough that its inhabitants could be adequately informed of community problems and participate freely in community affairs. The property necessary to social stability was agricultural real estate, which provided each owner with free and independent subsistence. The vast supply of public land assured everyone the right of ownership, as no landed aristocracy was the goal. From the soil came the worth and virtue of the natural aristocracy. "Those who labour in the earth are the chosen people of God, if ever He had a chosen people," Jefferson wrote in *Notes on Virginia;* "Corruption of morals in the mass of cultivators is a phaenomenon of which no age nor nation has furnished an example." Added to the superior virtue of the *aristoi* would be the superior talent, sharpened and polished by education. The tax-supported educational system was initially open to all, but only the better students would find their way to grammar school and college. Such education would not only help call forth talent but would also help assure freedom by qualifying the electorate to exercise political power.[17]

All in all, the agrarian synthesis of the dream of freedom and equality offered the maximum possible liberty within the framework of an organized society; an envisioned aggregate of small farmers offered approximate economic equality; a public, tax-supported educational system provided equal opportunity for all to develop to their highest potentialities. It was an appealing vision, and for its survival the Jacksonians were to include the stalwart city laborer among the virtuous chosen people. The Populists were to rally supporters of the dream under the banners of free silver, reform, and Bryan, but by 1920, an industrial society had appropriated the values. To be aware that the idealized society did not survive in its pure form, even to the death of its architect, however, is not to deny its attractiveness to generations of Americans. The dream of freedom and equality was redolent with the soothing airs issuing from the paradise that waited for the new Adam's return.

(In the year of the appearance of *Leaves of Grass,* a sturdy, self-sufficient, real-life cowboy only sixteen years old made a cattle drive from the Indian Territory to St. Louis. This hero of freedom was Clem Vann Rogers. In 1859, at twenty, he married Mary America Schrimsher and settled as a farmer and rancher on the Caney River, northeastern I. T. In 1879, at forty, he became the father of a son who would one day be perceived by millions as a hero of freedom and equality—an authentic American democrat.)

Within fifteen years after Appomattox, the elder Rogers had apparently realized the promise of the agrarian synthesis. He raised what he ate plus enough to sell and make him prosperous, and he participated in the political affairs of his district. His ranch home seemed to be a place appropriate for rearing American democrats in other ways, too.

To begin with, the human relationships in the Rogers household could have helped give the younger Rogers a trust in people and belief in their worth. Besides the affection he received from his family as the only surviving son, the boy found a world peopled by those who shared their lives, in trust and friendship, with the Rogerses so that the family circle was widened to include many neighboring families. "Between the Cherokee families," reports Betty Rogers, "there was more feeling of kinship than of just being neighbors. Everybody was 'Aunt' or 'Uncle.' Homes were hospitable, warm and friendly."[18] On Sundays, the mother often invited some neighboring family for dinner; because of the distances of travel and slowness of transport, the guests stayed the rest of the day and often through the night. At parting, visitors always received a special going-away gift of either baskets of grapes, peaches or apples from the Rogers orchard or else a delicacy from "Aunt" Mary's oven. For his own part, the hard-driving Clem Rogers would occasionally plan and carry out all-day fishing excursions to the famous Four-Mile Creek, which had perch and bass that at times would strike at the colored corks on the lines. Such gatherings probably impressed upon the Rogers boy something of their equalitarian milieu. In the Cooweescoowee country, says Ellsworth Collings, "A man was judged by what he stood for in his present community, his daily relations with his neighbors, not for what his family had accomplished in generations past."[19] Too, reports Betty Rogers, farmers and ranchers from miles around would come to talk over their problems with the elder Rogers during the time when he was a judge of the Cooweescoowee District and, later, when he was a Cherokee senator. Such an atmosphere, then, had not only idyllic moments but also times of shared troubles. In such relationships that include but go beyond happy instants, young Rogers could have found a source for his trust of people, a quality necessary for the American democrat.

That trust could have been extended by his knowing the worth of Negroes in Cooweescoowee. To be sure, the culture of the country included Southern mores and, to the Negroes who had gathered at the big house for young Rogers' birth, he was "the young master"; moreover, as the son of a former slaveholder, the boy undoubtedly felt like the young master. Treated with deference, the boy would "play horse" with Clement Vann Rogers, son of a man once owned by the elder Rogers. "We growed up together, if you know what I mean," Clement Vann Rogers was to tell Homer Croy years later; "He used to put a saddle on my back and make me pretend I was a bucking horse and he would ride me, spurrin' me with his bare heels. One time he gets mad with me and shoved a branding iron against my behind, but it wasn't very hot, scared me more'n anything else."[20] As a cadet at Kemper Military School, Boonville, Mo., Rogers would insist upon differences between the Indian and Negro races. He felt, almost surely, that he was superior to the race.

Still, there were "Uncle Dan" and "Aunt Babe" Walker, who shortly after their marriage had moved into a three-room frame house just over the hill from the Rogers home. In young Rogers' eyes, according to Donald Day, Aunt Babe was "the soul of kindness" and "an extremely religious woman."[21] As for Dan Walker, he was the best roper on the ranch and could lasso cattle around the neck, the four feet, or the horns. Dan Walker was experienced in doing the work that defined a man in the American West. When Walker showed young Rogers how to rope, the fact that he was a top roper and rider, and not that he was a Negro, was probably what mattered to the boy. Further, the boy probably respected Uncle Dan's worth because Clem Rogers himself respected his cowhand. Such intimate sharing of lives was what would prompt Rogers, years later, to say, "They're all folks," and to mean that they were, first of all, human beings.

Still another range of experiences probably helped to shape Rogers' concern for the worth, equality, and freedom of the human spirit. He probably considered himself a white but was also proud of his Cherokee blood. When, then, a classmate at Kemper called an Indian chief a "thoroughbred," Rogers quickly got to his feet to correct the error. The proper term was "full blood," Rogers explained, his voice full of anger; to use a horse term for a fine Indian, he said, spoiled his whole afternoon. On another day, he and a fellow cadet stood before a reproduction of a painting depicting the defeat of Custer at Little Big Horn. Rogers said he liked the picture and the other boy wondered why. It was, replied Rogers, the only picture showing that his race got the best of it. Later, Tom Mix would tell of Rogers' hurt at overhearing a girl in an eastern audience, upon reading his billing as a "Cherokee Indian," say that "she could stand being entertained by the darkest inhabitant in Africa, but an Indian went against her nature."[22] Later, too, Betty

Rogers would record his chagrin at knowing that her friends had teased her about her "Wild West Indian Cowboy." Thus, taking, or being given, the roles both of Indian and of white, Rogers probably had borne in upon him the operation of prejudice.

Experiences such as these could, then, have partially explained what was to happen in the years ahead, when Rogers would appear before three thousand Cherokees descended from those who had remained near the ancient tribal territory in the South. His audience would listen impassively while he spoke, until, as Ben Dixon MacNeil was to report, the part-Cherokee son of Oklahoma "went into a berserk rage for about three minutes and precipitated a demonstration that was unparalleled." Rogers was not to be angry with his audience; instead, his rage was to be directed at Andrew Jackson, hero of freedom and equality for whites, but the "Betrayer" to Cherokees, who viewed the forced removal of most of the tribe to Oklahoma as the "Betrayal." MacNeil was to report, "No enemy of Jackson was ever more bitter than Rogers. The Indians listened, and then the quiet was ripped by the screaming war cry of the tribe."[23]

Those who know the pain of discrimination become keenly aware of their rights as men and their dignity in the sight of their maker, whether they be American Indians or second-class citizens of the British Empire who a little more than a century before Rogers' time had revolted in the name of natural rights and equality of all men. From Rogers' trust in the goodness of people, from his knowledge of the worthiness of other races, and from awareness of his tie to a badly-treated minority group could well have come his own brand of equalitarianism and sympathy for the underdog.

Will Rogers was also a child of freedom. Horses and schools had a great deal to do with his free-flying spirit. Before he was old enough to sit on a horse, he would ride in his mother's buggy, drawn by a white horse that moved the woman and the boy across the space of the prairie, freeing them of being place-bound. Later, he would learn to ride one of Uncle Dan Walker's horses, and still later would come that magic moment in his sixth year when he found a just-right pony saddled and waiting outside the door of the ranch home. With his own horse under him and the world before him, "A wonderful feeling of exhilaration came over him," believes Donald Day (page 16).

If the horse gave Rogers a sense of liberty, schools gave him the sense of confinement. By the time he was in his thirteenth year, he was ready to enter his fourth school; his despairing father placed him at Kemper, hoping that the military discipline would aid the boy in getting down to the business of going to school. Young Rogers had good times at school, but they were more often connected with ropes, horses, and pranks than with the pleasures of the classroom. When he left Kemper in February of 1898, he declared his independence from schools for the rest of his life.

Will Rogers found his love of mobility and lack of restraint turning him toward the life of a free spirit. His identification with the ways of the American cowboy confirmed him as a disciple of the way of the liberated. From the day that young Rogers first admired Dan Walker's skill to the end of the humorist's life, his beau ideal was the knight of the range. He could see real ones right at home: "Most of the boys working on Clem's range were honest, generous to a fault, respectful to women and to the aged," Collings wrote in *The Old Home Ranch* (page 53). Riding his own pony, the son roped everything in sight; then came the day when he was given a role that would prove his worthiness as a squire on the range: The elder Rogers asked him and another boy to help with the branding of calves. Young Rogers was thrilled at being a part of the activities —the dust, heat, cursing, and smell of sweat of men were no doubt beautiful to him. For still, in the year before he was to die, Rogers would go on a vacation pilgrimage to the "Mashed O" ranch near Amarillo, rope and drag calves to the branding, and revel in the heat and activity. Betty Rogers would report, "He was hot, dirty and dog tired and the sweat was pouring down his face, when he overheard an old slow-talking cowboy say to another, 'Some folks sure got a hell of an idea about a vacation' " (page 58).

Reinforcing his boyhood identification with the cowboy was a trip to the Chicago World's Fair in 1893. The high point, perhaps, of the journey was his being seated in a huge

horseshoe amphitheater among twenty-two-thousand people and watching the four hundred riders from Buffalo
Bill's Wild West Show open the performance at a full chase;
then came the breathless moment of the triumphant entry
of that symbol of freedom, Buffalo Bill. Later followed Vincente Oropeza, the great rope artist from Mexico, grace-
fully spinning the lariat, leaping in and out of the circling
loop, then snaking it out and smoothly lassoing a dashing
horse by the front feet, then the back feet, then all four feet,
then by the saddle horn and even the tail! To close, the artist
probably amazed young Rogers by spelling "Oropeza" in the
air, one letter at a time, with the rope that seemed alive.[24]
It might have been here at Chicago, with the freedom of the
West luring millions to vicarious participation, that Rogers
first thought of showing his own westernness to the public.

Besides all the rest, one other man attracted Will Rogers
to the life of the cowboy—his father. The elder Rogers could
ride well in the saddle and could cover long distances on
horseback. The boy heard from his father's lips how, as a
teen-aged boy, the elder Rogers had taken the foremanship
of a long drive of two thousand head, first to Kansas City
and then to St. Louis, with the loss of only one steer. The
father must have seemed to the son a latter-day David winning over Goliath.

Through such experiences, young Rogers could have been
drawn to oneness with the American hero of freedom, the
cowboy. This symbolic freedom, coupled with his tendencies of dedication to ideals of equality, readied him for his
role as American democrat.

THE TIME for Rogers to fill that role came during the twenties and thirties. At the beginning of that fifteen-year period, women won the suffrage for which they had begun to
struggle almost three-quarters of a century earlier. The
Nineteenth Amendment was to be, however, almost the last
gleam of that zeal for reform that had grown under the
Populists and flourished through the first Wilson Administration. For the rest of the time of Will Rogers' ascendancy,
much of American life exhibited few signs that the Ameri-

can dream of freedom and equality was becoming reality.

Signs to the contrary, however, were still present. Well before Wilson articulated his concept of the "New Freedom," some Americans after 1870 had to, according to Nye, review "the whole question of the individual and society" (pages 234-35), as well as nature and the Supreme Being; pragmatism and its choices of action made in the *belief* of free choice offered only partial reassurance. All this occurred under the impact of scientific speculation that "moved inevitably away from the individual toward the statistical," of population increase and industrialization that tended "to nullify the individual," and of the new psychology that denied freedom of the will. Mark Twain, in the preparatory stages of declaring the meaninglessness of existence, pictured a life in which man had no freedom, new, old, or otherwise. Theodore Dreiser would describe an American tragedy, the fall of an individual through no fault of his own, but rather through the concatenation of circumstances that held him prisoner and foreordained his defeat. Even Wilson's enunciation of the New Freedom contained a negation of the libertarian freedom dreamed of years before by its prophets—Thoreau, Emerson, and Whitman. "I feel confident," the new President had said, "that if Jefferson were living in our day he would see what we see: that the individual is caught in a great confused nexus of all sorts of complicated circumstances, and that to let him alone is to leave him helpless as against the obstacles with which he has to contend." The role of the government in such conditions was to guarantee one aspect of the dream of freedom and equality. "Without the watchful interference, the resolute interference, of the government, there can be no fair play between individuals and such powerful institutions as the trusts." Fair play through interference might seem a contradiction of terms until one understood President Wilson's affirmation that "human freedom consists in perfect adjustments of human interests and human activities and human energies."[25]

Constraining as this kind of New Freedom might sound, even the pursuit of it seemed abandoned during the twenties in the nostaglic search for normalcy. Speaking of domestic reform as well as of international isolation, John

Hicks in *Republican Ascendancy* remarked of the period, "Immediately after the war the reaction set in, and the pendulum that had swung so far to the left headed backward toward the right."[26]

So far had public opinion in the country departed from the ideal of Wilson's New Freedom that the government virtually abdicated in favor of the business that it was supposed to keep in balance for the sake of fair play. Probably, most Americans approved. Hicks reports that farmers the whole country over were urging Congress in 1921 to accept Henry Ford's proposal to purchase control of what one day would become the TVA—including a government loan at low interest to finance the payment, which itself was to have been only a small fraction of what the government had already invested. So low had the liberal tide sunk that it was all that Senator Norris could do to prevent the sale, much less move the government to action in the development of the region. "The business of America is business," President Coolidge was to be reported as saying,[27] and through such measures as the Mellon tax revision of 1926, the government evidently meant to redefine in favor of the few rather than of the many the nature of the "perfect adjustments of human interests and human activities and human energies."

Another part of the adjustment of postwar America was the culmination of a long-lived reform movement in the enactment of national prohibition, which in turn called forth an affirmation of the dream of freedom that was revealing in its lack of idealism. "People who wished to drink had no notion of being deprived of their liquor, whatever the Constitution might say on the subject," concludes Hicks, "indeed, it became the smart thing to drink, and many who had been temperate in their habits before were now moved to imbibe freely as a protest against the legal invasion of their 'personal liberty'" (page 178). Will Rogers claimed a $25,000 prize for the best suggestion for prohibition enforcement: a law making drinking compulsory. "People would rebel against it so that they would stop drinking."[28] In the case of prohibition, disobedience of an unjust law probably brought Al Capone more to the American mind than it did Henry David Thoreau.

Perhaps freedom of discussion seemed limited, too, in some respects. Opinion of communism was apparently so polarized as to produce, on one hand, the national-scale "red scare" at the beginning of the twenties and, on the other hand, to cause Eugene Lyons to complain at the end of the thirties that freedom for criticism of the Communist movement was stifled by the standard epithet of "red-baiting." During the depression, freedom for the pursuit of happiness seemed more like the freedom to starve for so many Americans that the fortunate ones with livelihoods could not ignore them.

Nor did the hope of equality seem as bright for the fifteen years of Rogers' national stardom as it had earlier. The eighteenth-century notion of equality seemed obsolete to many: Popular magazines agreed on the scientific fact of inequality; some scientists posited racial inequalities; and the new humanism stood, in Russel Nye's words, for "a class-structured society which placed power in the hands of a superior natural aristocracy of talent, taste, and restraint" (page 342). Crozier had written of an America in which "a natural equality of sentiment" sprang from and rested on "a broad equality of material and social conditions." But even before the years of the unemployed, the evicted, and the hungry, the hoped-for gentle gradations of economic status yielded unmistakably to marked gaps in shares of national income. In 1926, the Mellon revision reduced income taxes from $600,000 to $200,000 for the person with an income of $1,000,000. On the other hand, observes Hicks, "Concessions to the small taxpayer were held at a minimum" (page 132). By 1929, the American dreamer of equal economic opportunity had to console himself by looking lovingly at his radio, automobile, or washing machine, which he hoped were the same brands that the rich man had. By that year, one-third of all personal income was concentrated in the hands of 5 per cent of the population. In many white-collar and labor families, then, wives and children held jobs to supplement family income in order to pay for new essentials; the farmer's shrinking share of the national wealth had already made its impression on those Americans. Crèvecoeur had, so long before, referred to the absence in America of "despotic prince, . . . rich abbot, or

... mighty lord" to claim a part of the American's own fruits of his own labor. By contrast, John M. Blum has conveyed the mood of the twenties:

> Men of wealth and their standpat representatives who had chosen to control the Republican Party even at the risk of its defeat collected their reward after 1918. Content to let the Democratic factions neutralize each other, they systematically nullified the effect of most of the reform legislation of the previous two decades by turning government over to ineffectual administrators, by reducing the income tax, by re-enthroning industry and its privileges. This regression to conditions as they had been was possible only because of the changes that had occurred. Though the bastions of reform had become paper fortresses, the tired progressive was content with the semblance of success. He had no stomach either for subsidizing agriculture or for effecting a broad redistribution of income and property. He was happily seduced by the prosperity of the golden twenties. The cornucopia of advancing industrialism overflowed to the unprecedented benefit not of its masters alone but also of their bureaucratic, legal, medical and aesthetic servants. Industry took care, too, to allot some of the increase in productivity to labor. Business paternalism for the time made the doctrines of a magnanimous stewardship amply satisfying. The organized labor movement receded, losing both membership and spirit, smug in the false comfort it drew from the restriction of immigration which it helped to effect.[29]

Between 1920 and 1933, Jefferson may have tugged the heartstrings, but Hamilton held the purse strings. The farmers, of course, had not quietly acquiesced in the triumph of industrial centralization of wealth. Under the leadership of a farm equipment executive, George N. Peek, the agriculturalists fought for government legislation to provide farm prices supplying a degree of buying power on a parity with other groups in the economy. Nevertheless, believes the historian of the movement, the underlying motive in the drive for passage of successive versions of parity legislation was deeper than better living standards. "Basically," writes Gilbert Fite, "it was a conflict between agrarian and industrial capitalism. In the 1920's farmers were making a last-ditch stand against industrial and commercial domination."[30] Thus, at bottom, it was a reiteration of the Jeffersonian dream. Following a typical line of argument, Peek would assert, "Some of the countries of Europe made their choice, electing to become industrial rather than agricultural, thus relegating their agriculture to a system of peasantry. The political results speak for themselves."[31] The fact was, of course, that agriculture had already become subordinated to industry. Just as the McNary-Haugen bill was a symbol of the Jeffersonian counterattack, its successive defeats provided an emblem of the successful challenge to the agrarian dream of freedom and equality. "McNary says he would like to be given another chance to draw up another bill," Will Rogers would comment. "He says he can draw up one without the objectionable features of the last one. If it eliminates the objectionable features it won't be any good, for it will eliminate the relief."[32]

Other banner events of the period might well have shaken Americans' confidence in their hopes of freedom and equality. The Ku Klux Klan, given the talents of promoter Edward Y. Clarke, grew steadily in influence from 1920 until 1925; not until 1928 was its power clearly on the wane. Utilizing the superordinate goal of hatred in the name of "Americanism," it appealed to the intolerance of some Southerners against the Negro, to chauvinists who resented new immigrants, to certain prejudiced Protestants who reveled in righteous hatred of Jews and Catholics, to persons of fundamentalist-prone personalities who were convinced that all "wets" were Sons of Satan, and to reactionaries who wanted to "get" radicals of any persuasion. Hicks estimates a voting power of four to five million Klansmen at the end of 1924.

Coming along with or remaining after the Klan were other movements ostensibly protecting true Americanism. The Scopes trial, in 1925, signaled another attempt to enforce legislated virtue; fundamentalists wanted to stop talk on evolution in the schools and thus attempt to keep youth in a state of naïve Adamism. Henry Ford attacked the Jews. Mayor William Thompson of Chicago established his America First Foundation as watchdog over patriotism and schoolbooks. The Daughters of the American Revolution and the American Legion deplored textbook treatments that were deviations from the traditional in American history.* The D.A.R., itself, may have implied a status system based on ancestry: "Membership in this proves that you did have a forefather on or about 1776," Rogers wrote. "Non-membership proves that your forefathers, if any, must have sprung up from somewhere in just practically the last few years." The election of 1928 demonstrated the ability of rum and Romanism to arouse individual voters to heights of intolerance on both sides of the fence, even though recent research indicates that the national result was uncorrelated with these issues. "All religions in this campaign," wrote Rogers at the time, "seem such handicaps that I think it's better to claim you are an atheist."[33] It may not be too unfair to the spirit of tolerance in the twenties to speculate that John Humphrey Noyes, founder of Oneida Community, might have been permitted less time for his experiment than during his own period.

Then, in the spring of 1932, veterans gathered in Washington to exert pressure for passage of the Patman bill, which would have immediately paid the remaining 50 per cent of the soldiers' adjusted compensation, or bonus. They took up quarters in unoccupied buildings and in a "Hooverville" shanty town on the Anacostia Flats. On June 17, the Senate killed the Patman bill. President Hoover then set about dispersing the Bonus Expeditionary Force by offering to pay transportation home, then by sending out police, and, finally, by calling out tanks and cavalry after two Bonus soldiers had been killed by the police. To millions of Americans who knew the light weight of their own pocketbooks and understood the motives of the Bonus marchers, it may well have appeared that the government did not exist for the good of the governed. A year before, Rogers had observed, "You can get a road anywhere you want to out of the government, but you can't get a sandwich."

*Of course, such efforts to control the content of textbooks had occurred before; moreover, prior to World War I, there is some evidence that the D.A.R. supported some reform causes; finally, we should note that there is some question as to whether the superpatriot or the debunker represented the dominant mood of the time. See Wesley Frank Craven, *The Legend of the Founding Fathers*, 155, 140, and 160.

Roosevelt came. Whether his election signified little else than that the people had nowhere else to go but to the Democrats, or whether it hinted at a national desire for a return to the Jeffersonian-Jacksonian-Wilsonian dream of "life, liberty, and the pursuit of happiness," hope was renewed shortly after the new President's election. During the famous "100 Days" Rogers would comment, "The whole country is with him. Even if what he does is wrong they are with him. Just so he does something. If he burned down the Capitol we would cheer and say, 'Well, we at least got a fire started anyhow.' "[34] Later, with inflation of currency, introduction of low-cost loans for homes or home improvement, the Civilian Conservation Corps, the Works Progress Administration, the National Recovery Administration, together with a multitude of other agencies, the government worked by many trials and a fair share of errors toward both relief and recovery.

By the summer of 1935, the NRA was dead, together with whatever hopes had been attached to it. Social Security was in debate. Men like Huey Long and Father Coughlin were perverting the dream. Long would make every man a king if every man would consent to making him a dictator and trusting him to carry out a nebulous, confiscatory "Share-the-Wealth" program; one estimate of his strength indicated that he could poll three or four million votes. Rogers had other plans for the man from Louisiana. From Budapest, he wrote that Hungary, a monarchy, was looking for a king. "I believe the old Kingfish will fit 'em. I can fix it for you, Huey."[35] Coughlin, who later would turn his virulence against any who opposed him, had in 1934 organized his National Union for Social Justice, boasted of having nine million adherents, and pushed for nationalization of banks, credit, utilities, and natural resources. On the other end of the political continuum, the American Liberty League, with an executive board of millionaires, was formed in 1934 to combat what it called "the tyranny of autocratic power." Such groups and movements, coupled with Upton Sinclair's EPIC plan and the Townsend pension plan, might have given the impression that the country was coming apart in great gaping sections from abuse by the left and right.

As was the case with the dream of the individual, an

antihero to the dream of equality was emerging. His components existed in the values expressed by H. L. Mencken.
Cooperating with George Jean Nathan in 1920 to produce a
biting commentary in *The American Credo,* Mencken rose
to his crescendo, perhaps, in his damning *Notes on Democracy,* in 1926. From the pages of the *American Mercury* he
attacked Babbittry, political illiteracy, weak-kneed educators, fundamentalism, Communists, Socialists, Redbaiters,
and Rotarians. "If he had in mind any other purpose in his
diatribes than for the elite of mankind to laugh derisively
at all lesser men," says Hicks, "he concealed it well" (page
185). Years before, Mencken had explicitly drawn the antiequality hero when he wrote his study of Nietzsche's philosophy. There the superman, who was dedicated to the good
only of future generations (and then only in the sense that
his own highest achievement of power would incidentally
improve the race), was the "aristocratic individualist." He
would "seek every possible opportunity to increase and exalt his own sense of efficiency, of success, of mastery, of
power.... All growth must occur at the top. The strong must
grow stronger, and that they may do so, they must waste no
strength in the vain task of trying to lift up the weak."[36] To
be sure, Thomas Wolfe was writing a series of novels that
together would picture a hero of freedom and equality, but
not until after his death in 1937 would posthumous publication confirm his credo of the necessity to believe in a dream
of freedom, equality, progress, and the dignity of the individual. William Saroyan seemed out of sight: His *Human
Comedy,* relating the necessity of a wise innocence in hoping for equality and democracy, would not appear until
1943.

All this probably caused most Americans to feel an uneasy stir about the state of the dream of freedom and equality. Yet baseball still came every spring, between crises
spaced months or years apart; after the rise of radio, "Amos
'n Andy," perhaps in the tradition of the blackface minstrel,
warmed American living rooms with the humor of the
resilient spirit. Rogers' "big Normal Majority" could for a
silver coin take a ride on the movie "time-machine" and see
William S. Hart's Indianized cowboy symbolize the hero of
freedom and equality in silent productions like "Singer Jim

McKee" or "Tumbleweeds." Later, they could hear as well as watch realistic cowboys, like Richard Dix in *Cimarron*, who got dust on their clothes, or could choose to see stylized cowboys, like the latecomer William Boyd, wearing white sombreros and riding magnificent white horses.

Despite such diversions, Americans knew that probably the dream of freedom and equality was subject to some degree of pessimism. They knew it if for no other reason than that the immigration law of 1924 reduced arrival of the world's wretched ones to a trickle of the former torrent. "The Statue of Liberty now lifted her lamp only for a favoured few," writes Hicks (page 132). Most Americans, living in the land Jackson and earlier spokesmen for the dream had named an "asylum where the wretched and the oppressed find a refuge and a support," probably approved restriction of immigration. If they felt any national sense of guilt, they would have welcomed an embodiment of the dream. The time was right for Will Rogers to be the American democrat.

AMERICANS could see and hear that embodiment in the publicity accorded Rogers; his behavior that the public saw, read, or heard about made him seem the ideal American democrat. News stories told in 1923 of Rogers' giving a speech in New York's Piping Rock Club as a welcome to the Crown Prince of England; papers in 1926 announced that he had visited the Prince in London. They told of his overnight stay with Coolidge at the White House in the autumn of the same year, and a society story in 1928 described his lunch with members of the Vanderbilt and Harriman dynasties at Newport. In such stories, Rogers was the symbol of the common man who could move with aplomb among the world's elite.

In the papers, too, readers could see stories depicting Rogers as a responsible democrat, interested in the affairs of his country. The part he played in attempts to conciliate Mexican leaders in 1927 was a regular inclusion in the reports dealing with meetings between President Calles and the new American Ambassador, Dwight Morrow.[37] Other news stories reported such things as his influence in 1928 on tentative selection of a federal hospital site; his policy huddle with Secretary of State Stimson in 1931; his being boomed by a federal official as a candidate for the California governorship in 1934; and his being asked to testify to President Roosevelt's commission on aviation in the same year.

Newspaper and magazine stories further enhanced Rogers' role as a hero of freedom and equality by telling of his place as a cowboy. Since 1915, stories giving the main outlines of his life had appeared; always they covered the roaming cowboy jaunt around the world at the turn of the century. The time and deed may have seemed appealingly simple and uncomplicated to readers beset by the complexities of industrial America, who no longer had new country to think about wandering to. At least one *New York Times* feature story, in 1932, emphasized Rogers' freedom as a cowboy. After noting that at seventeen he had been a "full-fledged" cowboy who soon after "owned a small herd of his own," the story continued, "When the wanderlust seized him he sold his cattle and went down to Argentina with another youth. . . . He punched cattle across the pampas for $4 a month and then worked his way to Cape Town, South Africa." In the same article, Rogers was the cowboy who rides out to set things right. Implying that he had gone to South Africa to get into the Boer War, it continued, "The fighting ceased the day after he arrived and Will, swallowing his disappointment, joined a travelling 'Wild West' show." Rogers had become the hit of the show with the suitable Western stage name of "the Cherokee Kid," had played the leading cities of South Africa, and then had moved on to England.[38]

Despite many inaccuracies, such as managing to send Rogers to England instead of to Australia and New Zealand as was the fact, the story was true in spirit to the image of the fancy-free, hard-riding, straight-shooting man on horseback. Moreover, in the reader's imagination, Will Rogers as the Cherokee Kid in a wild West show could gallop forth just as Buffalo Bill had on that memorable day in 1893 at the Chicago World's Fair. Another *New York Times* feature, fifteen years earlier, captured the nostalgia identified with the figure of the cowboy and attached it to the figure of Will Rogers. After pointing out that he was American "to the grass roots" because he was part Cherokee, the story reported, "He is a representative of that other typically American group, the cowboys of the plains, who, in no far distant future, will become a memory, as they are now only picturesque characters of fiction and the movies to the great public."[39]

The press also helped disseminate a cowboy-hero story involving Rogers. Will Rogers, believed the public, had once saved many lives in 1905 by roping a runaway steer in Madison Square Garden. In 1915, the recounting attributed to Rogers was relatively bare of detail: " 'I came to New York with a show and had the luck to rope a wild steer that broke away from the arena in Madison Square Garden and started to climb up among the audience.' " By the time of Rogers' death, the story had circulated widely and lost little in the retelling. A 1935 sample from an Oklahoma newspaper will illustrate:

> One day a steer, crazed with the heat, leaped over the barriers and charged roaring down on the shrieking audience. A weather-bitten cowpuncher leaped after the brute, swung a lariat, and dropped a loop over its horns and swung the rope's end about a pillar, doubtless saving a number of people from injury and even death. This weather-bitten cowpuncher was Rogers.
>
> The New York papers were full of the thrilling incident and public notice was centered on the hero and his skill with the rope in his stage performances aroused admiration.[40]

The emphasis on Rogers' heroism did no damage to his portrait as "knight of the range." Will James, the cowboy writer, spoke for his own cowpuncher acquaintances when in a memorial anecdotage he wrote, "They knew and admired him the same way I did, as a cowboy. By that I don't mean anything that wears a big hat and boots, I mean one with the ideals, courage, sentiments, heart and guts that's needed in the making of a real cowboy."[41] No hero of the pulp westerns could have asked for more.

In press releases for his lecture tours, many of the same motifs already noted appeared. A sample prepared for a projected 1928-1929 tour, chosen for its brevity and its typicality of others used on tours between 1926 and 1928, illustrates:

> He has travelled all over the earth, has been wined,
> dined and feted by royalty and great ones, yet withal he
> has preserved that modesty and simplicity that made
> him a friend of and endeared him to all the "nesters" he
> rode the range with back in Oklahoma when he was a
> kid. He was Bill to them then and he is Bill to them now,
> and they love him for the same things that they loved
> him for then.*

Such "canned" stories, used in whole or part by local papers wherever Rogers went, helped make available to Americans the picture of Will Rogers as American democrat. He was the American with aplomb moving freely among all classes, who nevertheless did not forget the folks back home; he was the cowboy hero, even if—as erroneously stated—he was keeping company with dirt farmers, or "nesters" as they were sometimes called.

Besides such coverage in the press, word-of-mouth publicity may have helped etch lines of equalitarianism in Rogers' public portrait. As already noted, a California governor recalled that Rogers "was always happiest while exchanging cordial courtesies with the common people whom he enjoyed so much and served so well." One such happening lives in the memory of former Senator Mike Monroney, who in 1927 was a reporter on an Oklahoma City paper with the assignment of covering a Will Rogers arrival. Waiting for Rogers at the train station were civic leaders, suitably attired and arrayed to "welcome Will in true and dignified fashion." When the pullman glided to its stop, the suspense of waiting ended with the appearance of the man himself, "with his slouch hat askew, his hair sticking out from beneath the battered headpiece." Rogers took in the crowd at a glance and gave its members, including the local digni-

*Miscellaneous Scrapbook #1, Will Rogers Memorial. This paragraph was prepared for publication for a tour in 1928-1929 that never occurred because of Rogers' substituting for Fred Stone in a Broadway musical, *Three Cheers*. It is reproduced here because it is short, yet quite similar in tone to stories that actually went out for publication in earlier tours.

taries, his usual "Howdy!" "Then," says Monroney, "he spied a shabbily dressed cowhand, standing alone and unnoticed in the rear. 'By Gosh, men, there's McGinnity,' Rogers exclaimed, 'he was the best rough rider in Roosevelt's company. Meet my friend McGinnity!'" The moment of climax in the drama symbolic of equalitarianism was at hand. "The official welcoming party stood back," Monroney recalls, "and Will and an old friend made the trip to the hotel, alone, for an old time visit."[42] Table talk in Oklahoma City of that arrival could hardly have omitted such proof of Rogers' identity as American democrat. Donald Day describes a similar incident of equalitarianism occurring later, during the years of the locust. Rogers had arrived on location for a new movie—with the usual assortment of town officials and Chamber of Commerce handshakers to greet him. "As he stepped off the train," Day writes, "he noticed off to one side a hundred disreputable tramps waiting to say hello. . . . With a hurried 'Howdy do' to the official party, Will sauntered over to the group of 'forgotten men'" (pages 335-36). A half hour later, Rogers continued his journey, having emptied his pockets giving a "hand up" to the newly-remembered men. The cowboy ambassador thus did affirm the dream of equality (and of the individual's worth) in a way that no wreath-laying ambassador could have done.

Another story, making the rounds in New York City, reenacted the drama of equalitarianism. Rogers, perhaps preoccupied or in a hurry, had suddenly left his seat at a soda fountain when a Negro boy had taken the seat next to him. The conclusion, for the boy, was obvious—and one that he had shared with the fountain attendant: Will Rogers had not wanted to sit next to a Negro in a public eating place. Later, when Rogers heard the story from the attendant, he waited for the boy to come in at his accustomed time. "Say, boy, are you busy?" he asked at his first opportunity. "Come on, let's take on a dish of ice cream." Then, seated beside each other, they had done just that. Croy, who tells the story as he heard it from another, concludes that Rogers "had great liking and respect" for Negroes (page 161). Whatever Rogers' private thoughts were, his actions as circulated by word of mouth were those of an American democrat.

In California, parishioners of J. Whitcomb Brougher, former president of the Northern Baptist Convention, could hear the minister tell of Rogers' help in raising money for such causes as orphans' homes or for black Baptists. In the eyes of Brougher, Rogers "did not have a shadow of intolerance or prejudice in his make-up. He was a brother to all mankind." On movie lots, stories circulated of Rogers' unwillingness to claim favors or prerogatives not available to everyone else, or his unwillingness to act the "star." Apocrypal or not, such stories had the truth resulting from congruency to a legend. "Will Rogers' visits," says Monroney, speaking of Oklahoma, "always showed his great love for the average man."[43]

Also, in his own words, carried by newspaper, magazine, and radio, Rogers merged himself with the dream of freedom and equality. "We will never have true civilization until we have learned to recognize the rights of others," he wrote, early in his newspaper career. Learning to recognize the rights of others lay at the heart of Rogers' concept of freedom and equality. He spoke directly of the principle of freedom in 1934 when the American Liberty League, with its executive board of millionaires, gave the name of "resisting autocratic power" to league activities. "Everybody is running around in a circle announcing that somebody's pinched their 'liberty,' " he reported in his daily wire, and thus indicated a great need for a correct definition of liberty. Any "half-wit," he said, could tell that anarchy would not work: "So, the question arises, 'how much liberty can I get and get away with it?' " The answer was pithy: "Well, you can get no more than you give."[44] But readers had their own liberty, he said, to define freedom for themselves.

Equality would result from such a freedom, for the two were interfused. Over the years of Rogers' national prominence, his rambling conversation with his public expanded and refined his identification with the twin hopes. His comments through the twenties and thirties projected to his national audience a belief in a government serving the good of all citizens, rather than the good of specially-privileged groups; he identified strongly with *laissez faire* for the spirit, allowing freedom of the press, speech, and religion.

In his words, the advocacy of a moral freedom showed itself in championing of minority rights as grounded on spiritual equality. His public statements also accorded with the dreams of social, economic, and political equality— with each being commingled with the dream of freedom.

No better epitome of all these expressions exists in Rogers' work than that appearing from time to time during the late twenties. A 1927 weekly article probably best showed his democratic sentiments, voiced at an hour when such movements as "America First" were seeking approval and claiming national attention. Maintaining a mask of irony throughout, Rogers pointed out that such societies had "grabbed our little civilization just when it was on the brink and hauled it back to normalcy," for they had awakened America from its erroneous ways of freedom and equality. Before the great war people thought "as long as they paid their taxes, tended to their own business, went to their own churches, kept kinder within the law, that that was all they were supposed to do." But the country actually was backward and did not know it: "What we had to learn was to be better Americans." Then, during the war, the country had been in such a hurry to "muster up five or six million men of every breed and color" and start them drilling, that there had not been time to put them "through a clinic and find out" what per cent American these soldiers were. But this was peacetime and now the people had time to see who was who, and why. It was true that under the one society set up by the Declaration and the Constitution, "if you was here and belonged to that why you was all members of the same Club. You dident know whether you was a 2 and ¾ per cent or what ratio you was." Also, being willing to work and fight for the country, "you could worship what you wanted to, talk any language you wanted to, in fact it looked like a pretty liberal layout." But the new societies had pointed out the error: "After 150 or more years, it was immediately seen that this plan was no good, that the old boys that layed out the Constitution dident know much, that the country should be divided up in various Societys and Cliques." It was time for them to show "just what to do to prove that we are not against the old fatherland."[45]

Then Rogers introduced his own "modest proposal" to ensure the denial of the dream:

> Now I have looked over all the clubs and none of them seem to have enough scope, or broad minded ideal. So that is why as I told you a few weeks ago that I wanted to get this Society going. "America First" is all right, but it allows somebody else to be second. Now sometimes a thing second can be almost as good as something that's first. So that's the thing my society avoids. Its with the whole idea of there being no one else. In other words, I am just taking the spirit and foundation of other clubs and societys and making them broader.
>
> They are against something (They got to be against something or they wouldent be formed). Well, mine improves on any of theirs; its against everything. . . . I am getting a lot of applications already, real redblooded go-gettum Americans, that have seen this country trampled under foreign feet enough, and they are right out in the open. Why I figure the patriotism in my organization when I get it formed will run around 165 or 170 percent American. It will make a sucker out of these little 100 percent organizations. Its not too late to send your $20 yet. Remember when you belong to "America Only" you are the last word in organizations.[46]

Though it is easy to overestimate Rogers' liberalism because of this message directed against the far right, he believed in that freedom and equality that allowed the millions of all "breeds and colors," whatever their "ratio" of Americanism was, to belong as members in good standing to the club set up by the Constitution and the Declaration of Independence, to go "50-50," and to be free in worship and speech.

Like the Jeffersonians who came to trust a strong central government after they had power over it, Rogers said in many ways that the cause of freedom was served by a government willing to work for the good of the people. (Because the measure of equality provided by such a government related to the idea of all the people being worthy, comments of this sort were also often appropriate to the dream of the individual's dignity.)

One of the unalienable rights of free men was that of life. Long before the days of the Great Depression, Rogers used property rights to help make his point on the right of children to life and the role of government in helping guarantee it. "You wire the State or Federal Government that your Cow or Hog is sick and they will send out experts from Washington and appropriate money to eradicate the cause. You wire them that your Baby has the Diptheria [*sic*] or Scarlet Fever and see what they do." The answer was bleak, in comparison with care of property: "All you will do is hire your own Doctor, if you are able, and there will be a flag put up on your front gate." The way to get help, he said, was "Don't tell them it is any human sickness. Tell them it is Boll Weevil or Chinch Bugs, and they will come a running." Then came the clincher, "Why can't we get the Government to at least do for a Child's protection what they do for a Cow or a Hog?" Rogers was concerned, too, for the needs of the aged: "You know, we are the last civilized, (chuckle) if you can call it that, to do anything for old people—all we do is just let 'em—we just watch 'em get older, is all we do." Or during the time of scourging, when a federal administration apparently seemed more willing to work for the good of the Hamiltonian elite than for the good of King Demos, he might say, with no pretense at irony, "If you live under a Government and it dont provide some means of you getting work when you really want it and will do it, why then there is something wrong." He made clear how wrong by stating an accepted premise and its related alternatives: "You can't just let the people starve, so if you dont give em work, and you dont give em food, or money to buy it, why what are they to do? What is the matter with our Country anyhow?"[47] Such statements came regularly enough from Rogers' lips and typewriter that his audience could identify him with the dream of a government serving the good of all; he had said it before the American earthquake (as Edmund Wilson would call it) and that cataclysm gave his later words timeliness.

One way to serve the good of all was to keep America free from domination by special interests. Since at least the days of Bryan, agrarians had inveighed against "the interests." Will Rogers spoke and wrote in a tradition that was relevant, itself, to the American dream. Noting the rise of stock market values after Coolidge's election, Rogers doubted that the rise was related in any real way to the production and consumption of goods and, therefore, asserted that the producer or consumer should be unaffected by special interest speculation: "You are interfering with personal rights. Then another class of men bet thousands of dollars every day on race horses, yet they don't interfere with the horse raiser in Texas." Most of the time, when writing against domination by special interests, Rogers avoided characterizing either party as a tool for the interests, commenting instead on individuals. But during depression times he did categorize parties on occasion: "Now with a Republican there is just something about his makeup, that the richer the man, the less he should be watched, the bigger the industry the wider open it should be run." Rogers made clear this was wrong: "Its just against their principles to stop a guy from making a big killing, even if he is robbing a bank. They claim you are 'Hamstringing big Business.' "[48]

In thus urging the case against domination of the country by the interests, Rogers as the American democrat was becoming coessential with the dream of freedom. He merged himself with that vision, too, by defending in his commentary the freedoms of press, speech, and religion. "We got lots of fleas on us," Rogers wrote, "and everybody is scratching to get 'em off, but there is one insect that bothers most of the world that we are at least free from, and that is a newspaper press that is not free." One of Rogers' targets—as a working newspaperman—was censorship of books by organizations ostensibly promoting patriotism and Americanism. When a mayor of Chicago sought to root out what he thought to be unwholesome foreign influences in the book stacks of his city, Rogers threw his typewriter at him. "It seems that the Chicago Library has been subsidized by the King of England. He had been sticking a lot of Dick Turpin novels in there and replacing the lives of Hinky Dink and Bath House John." An adumbration of what would later be happening in Germany followed:

Chicago become famous over one fire and Bill [Thompson] wants to personally conduct another. He wants to strike the flint that will light the torch of Liberty as they burn to a cinder every page containing reference, hint, suspicion, heresay [sic], or even inference between lines of the British Empire, King George or any of his forebears, or offsprings. Even to any picture

depicting the eating of roast beef, Plum Duff, Yorkshire
Buck, or the drinking of Lime Juice. All such periodicals
will be burned at the stake on the filled-in-Beach, just
before the next election.[49]

He noted another time that, though one's mind naturally
turned to "higher things," during the week of his visit to
Boston, *An American Tragedy* could not be "sold over the
bar." He further noted that "the Committee was then reading Pilgrims Progress, to see if there wasent some underlying meaning to it."

Freedom of the press, however, approached irresponsi-
ble anarchy when newspapers violated the rights of the
individual. Because of the problem of attracting reader interest, Rogers felt that the press abused its freedom not only
by sensationalizing crime stories but (and more to the point
of the dream of freedom) at times it also violated the individual's dignity. In hyperbolic terms, Rogers might insist
that "the last right of a citizen has been taken away from
'em. You can't even commit suicide in private any more."
The press asked all sorts of prying questions in its role as
coroner:

> "What's the idea leaving a note that nobody but your wife
> can understand?" "Don't you know this is a free country
> and the public has got as much right to know everything
> as your family?" "Who did you love, and when, and
> why?" "Have you got any old love letters, or birthmarks
> on you that we haven't seen? We'll teach you to try and
> sneak off and die and not let us in on all the reasons.
> Now get up and pose for the photographers, and give us
> the whole confession, and don't let it happen any more."

Overall, however, Rogers rejoiced in the part the press
played in making America an open society. "Every day just
shows us what a lucky country we are," he wrote in the lead
paragraph to a dispatch on the benefits of a free press.[50]

Rogers also expressed devotion to free speech in an open
society. No more explicit pointer to this part of his public
portrait exists than his statements on free speech for Communists during the late twenties and the thirties. As late as
1935, Rogers was praising institutions of free speech in England, such as Hyde Park; as early as 1925, he dealt with
events surrounding an earlier meeting of "these Reds, or

Bolsheviki, or whatever they call themselves" in Madison Square Garden. "Now some say that a thing like that should not be allowed. Why sure it should be allowed!" he insisted. Then he applied an analogy establishing one reason for freedom of speech and at the same time making clear his lack of agreement with the Communists: "It's just like an exhaust on an Automobile. No matter how high priced the Car, you have to have an exit for its bad Air, and Gasses [sic]. They have got to come out." Eighteen months after the stock market crash, Communists seemed to be on the march. They had what may have seemed to be plausible, enticing explanations for the bewildering economic chaos; they thus seemed to many Americans a greater threat than they had appeared to be five years before. Rogers still applauded efforts to give the Reds a hearing. "Yesterday when thousands of police from the White House to Claremore were fighting the Reds to keep them from marching, Mayor [James] Rolph [of San Francisco] helped 'em form in line, had his men show them where the city hall was, fixed a stand for 'em to speak on, thanked 'em for coming to see him, and a good time was had by all, except the women who were unable to get arrested." At other times, Rogers used restrictions on free speech in Russia to sharpen the contrast; thus the closed society became the foil by which the dream of free speech glittered for the jewel that it was. "Russia is a country that is burying their troubles. Your criticism is your epitaph." Listeners to a 1934 Rogers network broadcast series wanted to know whether the Russian people had "anything to say" about their government. "I have an answer to that," the American democrat drawled. "Yes, they have, but they must say it to themselves and under their breaths."[51]

Rogers defended free speech at other times of high audience attention, too. When in 1934 an accuser asserted that Rexford Tugwell and others at a dinner party had plotted a Communist takeover, a congressional investigation followed; at its conclusion, Rogers had a pungent comment. At good dinner parties, people didn't say sensible things, anyhow; besides, "you know there is two places where what a person says should not be held against 'em in a court of law. One is at a dinner and the other on the witness stand of a Washington investigation. Both affairs are purely social

and should be covered only by the society editor." Aware
that an investigation often was a two-edged sword, he wrote
in the waning days of 1934, "From the record of all our
previous investigations it just looks like nobody can emerge
with their nose entirely clean." The reason was clear and
not necessarily related to guilt: "I don't care who you are,
you just can't reach middle life without having done and
said a whole lot of foolish things." Rogers, a critic once said,
had early claimed "a license of free speech"; as the wisely-
innocent American democrat of the mass media, he also
claimed it for all Americans. (Between times, he might sol-
emnly inform his audience that he had just addressed a
state legislature in order to "inject some seriousness" into
the proceedings.)[52]

No less important to the dream of freedom was the ideal
of liberty of conscience. When Rogers, in the character of
the wise new Adam, remarked after mixing with so many
people all over the world, "I can honestly tell you that I dont
think that any one religion is the religion," he was also
stating his commitment to the dream of religious freedom.
Every time he "argued not about religion," he identified not
only with the action corollaries of the dream of the individual's worth, but also with one category of the dream of
freedom. As with free speech, he sometimes used Russia as
a contrast: "I don't care what you believe in, but you certainly got a right to that belief, and you shouldent have to
give it up to take part in the Government of your Native
Land. If the Bolsheviks say that religion was holding the
people back from progress, why let it hold them back. Progress ain't selling that high." More importantly, perhaps,
when national attention fastened to the Scopes trial, Rogers
chose to relate intellectual freedom to religious liberty and
defend them both during simplistic fundamentalism's last
great stand. Bryan's conduct of the prosecution was wrong,
first, on the ground that it violated intellectual freedom,
"You can't stop a man thinking; neither do I believe Bryan
could start a serious man thinking." Those who believed
that their ancestors "were as proficient with their toes as
with their fingers" had as much right to that idea as did
Bryan to "believe he is a second messiah and that Nebraska
was the modern manger." Softening his attack by saying

that he liked "Bill," Rogers disapproved, in the second place, because Bryan was trying to make political hay: "Now he is going to try and drag something that pertains to the Bible into a political campaign. He can't ever do that. He might make Tennessee the side show of America, but he can't make a street carnival of the whole United States." Finally, Bryan was wrong because of Constitutional guarantees, which could not be amended away.

> As for changing the Constitution that has been done
> every day. They have juggled it around until it looks like
> a moving picture of a popular book (it's so different from
> the original). But when those old boys who blue-printed
> the first Constitution decided that a man can believe
> what he likes in regard to religion, that's one line that is
> going to stay put.[53]

Rogers gained credibility in such a message because he "liked" his adversary and, as "reluctant witness" for the defense, he did not think "we came from a monkey." He also identified his stand on the issue with the face of freedom on the great American god-of-many-faces. Thus, in his religious ecumenicity, he implied a spiritual equality of mankind.

In other statements he made himself explicitly one with the dream of equality: "I believe the Lord split knowledge up among his subjects about equal after all," Rogers once wrote, and in saying it related himself to the equality dream. At great length, in his speeches and newspaper articles, Rogers merged himself with the visions of spiritual, social, economic, and political equality.

His chief mode of identification with the dream of spiritual equality was to speak up for members of minority groups in America. Not many years after he had become a national institution, Rogers gave a slap to all minority baiters in general, but to United States Senator Thomas Heflin in particular; the daily wire printed in February, 1927, bore the dateline of Montgomery, Alabama:

> Senator Heflin of Alabama held up all Senate business
> yesterday for five hours. That's a record for narrow
> views.
> Tonight in his home capital I am pleading with

> Alabama to please not exterminate all Catholics,
> Republicans, Jews, Negroes, Jim Reed, Al Smith,
> Wadsworth, Mellon and Coolidge and the Pope.[54]

Rogers had much fun with Heflin as a symbol of all minority baiters, "Tom will be wanting to abolish boulevards that make direct right angle crossings (claiming that it was some sort of papal sign), and make 'em cross each other slantwise." Or he could hold up the mask of irony and, describing himself as "a Senator in waiting," promise to denounce Catholics on Monday, Baptists on Tuesday, Methodists (both North and South) on Wednesday. Thursday would be for Presbyterians and Friday would be society day, reserved for Episcopalians. Saturday was reserved for summing up and hitting any groups that he had overlooked during the week. When Al Smith, the boy from the sidewalks of New York, felt compelled to make a policy statement in 1927 to ease apprehension regarding his Catholic candidacy, Rogers applauded it and scored the country: "It's no compliment to a nation's intelligence when these things have to be explained."[55]

Members of the Jewish, Negro, and American Indian minorities also had a friend in Rogers. "There is a Jewish fellow running," he wrote of the 1928 gubernatorial race in New York, adding a sly dig at bigotry, "and if he gets it and makes a good Governor for four years, why, the religious issue won't come up again for President till 1936." When the trouble between Henry Ford and Jewish Americans was at its height, Rogers turned the stereotype of Jews as money grabbers against the gentiles by implying that the root of the trouble was Ford's need of a profit. "I am in Detroit in connection with trouble between Henry Ford and Jewish people," he advised his readers. "Think if every one of them will agree to buy one of those things at cost plus 10 per cent, trouble will be patched up all around." Later, when the feud was settled as far as public profession was concerned, the American democrat was serious both in his praise of Ford's public statement and in his being aware that Ford had been wrong. Rogers was to die before Hitler's Germany moved to its "final solution" of its "Jewish problem," but he knew of Hitler's persuasive techniques, which cast Jews as the scapegoat for German failures. In 1933, Rogers filed a wire from Washington, D. C., that punched at the myth of Aryan superiority by holding up a Jew as being superior to the Führer himself: "That fellow Hitler kinder prides himself on his oratory," he wrote. "Say, if he could have heard Rabbi Wise of New York at a great Jewish convention here today Hitler would have been speechless. Wise had everything." Wise, himself, told of more than one occasion on which Rogers had contributed to Jewish causes. At one banquet, Rogers had presented an offering saying, "This is my contribution to the good cause of the American Jewish Congress in defending Jewish rights wherever invaded or assailed." Will Rogers' public portrait had no swastika on it: Shortly after his death, national headquarters for Hadassah announced that the San Francisco chapter was planting a memorial tree in Palestine in recognition of Rogers' "sympathetic understanding" of the Zionist movement.[56]

In his public statements, Rogers also recognized the black American's rights as a human being and a citizen. He wrote of Negroes on their merits as men; he neither approved nor disapproved of them simply because of their skin color. An outstanding Negro cowboy had taught him to ride and rope, and Rogers wrote admiringly of other Negro cowboys' exploits, as in the following: "A little small, good-natured, likeable Negro died last week in Oklahoma, named Bill Pickett. Don't mean a thing to you, does it?" And then Rogers explained why it should. "Well, he was the originator of a stunt that has thrilled millions. It was the rodeo stunt of 'bulldogging.' "[57] In Rogers' columns, a white man recognized the contributions of Negroes to the subculture of the man on horseback. Today, Will Rogers would be no hero of equality for Negroes. He frequently called Afro-Americans "darkeys," "coloreds," and "senegambians"; his often-expressed admiration for *Birth of a Nation*, universally regarded now as a racist movie, would be repelling today. In his film appearances with "Step and Fetchit," a black artist who capitalized upon the stereotype of the Negro as lazy, vacant, and fearful, Rogers did nothing to revise the stereotype. Although the times of his ascendancy in the mass media, roughly from 1922 through 1935, were years of relative racial calm, Rogers ignored in his columns the Harlem riot in March, 1935.

By the standards of his own time, however, Will Rogers' imaged face probably was a friendly one to the hopes of black Americans. During the great Mississippi flood of 1927, with ten thousand square miles washed into barren mud flats, Rogers saw the suffering of Negroes and reasoned that God saw them as being equal to whites: "The Lord so constituted everybody that no matter what color you are you require about the same amount of nourishment." In a moment when being poor and homeless was almost a badge deserving of honor for white dwellers along the Mississippi, the man from the Verdigris included black Americans:

> When you talk about poor people that have been hit by
> this flood, look at the thousands and thousands of
> Negroes that never did have much, but now its washed
> away. You don't want to forget that water is just as high
> up on them as it is if they were white.[58]

Indeed, Rogers could sound somewhat like a modern campaigner for poor people's rights, as he did in 1931 when he commented on a much-trumpeted rise in the stock market: "United States Steel can go to a thousand and one, Auburns to a million, but that don't bring one biscuit to a poor Negro family of fifteen in Arkansas, who haven't got a chance to get a single penny in money till their little few bales of cotton are sold way next fall." And, in 1927, when a Supreme Court decision on southern primary voting seemingly promised wider Negro participation, Rogers not only had his usual fun ("First thing you know they will be allowing a white Republican to associate with a white Democrat in the South.") but signed himself approvingly of the decision: "Yours for quality in politics regardless of quantity and color." Later, when some whites disapproved of Mrs. Hoover's entertaining the wife of a Negro congressman, Rogers defended the First Lady and the rights of Negroes as voters:

> A week or so ago there was quite an attempt to try and
> make something out of the fact that the colored
> Congressman's wife got so far in the White House that
> she got three saucers of tea before anybody knew it.
> No, wait a minute, lets get this straight. . . . Its all right

to say the Coolidges, the Hardings, the Wilsons, and all
those dident do it, but the opportunity was not put up to
them. There was no colored Congressman in their time.
Dixie hadent reached Chicago.
  Now Mrs. Hoover knew what she was doing. If it was a
custom for the First Lady of the White House to
entertain all the Congressmans' Wives, then when a
colored one come along there was nothing else to do.
When he was elected and ready to be seated there was no
one in a position to say they wouldent sit with him in
Congress. No, it was a custom and nothing was thought
of it.

Then Rogers concluded his discussion of the matter with a
view consonant with the mainstream of American politics:
"Neither party refused their votes, and you got to give 'em
a little consideration."[59]

When Rogers told the nation, in 1925, of the integration of
memorial services in Oklahoma for his sister Maude, he
possibly was not a favorite with the Ku Klux Klan, but he
was, in what would be Sandburg's later description, embodying the "best of the Constitution and the Declaration of
Independence" for his time. "Today, as I write this, I am not
in the Follies, the carefree Comedian who jokes about everything. I am out in Oklahoma, among my People, my
Cherokee people, who don't expect a laugh for everything
I say," wrote the sorrowing cowboy philosopher. "Now we
are in the South, of the South, and according to Northern
standards we don't rate the Negro any too high." In refuta-
tion, Rogers quoted his sister's words: "They are all folks,
they have helped me for years, they are all my friends.
When I am gone I don't want you Children at my Funeral
to show any preference." Then he underlined the statement: "That's the real South's real feelings for its real
friends. Death knows no Denomination. Death draws no
Color line."[60]

If, in his public image, Will Rogers was no crusader for
Negro causes, he at the same time was no bigot. He chose
to regard the Negro on the very basis that the black American claims today: as human being, man, and American in
his own right. Admittedly, Rogers' dispatches on behalf of
the American Indian were more militant than those for

blacks, just as contemporary Negro spokesmen have said more on behalf of blacks than of Indians.

A favorite but biting joke that Rogers may have repeated many times was that his Indian ancestors had welcomed the *Mayflower* and had been sorry ever since. He could not always contain his judgment in the mask of humor, however. Perhaps the trigger for his anger would be his understanding of oil "royalty arrangements" on Indian lands, as in 1927:

> They struck oil on the Navajos' land three years ago. I foolishly asked how often they get their payments for their oil royalty. Well, they hadn't any yet. They took a million of it to build a bridge across the Little Colorado River so tourists wouldn't have to drive so far around to see the Grand Canyon. The Navajos paid for the bridge and there has never been a Navajo crossed it yet.
>
> If the Indian's oil royalties hold out they will have enough to build the Boulder Dam for the Whites.

When the dam was built, by whatever actual means of financing, Rogers took an historical look at the meaning of the event for readers of his weekly column:

> We were out there on Indian land dedicating a Dam to get water for white people to come out and use and gradually take more Indian land away. There is going to be nothing different. It started with Lief Erricson [*sic*] in 996, then skipped over Columbus in 1492, for he couldent find this Country in four trips. Then come the Spanish settlers, then the Mayflower was the last straw.
>
> They dident have any Ex-President at the dedicating at their taking land from the Indians but they got it just the same, and they have kept right on doing it up to last week. So you see history repeats itself, the same as it has in wars.[61]

Rogers could wheel his satiric scorn into action at any time: "See by the paper this morning where the Department of Indian Affairs have promised that they will have their Indian agents do better this year," he might begin innocently enough. Then would come the snap of the whip: "I mean do better for the Indians, for a change." Rogers might tell his readers about a book that revealed the perfidy of the white man, or state in hyperbole, "The Pine Ridge Agency Siouxs [*sic*] have to eat so much horse meat, that they are wearing bridles instead of hats." Always suspicious of the outcomes of diplomatic conferences, Rogers could rejoice at a conference "that got somewhere":

> The Navajo Indians held a conference and decided that they could get along without the services of about twenty-five white officeholders that had been appointed to help look after them. The Indians said they were doing it to save the white man money. Who said the Indian didn't have any humor?

In the spring of 1935 Rogers, under the impression that a national women's organization was about to pass over a qualified Indian candidate for the national presidency, wrote in a way that must have, by that time, been predictable by his audience: "You would expect intolerance from some organizations, but not from the most civilized one we have." Even one of the great uncivilized tribes, the Republicans, had elected a part-Indian as Vice-President. "So I don't believe these ladies are going to get bias. Of course, there is some of 'em that would love to meet around the convention campfire and shout: 'Well, sisters, we scalped another Indian. We have to keep this club 100 per cent American.' "[62] Rogers apparently felt strongly that "they couldn't afford to do that"; less than a week later, he issued a similar pronouncement in his weekly radio broadcast.

Part of Rogers' stance as American democrat, then, was this sort of defense of minority Americans in which, in the good company of Edmund Burke, he discussed general principles with reference only to specific rights. "Every human and every place is equal after all," he wrote in 1933, considering everything on balance. To those who may not have been attracted by his concern for every human, another kind of message could well have given him his homespun toga as true equalitarian. On the occasion of publication in 1930 of the annual Social Register, Rogers developed at some length a motif relating to social equality that appeared often in his columns: "Of all the undemocratic things you can think of just off hand that is the prize 'Hooey,' a book to tell you who is a good Parlor Hound and who is a sort of mongrel around the tea table." Explaining that society was "any band of folks that kinder throw in with each other, and mess around together for each others discomfort," he pointed out that the only thing distinctive about "high society" was the money spent in "messing around" and hereditary membership. "No matter who you raise up in your family zoo why they naturally inherit your space in the 'Social Register.' Your personal accomplishments have nothing to do with it." Missing, Rogers noted, was polar explorer Byrd: "Guess he had been running around these poles when he should have been at home taking care of his duties in the drawing room." Missing, too, was Henry Ford: "Transportationally he is a Giant, but socially he is a Gnat. I can just imagine his embarrassment when he found that out." In this piece, more than envy by a latter-day Buckskin was involved. Embedded in its texture was the equality idea that every man should be accepted for what, rather than who, he was. At the conclusion, Rogers used a variant of a standard deflater of stuffed shirts: "So for downright amusement in reading matter that Register will compete with the Congressional Record." With Boy Scouts, Four-H, Future Farmers of America, and other organizations emphasizing achievement (as he saw it) for acceptance, he dealt lovingly as being "purely democratic," requiring "no accident of birth, no pull, no nothing but just merit."[63] Thus, on these and numerous other occasions, Will Rogers' public image coalesced with the dream of social equality. His and America's vision was of an open society.

In words that served to unite him with the dream of economic equality, Rogers espoused no communal vision of a seamless society composed of a gray sameness of station for all. Instead, the message he expressed was one advocating as nearly-equal opportunity for financial gain as was possible and one calling for fairness to all in distribution of the national wealth.

A 1926 dispatch outlined the grounds for providing a degree of equal financial opportunity for all: Wealth arose from the efforts of the entire community and, therefore, no segment of the community should be permitted an eternal monopoly upon it. Specifically, Rogers was referring to a proposed tax revision relieving the "suffering" of the country's wealthy beneficiaries: "They claim that sometimes

there has been cases known when they had to sell one of the
Yachts to pay the Government the Inheritance Tax and in
one extreme case I remember reading where a Son had to
give up his membership in over half of his Golf Clubs."
Such pitiful tales had convinced the "Proletariat Senators"
that "if the Father died with a hundred million that he had
wormed out of our country, that the spoils all belonged to
the Children and no part of all to the Community that had
made it possible for him to accumulate this heavy jack."
Rogers made the conclusion absurd: "In other words they
claim his Descendants were more responsible for him making it than the state he made it out of."[64]

In other telegrams and speeches, Rogers spoke directly of
the need of equal economic opportunity. True to the Jeffersonian agrarian tradition, he placed the financial aspirations of the worker or farmer on a par with those of the
Hamiltonian elite. The idea that Roosevelt's Administration was attempting to give economic opportunity to the
little man as well as the big formed the basis of Rogers'
approval in a nationwide radio speech in 1933, "I tell you
folks, I came away from Washington last week with the
idea that the little fellow had got somebody in his corner in
Washington." The Administration wasn't against Big Business, and many business leaders were working hard with
the Government, he pointed out, "but for the first time in
years, the big man comes to Washington the same as the
little man." Rogers added an epitaph, a favorite device with
him: "If this administration ever goes under it should have
written on its tombstone: 'Perished through trying to give
the little fellow a square deal.' "[65] The years of the locust
required an affirmation of the American dream in general
and of the vision of equal economic equality in particular.

A measure of that economic equality thus depended upon
an equality of opportunity and an equitable distribution of
the nation's wealth. In his network broadcast with President Hoover in the fall of 1931, Rogers put the question of
economic equality into perspective in relation to other issues of the day:

Now here we are worrying and reading in the papers
about a hundred different problems that they got us all
excited and making us believe they amount to something.
This country has just got one problem, it's not the

143

balancing of Mr. Mellon's budget, (that's his worry, not ours), it's not the League of Nations, that you read a lot about, it's not the silver question—not a one of these problems mean a thing in the world to us, as long as we have seven million of our own out of work, that's our only problem, and to arrange the affairs of this prosperous country, (yes, prosperous right now) to so arrange it so that a man that wants work can get work, and give him a more equal division of the wealth that the country produces.

Deluged with requests for copies of the speech, Rogers may have been getting votes because—as some political strategists might suggest—he was tying himself not to some specific proposal but rather to a principle that could generate proposals. Too, of course, Rogers appeared as a voice of the American dream in that he expounded his doctrines of freedom and equality in the concrete contexts of current events. "This panic has been a great equalizer," he wrote, tongue in cheek. "Its done away entirely with the smart man."[66] Thus on the ideological, directly material level, Rogers identified with the dream of freedom and equality.

On the next level, his actions, as revealed in what he said and wrote, were similar in content to the twin dreams. "If we dident have to stop and play politics any administration could almost make a Garden of Eden out of us," he wrote in his democrat's role of being independent of political parties. He also performed over the years the action corollaries of being a practitioner of fair play and defender of the underdog. In so doing he was naturally being the responsibly free American. He showed his equalitarianism by unabashedness in the presence of the mighty, mingling with people of all estates, and championing manners that were civilized without being foppish. What all of this may have said to his national audience was that he practiced what he preached; like Chaucer's country parson, Rogers would have thus gained affection and believability.

"The floating, uncommitted electors, clerks, mechanics, the masters of parties—watching aloof, inclining victory this side or that side—such are the ones most needed, present and future," Walt Whitman had written in his plan for Americans to conserve freedom by being interested in poli-

tics but above parties. Will Rogers, through his public statements, seemed to do just that. "I am as independent as any
one writing," he told a reader in an open letter. "I have as
many Republican as Democratic papers, as many readers
that cant read as can. The editorial policies of these great
dailies mean nothing to me, I am going to call em like I see
em."[67] In practice, this realistic approach meant both com-
plimenting worthy things and "taking a shot" at "hooey."

In many daily wires, Rogers paid homage to political leaders whom he perceived as not being party men—William E.
Borah, in particular. "What's best for America is best for
Borah," he said by daily dispatch in 1927. After the Democratic loss in 1928, he conducted his own post mortem in the
guise of a toastmaster talking to a Democratic gathering
through the columns of *The Saturday Evening Post.* What
the Democrats needed to do was play fewer party politics
and better represent the interests of the country. "In other
words, get in there and act like you was working for the
taxpayer instead of exclusively for the Democratic Party.
Vote 'YES' on something besides widening the Chatahoo-
chie." Democrats should eliminate secret caucuses: "If you
haven't got the nerve to let the people know how you stand
on anything, have a sick friend, and go home and sit up with
him on the day of the vote." Democrats, he opined, would be
surprised to learn how quickly people would find out that
such politicians were nonpartisan:

> If the Senate wants to take a secret vote, let it be known
> that Democrats were against it to a man. In other words,
> you got to shame the Republicans into decency. . . . It
> wouldn't take a Party any longer to show that it was
> Progressive than it would an individual. Borah, just for
> Campaign purposes, was listed as a Republican. But look
> how quick he lived it down. Now, you would be surprised
> at the amount of people that think he is working for the
> people.[68]

As late as 1934, Rogers was praising Borah as politician
above party.

Much of the "hooey" at which Rogers aimed his barbed
wit was blind party loyalty, "wets" and "drys" as well as
Democratic and Republican. To counteract the sometimes
reluctant embraces of party men for sake of party unity,

Rogers came out for himself (at the suggestion of Robert Sherwood and the old *Life* magazine) for President in 1928. As the "Bunkless Candidate," free from "party hooey," he "campaigned" not only in the pages of *Life,* but also through the vast resources of his national newspaper syndicate:

> McAdoo finally came out for Smith, and to offset that Democratic gain, why Coolidge came out for Hoover.
>
> So that leaves only myself in the open.
>
> I have been studying the two parties and here is the difference: Hoover wants all the drys, and as many wets as possible. Smith wants all the wets and as many drys as he can get.
>
> Hoover says he will relieve the farmer, even if he has to call congress. Smith says he will relieve the farmer even if he has to appoint a commission.
>
> Hoover says the tariff will be kept up. Smith highly indorses prosperity.
>
> Hoover wants no votes merely on account of religion. Smith wants no votes solely on religious grounds. Both would accept the mohammedan vote if offered.
>
> Hoover would like to live in the white house. Smith is not averse to living in the white house. And in order to get in there either one will promise the voters anything from perpetual motion, to eternal salvation.
>
> So I am out openly for myself. . . .
>
> I have promised nothing, and am the only one of the three that can make good on the promises, so to offset Coolidge and McAdoo I come out for myself.

In his 1928 role of politician without party, Will Rogers performed an action corollary of the dream of freedom and equality. Such an identification was probably at least partly responsible for the report in *Nation* that headquarters for the "Anti-Bunk" party were besieged by large numbers of persons "desirous of voting for Rogers and anxious to find out how to do it."[69]

Another action corollary of the dream of freedom and equality was to practice fair play and defend the underdog. In 1924, Rogers addressed his readers in a way that showed him not only to be free from party domination but also to be writing with a sense of fair play: "I generally give the Party in power, whether Republican or Democratic, the more digs because they are generally doing the Country the most damage, and besides I don't think it is fair to jump too much on the fellow who is down." Nearly a decade later, Rogers was still describing fair play at a time when political fever fired the nation, "You must never disagree with a man while you are facing him," he wrote, applying the Indian principle of looking back over the shoulder in order to avoid getting lost on the return trip. "Go around behind him and look the same way they do when you are facing him. Look over his shoulder and get his viewpoint, then go back and face him and you will have a different idea."[70]

Rogers gave fair treatment to all, whether big or little in importance, including politicians. He spoke directly to Hoover during a radio broadcast after the 1932 election: "You just happened to be the man that was left watching the dam when the dam busted, and we expected that you would put the water back. Not a soul in America will ever crow to you. They will moan with you, but they won't exult over you." In later years, he evidently felt the need to treat Hoover's conqueror with the same fairness, at a time when the honeymoon between Roosevelt and the people was over, "I could sit down from now till morning and tell you what he should not have done, but if you give me five minutes continuous time, I couldent tell you what he should have done, and neither can any of the rest of 'em."[71]

Rogers was fair both to bonus-collecting veterans and to bankers charged with redeeming bonus certificates, to farmer and consumer, to the advantaged and the disadvantaged during the depression, to employers who realized that all labor unions were not Communist-dominated and to labor leaders who knew that not all bosses were exploiters of human resources. He rejected the extremes, though: "So we got radicals on both sides, 'Reds' on the one and 'Greens' on the other. Both of 'em ought to be run out, and leave it to men that know and feel that there is such a thing as a fair union and a fair employer."[72] By these and other acts of fairness, Will Rogers embodied the American democrat giving Americans a "square deal."

Defense of the underdog was another facet of fair play. Rogers stood up for the fellow at the bottom of the heap, whether nation or individual. During the time of his ascendancy, Rogers spoke often and clearly for the self-determination of nations, in a mood of indignation over the "big dogs" keeping the "little dogs" down. "Why don't nations let People alone, and quit trying to hold what they call a protectorate over them?" he asked. "Let people do their own way and have their own form of government." Nothing was so funny as something done in all seriousness, he often said, and he found a case in point in the Nicaraguan intervention, "You want to know why we are so funny to the rest of the world? Here we are sending warships to tell Nicaragua who to seat after their election and we haven't got a Senator that was elected here last Fall that will be allowed to sit down." He spoke consistently for a policy of fair play for the underdog in Latin America, for "fairer treatment to our sister republics, then we won't have to hold conferences."[73] In Asia, as well as Latin America, the American democrat said, underdog nations deserved consideration: "Give the Philippines their freedom and take that godfather clause out of our Cuban treaty, and the first thing you know we would be called 'brother' and not 'big brother'." Several years earlier Rogers had directly referred to the dream in defending smaller nations. What, he wanted to know, if England had asked the Americans if they were ready for the freedom of independent government? "Why, we wasent ready for anything, and because we finally did struggle through and starved and fought among ourselves and finally got away with it, now we think no one else could possibly be as smart or as deserving as us." As the American democrat, Rogers also defended individuals who were underdogs: "I can applaud a winner as loud as anybody, but somehow," he wrote, "a loser appeals to me." So it was that he started a successful drive for a trophy fund for the "world's most cheerful loser," Sir Thomas Lipton, who had failed in several challenges for the America's Cup, symbol of yachting supremacy. Rogers wanted to give a wrong-way football runner a medal for avoiding a standardized mind; he defended a mother of ten in Michigan who he thought was to get life imprisonment for a fourth bootlegging offense; he upheld the leader of a peaceable revolt who was struggling against great odds.

They got Gandhi in jail in India. He preached "liberty without violence." He swore all his followers "to truth and constant poverty." He wanted nothing for himself not even the ordinary comforts. He believed in "prayer and renunciation."

Well, naturally a man that's holy couldn't run at large these days. They figured that a crazy man like that was liable to get other people to wanting those fanatical things. The whole thing just gives you a pretty fair idea of what would happen to our Saviour if He would come on earth today.[74]

As the American democrat, Rogers also served the vision of equality, as well as that of the individual's worth, by remaining unabashed in the presence of the mighty, mingling with people of all estates, and championing manners that were civilized without being foppish. Rogers' audacity and irreverence toward bigwigs was almost legendary. Whether imitating the Coolidge twang, pretending to have to check up on Hoover to be sure that an appearance with the President would not harm the Rogers reputation, or genially insulting lords of finance as "loan sharks and interest hounds," he was the embodiment of Whitman's ideal American who took off his hat to no man. He played the part well, as when he drawled to candidate Roosevelt, whom he had just introduced to many thousands in the Los Angeles Coliseum in September of 1932, "This introduction may have lacked enthusiasm and floweriness, but you must remember you are only a candidate yet. Come back as President and I will do right by you. I am wasting no oratory on a prospect."[75] The audience liked that sally; Roosevelt threw back his head and laughed. Equalitarianism ran high.

When Rogers told of his doings among prominent people of his time, his behavior categorized him as a doer of the dream of equality. After visiting President Coolidge at the White House and describing the visit for newspaper readers, the "lowbrow comedian" commented, "Now if any Nation can offer any more of a demonstration of democracy than that, I would like to hear of it." Rogers met the Prince of Wales in a London mansion: "We just talked like a couple of old Hill Billies about neighbors and friends." He was the guest of F.D.R. at the White House: "Having dinner in the White House is more fun and laughs than any place I know, and it has just about as much formality as dining with a neighbor." The man from Oologah never, however, lost touch with other strata of American society. Even in such accounts as those mentioned, he always kept the character of the country boy, and he could write as delightedly of his encounters with plain people as of those with powerful folk. He liked to talk to the "regular Bird," to get his "angle," and he would urge Americans of all stations to talk to people outside their milieu. Any casual meeting might become the topic for a column, as when he and his mail pilot were forced down near a prairie lighthouse erected to guide night fliers: "I found this lighthouse keeper's wife a mighty cheerful and wholesome middle-aged woman. She wasn't interested much in a permanent wave, or reducing, but she did bake some of the best bread and make some of the best coffee I have had in years. They have two sons in college and are two of the finest folks I ever met."[76] Thus, moving freely among all kinds of people, Will Rogers lived the life of equality.

The cement, figuratively, that held Will Rogers in a cohesive relationship with all those he met, came from his poise, his natural manners—his Whitmanian "aplomb." The cowboy philosopher stated the idea, himself, early in 1927, after the impending arrival of Romania's Queen Marie had caused official American welcoming parties to practice bowing and dressing properly. After remarking that two weeks had been required to "train them from acting like Americans," he added, "You know, when you have to be told what to say when you meet anyone, you are not the one to meet them." Rogers did not limit his comments on manners to meetings with royalty. Adopting the wise innocent pose, he reviewed a book on etiquette by Emily Post and found that there was considerably more etiquette than he had ever supposed—seven hundred pages, in fact; he predicted that books on etiquette would fall "on fertile soil." Having had no idea up to then that "inflection of the voice was such a big factor in introductions," he managed the appearance of unintentionally making the rules sound undemocratic:

She says that the prominence of the party being
introduced determines the sound of the voice, as she says
for instance, "Are you there?" and then on finding out
you are there she says, "Is it raining?"
Now the inflection that you use on asking any one if
they are there is the same inflection that you are to use
on introducing Mr. Gothis, if he is the more prominent of
the two. Then for the other person, who Mr. Gothis
probably got his from, why, you use the, "Is it raining?"
inflection.[77]

By the time Rogers finished that "book review," the formal
structure of etiquette was in a genial shambles. He had
tried to use the proper inflection, himself, but had had trouble deciding which was the more prominent party; and besides, when the family dogs and cats rushed through the
door as a guest was admitted, he found that nothing in the
book told how to remove the dogs and cats and remain "non
challant." Another time, ruminating on manners during a
trip to Europe, he remembered people who in spite of social
graces were still not really civilized and others who were
courteous in spite of lack of "advantages": "I know Englishmen that have had the same well-bred Butler all their lives
and they are just as rude as they ever were," he recalled.
"Why, do you know, one of the most cultured men I ever saw
come from Texas, and where he learned it the Lord only
knows. It's just one of those freaks of Nature like a Rose
among Prickly pears."[78] In what he wrote about what he did,
Rogers projected the image of the American democrat who
managed to be civilized without being foppish. His
equalitarian behavior qualified him as unprejudiced and,
therefore, free in the larger sense dreamed of by Thoreau
and Whitman.

In another heroic character, Rogers strengthened his impression of freedom of spirit: He was the cowboy hero, mo-
bile in space, free of a complex mind-life, and generous of
nature. The flavor of the cowboy was present in the background of nearly everything he wrote, as it was in his
"philosophy" that held that satisfaction "on the range" was
necessary for "fat beef cattle at the end of their existence."
In addition, his persona as the cowboy was often in the
forefront of his messages in two ways: He continued to

show an interest in the life of the cowboy throughout his life, and he told of his own experiences as a cowboy in the Texas Panhandle before the turn of the century.

Dispatches on his latter-day pilgrimages to ranches were redolent with the cowboy's sense of freedom. "Been away up above the timber line for the last few days on Jim Minnick's horse ranch, so can't tell you what I have read in the papers for I haven't had any and I am just plumb in ignorance as to who murdered who, who robbed who, who married who, who divorced who and why," he might write, picturing a life free of the complexities of modern society. Even when he took an international trip, part of his commentary was often related to the life of the cowboy. From Argentina, for instance, came this story of a day's fun: "Well, I had a great day today. Saw the real Argentine gauchos do their stuff right on one of the big estancias." Rogers, as was often the case, had been a participant: "Those bolos that you hear about 'em throwing they use for ostriches. We chased ostriches all afternoon. They are the fastest thing I ever saw run."[79] Thus, the appeal of the man on horseback could combine with the lure of the faraway to emphasize the free mobility of the cowboy.

On occasion, Rogers' stories grew nostalgic about the glories of a day forever gone; in such comments he aroused all the associations surrounding the cowboy as a symbol of man's freedom in his natural state. He told his national audience of a sentimental journey to Texas in the summer of 1934, "We was driving over a Country where 36 years before as a boy 18 years old I had helped drive a bunch of cattle from that very place to Western Kansas, and there wasent a house or a chicken in the whole country." Then came the appeal to memory:

> That plains was the prettiest country I ever saw in my life . . . and prairie lakes scattered all over it. And mirages! You could see anything in the world—just ahead of you. I eat out of a chuck wagon, and slept on the ground all that spring and summer of 98. . . .
>
> No greater, no happier life in the world than the cattle man.[80]

It was this kind of youthful exploit that had qualified
Rogers to be honored, together with many others, as an "old
trail driver," in 1926. The names and deeds of the older men
evoked the past for Rogers: "Their names were to me like
you look on Presidents." The generous principle of accepting a man for what he was, rather than what he had, applied in that gathering of old trail drivers, some of whom
had become wealthy. Rogers' peroration pictured the cowboy as a defender of right, a criterial attribute of the hero
of freedom. It was "getting kinder late in the afternoon" for
many of the old cowboys; soon they would be "catching their
night horses for the last time."

> When they are waked up with a kick to go on guard by a
> Golden Slipper, instead of a shop-made boot, why they
> will roll out of there and face their new Range Boss, and
> when he asks them "Boys are you ready to go with me?"
> They will look him right in the face and never bat an eye
> and say, "We are ready to go with anybody that is
> right."[81]

Will Rogers, by deed and by association, appeared as one of
these western heroes to his national audience.

In brief, besides speaking directly for freedom and equality in his writings, Rogers also identified himself materially
as a hero of freedom and equality by being interested in
politics but above party, by practicing fair play for the underdog, by "going freely" among all classes of people, by
being poised yet not "admirably schooled in every grace,"
and by being the American cowboy.

Rogers also made himself coessential with the vision of
freedom and equality by formal appeals. In his language of
gesture and word, he took on the form of the American
democrat. If the American Adam's essential formal quality
was an aura of newness and freshness, the American democrat's was one of breezy casualness and "just plain folks."

Much about Rogers' appearance, posture, and gestures
gave him the image of the breezily free individual and
equalitarian. Speaking styles of his period, to a degree, followed traditions of the grandiloquence of the golden age in
American oratory. Early in Rogers' stardom, William Jen-

153

nings Bryan was still active on the lecture circuit; the elegant Chauncey Depew once stood after a Rogers introduction and announced, with an obvious reference to the rope-twirler from Oklahoma, "I've been making speeches for over fifty years, but I've never found it necessary to use a rope to hold an audience."[82] In such a context of speaking conventions, Rogers' own stage presence took on the aspect of casualness that was freedom and the aspect of approachability that was equality. Early in his vaudeville career, he had begun chewing gum in order to reduce nervousness; the habit became a trademark, and he would casually violate conventions of speechmaking by happily working his jaws, during pauses, on the cud of gum. Occasionally, to the delight of the audience, he would "park" the gum on the proscenium. Further, in a carry-over from the days during which he wore his small cowboy hat as part of his "cowboy philosopher's" costume, he sometimes spoke with his hat on —a literal image of the man who takes off his hat to no one. Far from striking a dramatic pose, or even of standing erect, shoulders squared, Rogers lolled first on one foot and then another, the idle leg thrust slightly forward and away as he rested on the other; he jammed his hands into his coat pockets, and made an acute angle with his shoulder line. Thus placed, he looked the part of the convention-free, friendly, at ease speaker. When he could not stand still any longer, he would walk back and forth on the platform, take a piano stool and sit on it, or lean on a piano or anything at hand. Sometimes, if a talk went well, he would go to the edge of the platform and sit down, dangling his crossed legs over the apron. Here he would finish his speech, having won his audience completely with his folksiness as well as his wit. Such details of appearance and bodily action in Rogers' speaking behavior, violating all rules of speech except the one requiring directness and communion with the audience and occurring countless times in the context of witty words that "smiled as they said it," could have become sufficiently conventionalized for his audience that the actions gave him an iconic quality as the American democrat.

In his written and spoken language, Rogers also used formal devices to identify with the dream of freedom and equality. Hyperbole suggested, by means of its overstatement, a breeziness that was free. When Rogers coupled the figure of speech with thoughts appropriate to the dream of freedom, the effect was to intensify his invitation to assent. He was using hyperbole when he remarked that Mayor Thompson's campaign to rid Chicago of Anglicizing influences extended so far that it included "any picture depicting the eating of roast beef, Plum Duff, Yorkshire Buck, or the drinking of Lime Juice." He used exaggeration, also, to heighten the effect of his awareness of Communist reactionary behavior that denied freedom for the reactionary, himself: "I was surprised," he told a national radio audience upon his return from a trip to the U.S.S.R., "they didn't walk on their hands instead of their feet, just to be different from capitalistic nations." On the other hand, Rogers used hyperbole to state that Communists should enjoy free speech: They "should have a place where they can get up and denounce anything from Washington's wig to Hoover's fish bait," he wrote.

The formal appeal of hyperbole also aided him in his coalescence with the dream of equality. By applying the heightening inherent in the exaggeration, Rogers could level distinctions and thus identify with the dream of equality. In a statement not only showing him as a political independent but also serving to level party distinctions, the role of hyperbole is clear. Referring to the issue of prohibition repeal, he wrote, "Both sides are going to do exactly the same thing, they are going to straddle the thing, if they have to split their carcasses clear up to their neck to do it." Of a Senate that could give itself airs over its legislative power, he could remark tellingly, "Confucious prespired [*sic*] out more knowledge than the U.S. Senate has vocalized in the last 50 years." By means of exaggeration, Rogers could also level distinctions between a visiting Balkan Queen and cowboys in Oklahoma at the famous One Hundred and One Ranch. "She will love it," he wrote. "It's just the size of Rumania, only more conveniences. There is a bathroom here to every revolution there. Cowboys sleep in silk pajamas, round-up in Rolls-Royces and dress for dinner."

On other occasions, he wished to exaggerate distinctions in order to clearly differentiate between the American dream and reality. He used hyperbole, for instance, to say dramatically that unequal distribution of wealth in the country was denying the American dream: "You are either at a banquet in this country," he wrote in 1932, "or you are at a hot dog stand." Showing how wealth "trickles up" to the specially-privileged Hamiltonian elite, he wrote at his typewriter, "You can drop a bag of gold in Death Valley, which is below sea level, and before Saturday it will be home to Papa J. P." Thus, Rogers could use the formal resources of hyperbole to portray equality in two ways: He could lower the high and mighty or raise the lowly so that their equality as human beings appeared; he could clarify the disparities between the American dream and the realities.

CONCURRENTLY, then, with his Adamic image-making, Will Rogers created the persona of the American democrat. He identified with the dream of freedom and equality in a direct material way by speaking for the right of all Americans to belong to the free and equal "club" set up by the Declaration of Independence and the Constitution. He also recommended a government for the good of all the people and advocated freedom of press, speech, and religion. Spiritual equality, with a consequent commitment to social, economic, and political equality, were additional beliefs. He merged himself with the twin visions in an indirect material way by being the politically interested person without being the party man, by practicing fair play for all and defending the underdog, by "not taking off his hat to any man," by mingling freely with people in all stations of life, by exhibiting "naturally" civilized manners, and by being a cowboy hero. When Americans saw him, his appearance and gestures were appropriate to the appearance of the American democrat—free and equal. When Americans simply heard or read his words, he invited their assent by the formal properties of language.

As American democrat, Rogers' role was clear in a 1930 *American Magazine* article:

> If the President of the United States says a thing is so, the Democrats may doubt him. But if Will Rogers backs him up, even the Democrats believe. In Washington they say that the Senate fears Will Rogers more than all the

editors in America, for Rogers, in a hundred words, can laugh away the effect of hours of oratory.[83]

As the people's tribune and as American democrat, Will Rogers did not put himself on a pedestal, nor did he have to. He had already identified himself with the dream of freedom and equality.

Will Rogers, Self-Made Man

"Success," pronounced that eloquent spokesman of the American experience, Henry Ward Beecher, to his faithful congregation at Plymouth Church shortly after mid-century, "is full of promise till men get it; and then it is a last year's nest, from which the bird has flown." Beecher may have been offering consolation to those Americans whose dream of success had faded, but he did not let his observation deter him from seeking success for himself. To many Americans the pursuit of happiness has been simply the pursuit of success. The charm of American life, Tocqueville once observed, lay in the anticipation of success; much later, Will Rogers was to write, "The old dollar might be filthy lucre, but there is quite a bit of energy and spirit yet in earning one." Although, broadly defined, success could reasonably be equated with a favorable outcome of Americans' hopes for their greatest possible self-fulfillment in a free and equal society, most Americans have envisioned it as a securing of fame and power to some degree, but primarily as the acquisition of money.[1] As it was when it arrived with the first settlers, the dream still seems but a simple vision—drawing strength from the Puritan theology that viewed success as the reward of virtue, and blossoming during the period of national expansion to the West. Actually, it was more nearly a new rendition of the complex of ideas in the great dream of Paradise to be regained.

To begin with, the vision of success modulated to a different key the dream of the infinite possibilities of the common man. That man in Europe too often had been in rags; if given opportunity in America—so went the success vision —he could rise to riches. More specifically, the success legend affirmed its belief in the common man by elevating the average man. Genius was suspect. In a lecture published for edification of young men, Henry Ward Beecher affirmed, "Genius is usually impatient of application, irritable, scornful of men's dullness, squeamish at petty disgusts:—it loves a conspicuous place, a short work, and a large reward." Indeed, although (as Irvin G. Wyllie has shown) the onus would drop from the college graduate when the modern

161

corporation grew, the spokesman for the success dream might carry distrust of intellectuality to active dislike. Picturing "actual" geniuses in accordance with the beliefs of the times, Beecher found that "they abound in academies, colleges, and Thespian societies; in village debating clubs; in coteries of young artists, and among young professional aspirants." In such settings they showed their true nature: "They are to be known by a reserved air, excessive sensitiveness, and utter indolence; by very long hair, and very open shirt collars; by the reading of much wretched poetry, and the writing of much, yet more wretched; by being very conceited, very affected, very disagreeable, and very useless."[2] True to the dream, that husbandman of little acorns, William Holmes McGuffey, expressed for generations an opposing faith in the common man's ability to succeed:

> Thus, plain, plodding people, we often shall find,
> Will leave hasty, confident people behind:
> Like the tortoise and hare, though together they start,
> We soon clearly see they are widely apart.[3]

If there was anything uncommon about the common man, it was drive and close application to work in order to succeed. But genius, itself, was unnecessary, as did testify other American spokesmen such as Theodore Parker and Ralph W. Emerson.

The success dream also affirmed the goodness of the common man, even though Russel Nye has shown that leading nineteenth-century philosophers of *laissez faire* believed that God, not selfish men, brought good by means of the system. From the viewpoint, however, of the writers of success manuals, the dream Adamically glorified the rural influences on those traveling the high road to success. "Fresh air and good food kept the country boy in good condition, and his daily round of work left him little time for the mischief that distracted his less busy city cousin," writes Wyllie of this phase of the success dream. "Whereas city boys wasted their lives and their substance in saloons, gambling dens, and houses of prostitution, country boys supposedly led a Spartan life that prepared them for the hard struggle of the business world," he concludes (pages 27-28). So effective was the country in eliciting virtue that the farm boy was a paragon: Work was sacred; perseverance was natural; frugality was a pleasing form of simplicity; sobriety was a characterization of the whole moral deportment. Other virtues included obedience, loyalty, and initiative as tempering for the armor of character. Thus, Emerson, in his essay on "Wealth," said, "Open the doors of opportunity to talent and virtue and they will do themselves justice, and property will not be in bad hands." Goodness led to success. "Experience has shown," observed Beecher, "that the other good qualities of veracity, frugality, and modesty, are apt to be associated with industry." That to Beecher the virtue of industry could substitute for genius is not surprising. Mothers, as well as rural surroundings, summoned the goodness waiting within sons. "The instruction which the American mother gives her son is a training in honor rather than in success," wrote Albert J. Beveridge in the early part of this century, but success depended on that training, and character led the list of requirements for success. Granting that nature set some limits to the possibilities of character development, rural surroundings and American mothers still imparted such possibilities in the development of good character that all candidates were free and equal.

The success dream was also a specific version of the dream of self-fulfillment. Self-realization of a sort came merely through the process, or the motions, of winning wealth—the "chief aim" of individualism after the 1870's, believes Nye. But the success legend did not mistake the short-run good for the ultimate one: "I am anxious," wrote Beveridge the self-made man, "that every young American should win in all the conflicts of life—win in college, win in business, etc.; but I am even more anxious that through all of his triumphs he should grow ever broader, sweeter, and more kindly."[4] Moreover, the acquisition of wealth made possible greater avenues to kindliness, for as Wyllie remarks (page 5), "The central precept of the folklore of success . . . says that money has no value except in relation to its uses." So it was that great numbers of Americans listened happily to Russell Conwell's words, uttered thousands of times, emphasizing the duty of Americans to make money: "Money is power; money has powers; and for a man to say, 'I do not want money,' is to say, 'I do not wish to do any good to my fellowman.' It is absurd thus to talk." The stewardship of wealth led to self-fulfillment. Good steward-ship was a way of laying up treasures in heaven, and though some of the country's successes possibly construed such a view as a new theory of divine right for their economic reigns, the dreamers of success went not so far. Emerson spoke for those dreamers when he said, "They should own who can administer, not they who hoard and conceal; not they who, the great proprietors they are, are only the greater beggars, but they whose work carves out work for more, opens a path for all."[5] All the great distributors of largesse, including Carnegie and Rockefeller, would have liked the name of good stewards.

The dream of success had its own brand of freedom, too. The successful man, like all other Americans, was to recog-nize that he must live a responsible freedom. True, he was to be largely free from interference by other forces in his affairs, but he was to justify this freedom by regard for the good of the community. The cornerstone of the success dreamers' social faith, believes Wyllie, was the idea summed up by Timothy S. Arthur, in 1848: "The common good ought to be regarded by every man, and whoever seeks to secure the common good most effectively secures his own." A judicious restraint, however, would characterize the responsibly free success figure, "This does not mean that a man should throw all his earnings into the treasury of the commonwealth, or do any act of similar kind." The dreamer of success was free in another way—he was free to will success for himself. To such a spokesman as Beve-ridge, the success candidate should pick out a function he could do well and stick to it.

> Then let your dreams become beliefs; let your
> imaginings develop into faith. Complete the process by
> resolving to make that belief come true. Then go ahead
> and *make it come true.*
> Work—that is the magic word. In these four letters all
> possibilities are wrapped up. "Seek and ye shall find;
> knock and it shall be opened unto you." Or let us
> paraphrase the sacred page and say—Work and you will
> win (page 9).

Conwell, the apostle of diamonds in the back yard, might say, "Never in the history of our country was there an opportunity so great for the poor man to get rich as there is now. . . . The very fact that they get discouraged is what prevents them from getting rich." The posture of the free individualist able to will his own fortune accords well with the stance of the new, free American Adam, even if on other intellectual levels some Americans recanted their belief in free will.

Too, the dream of success, in its rags-to-riches motif, was an affirmation of the dream of equality. The national experience, Daniel Boorstin has explained, began early with the concept of a "circulating current" of the laboring population, "of men on the move rather than in the groove"; so that such upward mobility and job mobility via the American factory system promoted "vagueness of social classes."[6] Thus, prior to the Civil War, any form of aristocracy seemed vulnerable to assault by the rags-to-riches conception. "There was a democratic ring in its assurance that every ordinary man could aspire to wealth, and through wealth to the power and prerogatives previously monopolized by the high- and well-born," writes Wyllie (page 152). A residue of this feeling surely remained after the war, when the success legend became additionally useful to consolidate power against infringement and to provide social control. Also of importance was the fact that philosophers of the dream affirmed a basic equality of aspirants. Talents obviously varied; but since industry and other marks of character were the main ingredients of success, chances for the crown of the capitalist's silk hat were equalized: "In respect to character," says the historian of the dream, "presumably, all started as equals" (pages 34-35). A third element was that the legend of success had a built-in corrective for the inequalities that might eventually arise because of superior character development. It was the doctrine of shirtsleeves-to-shirtsleeves in two or three generations. The effect came about in two ways. Russell Conwell, ministerial legitimizer of the dream, described the first when he said, "I pity a rich man's son. A rich man's son in these days of ours occupies a very difficult position. They are to be pitied. . . . They are raised in luxury, they die in poverty." Earlier, in "Wealth,"

Emerson had testified, "In a free and just commonwealth, property rushes from the idle and imbecile to the industrious, brave and persevering." Thus, if by inheritance money remained concentrated, prodigality or ineptitude in the second or third generation redistributed it. The second way, deducible from the motifs of philanthropy and good stewardship, was to bequeath to the second generation more in the way of honor and character than monetary wealth. Even though some great fortunes, such as that of Rockefeller, remained largely intact in spite of large benefactions, the dreamers of shirtsleeves-to-shirtsleeves saw in their doctrine provision for a continuing equality of opportunity and a perpetually renewed natural aristocracy in the best manner of the dream of freedom and equality.

To the eyes of foreign observers, the American dream of equality could take on a literally golden glow of reality. One British paper in 1882 found it so:

> What is especially remarkable in the present development of American energy and success is its wide and equable distribution. North and south, east and west, on the shores of the Atlantic and the Pacific, along the chain of great lakes, in the valley of the Mississippi, and on the coasts of the Gulf of Mexico, the creation of wealth and the increase of population are signally exhibited.[7]

The paper admitted that "some sections of the Union" had "advanced relatively to the rest," but the fact was that "the present tide of prosperity" had "risen so high" that it filled up even the "backwaters," and had "established something like an approach to universal success." A place of universal success was indeed a paradise to the success dreamer.

Moreover, success was supposedly related to progress. As Russel Nye explains, the "greatest good for the greatest number" resulted from an arrangement in which vendors competed for consumers' favor. "Progress is therefore built into the system."[8] For followers of social Darwinism, too, survival of the fittest also guaranteed progress. Thus, the dream of success provided variations on all the themes in the great American dream.

The disciple of success was in the mold of the American

Adam, who—being full of boundless possibilities and naturally good, besides seeking self-fulfillment in a garden where freedom and equality reigned—was more the doer than the thinker; but when he strove for the crown of the capitalist's silk hat, he was activism personified. The result was that the dream of success was identical with a strategy of behavior for its realization. Because, however, the success dream carried with it a new doctrine of *noblesse oblige,* a glance at this aspect of the strategy of success seems appropriate.

The American Adam practiced a wise innocence. Applied to the dogma of success, this innocence produced an American logic in the success dream. "Be intelligently good and you will be successful," it could be summarized.[9] "Never try to create a deeper impression than Nature creates for you," counseled Beveridge, a success figure for many Americans. "For example, never try to look wise. Many a front of gravity and weight conceals an intellectual desolation" (pages 2-3).

This touchstone of intelligent goodness and naturalness was the key to the obligations of the successful American. With his subordinates, he was a modern ideal liege lord, requiring from them unwavering loyalty and having, in return, great responsibilities for their well-being. Naturally, subordinates were to have a living wage that would "take care of every physical necessity and . . . assure peace of mind," summarized Wyllie (page 82). Moreover, the successful man had to be intelligently good in his wages of human dignity. Recognition, praise, and promotions for work well done formed a part of the kind treatment to be given employees. "The honorable employer, understanding that his men were equals in the sight of God, would treat them as self-respecting human beings, not as animals or machines" (pages 282-83).

Earning quick fortunes by speculation might have been intelligent but not good, for speculation was almost equal to gambling. Beecher, never averse to accumulating dollars, saw speculation as a defect of character:

> Scheming speculations . . . have produced an aversion
> among the young to the slow accumulations of ordinary
> Industry, and fired them with a conviction that

shrewdness, cunning, and bold ventures, are a more
manly way to wealth. There is a swarm of men, bred in
the heats of adventurous times, whose thoughts scorn
pence and farthings, and who humble themselves to
speak of dollars. . . . The young farmer becomes almost
ashamed to meet his school-mate, whose stores line
whole streets, whose stocks are in every bank and
company, and whose increasing money is already
well-nigh inestimable. But if the butterfly derides the bee
in summer, he was never known to do it in the lowering
days of autumn.[10]

Fortunes, rather, were to arise from honest, not merely legal, dealings with competitors and customers. With the former, competitive jousts were not to be marred by advan-
tage-taking. With the latter, full measure, honest representation, and fair pricing were requisite. This was an
enlightened goodness for, according to the success legend,
the self-made man's continued success depended upon it.

In his stewardship of wealth, the philanthropist was also
to use wisdom in choosing objects of his generosity: Generally to be preferred would be the endowment of universities
and institutes or the patronage of arts. "These agencies,"
says Wyllie, "offered broad opportunities for self-improvement, and through them the self-made men of one generation tried to prepare the way for their successors in the
next" (page 92). But philanthropy for relief of suffering was
also acceptable evidence that the successful man lived up
to his *noblesse oblige.*

Thus, through his intelligent goodness, the self-made
man proved that he possessed those inward virtues for
which success was the reward and, consequently, that he
deserved the crown of the silk hat. That this idealized picture of the successful man often departed from reality did
not destroy his appeal. He became a legendary hero for
Americans.

"Under his different guises," writes Marshall Fishwick,
"the self-made hero is always the Cinderella of our bour-
geois society, the personification of the equalitarianism of
our political structure."[11] Thus, not only is Andrew Jackson
an emblem of freedom and equality, but he is also a symbol
of success. A self-taught lawyer and military tactician, he

rose from obscurity to the highest office in the land. His connection between success and equalitarianism is natural in view of Americans' dream that the real criteria of worth are a man's deeds rather than his birth. The free cowboy, rugged individualist who combined self-reliance, loyalty, honesty, and talent, was also a self-made hero. In a sense, too, the ideal American portrayed in the pages of *Leaves of Grass* is a self-made man. But the gallery of American heroes also has an extensive wing devoted to the heroes of self-earned wealth, who in their persons present a synthesis of success dogma.

Benjamin Franklin is one of these. Influenced, possibly, by that progenitor of the American success dream, Cotton Mather, Franklin rose to affluence by diligent application to work and—so goes his story—by his virtues of thrift, honesty, cleanliness, and frugality. His was an honestly acquired fortune. His origins had been urban; but to nostalgic memory, even the cities in colonial America may have provided a rustic simplicity of environment. By 1857, Franklin's statue stood in Boston, and his identification as a success of the self-made variety was explicit. On the occasion of the unveiling, Robert Winthrop rehearsed the themes of the success dream and sought to inspire others to emulate Franklin. "Behold him, Mechanics and Mechanics' Apprentices, holding out to you an example of diligence, economy and virtue, and personifying the triumphant success which may await those who follow it!" Franklin had been one "who rose from nothing, who owed nothing to parentage or to patronage, who enjoyed no advantages of early education" not open to the average American, yet a man "who lived to stand before Kings, and died to leave a name which the world will never forget." That Franklin was a self-taught scientist and diplomat only added glory to his rise; that he may have been a genius received no mention: It did not fit the paradigm of the dream.

Another American hero who was trimmed to fit the pattern of the success dream was born a half-dozen years after the dedication of Franklin's statue in Boston. Henry Ford, unlike Franklin, was a farm boy of humble origins; and if he were a genius, the ability lay along lines that were easily recognizable and not suspect—he was a mechanic. Marshall Fishwick has outlined the legend of the "Henry B" created by such publicists as William Cameron. There was the dramatic, single-minded devotion to producing cars. Legend makers "made as much of the last hours of preparation as of the hours when . . . Lincoln was awaiting word of the chance meeting of the Northern and Southern armies at Gettysburg" (page 121). Ford had worked around the clock; it was nearly two in the morning; suspense grew; rain fell in the darkness; but Ford was determined. At last, with Mrs. Ford ahead of him with a lantern, the indefatigable Ford began turning over the engine. Nothing happened. Then he found the trouble—a missing screw. In the rain-swept darkness, the sound of the engine announced the beginning of the automobile age—success!

And after the country boy—through virtue and hard work —became wealthy, he was a good steward with his riches, providing not only a living wage for his workmen, but guiding them along the paths of his own virtue. The famous five dollar minimum pay for a day's work provided the necessary inspiration to character formation. "Only workmen who were morally fit qualified," says Fishwick. "Married men had to be living with and supporting their family; single men over 22 had to be living 'wholesomely' and displaying 'proud thrifty habits' " (page 121). Through the words of publicists, the remote and inaccessible Ford became a warm and engaging liege lord: "Cameron pictured him as lovable 'Henry,' the workingman's friend, moving about his plant in shirtsleeves, figuring out ways to make life better via higher production" (page 128). Ford was being intelligently good, as the success dream specified.

Moreover, his fortune, as James Truslow Adams remarked, was often cited as being an honest one. This made him suitable for the success pantheon; all the same, he kept a sufficient gap between cost of production and prices to accumulate $1,000,000,000 for himself. Not only was Ford's success the result of production rather than speculation; he was—in the public mind—an antagonist of that symbol of sinful speculation, Wall Street. "Proof" lay in that entity's attack on Ford through the *Wall Street Journal.*

Finally, Ford kept his success image bright by seeming to be the unspoiled child of fortune. True, there were rumors that may have clouded the public reflection: use of police spies to keep all employees under surveillance and fabulous, princely estates in Michigan, Georgia, and London. "Yet," comments Fishwick, the legend said that "he was as simple and sturdy as when he plowed his corn fields or tinkered in his tiny garage" (page 121). For Ford loved country dances and rustic pleasures like hiking. How could one so close to the virtue-giving soil be otherwise than unspoiled? Thus, with the aid of publicists who understood the appeal of the success hero, Ford had little difficulty in remaining one of America's supreme symbols of economic equality. That his efforts at diplomacy succeeded less well than Franklin's really mattered little.

When writers of novels produced success heroes, they did not have to contend with the weak flesh of real persons. They could make their demigods perfect embodiments of the dream, with no embarrassing aberrations to disguise. The apeiron of such heroes of fiction is Horatio Alger's Ragged Dick. Climbing the pyramid of success through scores of novels, he may have changed his name and some details of outward appearance, but his was a consistent characterization that kept him Ragged Dick. A poor city boy, he nevertheless had all the country virtues of honesty, thrift, industry, and sturdiness of moral fiber. He had an inspiring optimism that required no help from strong drink. Fatherless and isolated from enjoyment by the necessity of supporting his mother, he cheerfully accepted his lot as ragged newsboy, earning honest pennies and further chastening his spartan character. When opportunity came for him to work for a liege lord of success, he demonstrated his unwavering loyalty not only by repeatedly volunteering for overtime effort, but also by foiling attempts to subvert the company for his own decadent uses by a villainous figure representing the shirtsleeves-to-shirtsleeves-in-three-generations myth. The reward for such works and such character was always material success—further sweetened by the hand in marriage of his employer's daughter, who had earlier laughed at his ragged clothing, unaware of the real worth of Dick's character. At last, Dick's cup was full, his rise complete and satisfying to himself and his readers. As the prototype of the self-made man, he kept a strong hold on the American imagination. "Time has transformed but not destroyed his rugged image," concludes Fishwick of the self-made man, "Detractors have ridiculed him in vain. He still shouts 'Invictus,' . . . and plunges into the open market place. He is, and has long been, the nation's *beau ideal"* (page 142).

Contained in the legendary Alger hero is a brilliant fusing of values in the great American dream although, as Kenneth S. Lynn has remarked, the expression of the values finds a level appropriate to the dream of material success. "The belief in the potential greatness of the common man, the glorification of individual effort and accomplishment, the equation of the pursuit of money with the pursuit of happiness and of business success with spiritual grace: simply to mention these concepts is to comprehend the brilliance of Alger's synthesis," writes Lynn (page 7). The Alger hero thus represented a kind of secular synthesis of the dream of success. There remains for brief consideration another kind of synthesis: the theology of success.

At least one prophet of the success dream interfused it with the Adamic myth. Writing in *Hunt's Merchant's Magazine,* Matthew H. Smith insisted that business was divinely foreordained, making Adam his rhetorical example. "The race were made for employment. Adam was created and placed in the Garden of Eden for business purposes; it would have been better for the race if he had attended closely to the occupation for which he was made."[12]

If Adam's sin had been his aspiring toward godhead, the theology of success, as described by Wyllie, allowed him the role denied him after the eating of the forbidden fruit. True, during his rise to opulence, he stood under the constant judgment of a Jehovah figure, thus maintaining the relationship in the garden. But after his arrival at the peak of the holy mount of success, he was the god of the world of business. A just god, he awarded the salvation of success to those who willed it and who chose, in the words of Wyllie, the virtuous, narrow way of "industry, frugality, sobriety, perseverance, punctuality, loyalty, obedience, initiative, and a host of kindred virtues" (page 54). For those who chose damnation by not encouraging in themselves those qualities of soul, he recorded their sins as carefully as he had the virtues of the self-determined elect and dispensed hellfire-hot failure in just proportion to the sins. The later vogue of social Darwinism provided an up-to-date expression of such a theology of success, as Blum makes clear: "Belief in the manifestation of grace in wealth was now assimilated into belief in the survival of the fittest, with its corollary dictum that the laws of evolution, decreed by God, assured the triumph of the best."[13] Since at least the days of Mather, acquiring money has been grounded theologically as well as economically.

It is little wonder, in view of the re-rendering within the success dream of other values in the great over-all vision, that Emerson and Whitman could include it in their personal hopes for America. Emerson saw in success the natural law of the universe:

> Success consists in close appliance to the laws of the
> world, and since these laws are intellectual and moral,
> an intellectual and moral obedience.
> ....
> The counting-room maxims liberally expounded are laws
> of the universe. The merchant's economy is a coarse
> symbol of the soul's economy.[14]

Whitman, whose views on the connection of material success and progress will appear in more detail later, also included the success dream in his grand scheme for democracy. "For fear of mistake," he wrote in "Democratic Vistas," "I may as well distinctly specify, as cheerfully included in the model and standard of these Vistas, a practical, stirring, worldly, moneymaking, even materialistic character." The dream of success was a high road to paradise.

(By the time Will Rogers was seven, he could look upon a success hero in person. By "hard work, perseverance, and taking advantage of his opportunities," Clem Vann Rogers, former Confederate officer, had rebuilt his fortune to the point that he was considered one of the most prosperous men in the Indian Territory. Thus, by the decade of the eighties, with the success dream burning brightly in America, Rogers fell under its influence in his own home.)

SUMMER mornings, when the eyes of young Rogers traveled around the breakfast table in the rambling home near Oologah, they fell upon his sisters—Maude, May, and Sallie —upon his mother, Mary America, and upon his father, at the head of the table. The elder Rogers was impressive: A big man, his handlebar mustache and his heavy eyebrows gave him an aspect of dignity. He looked important, and he was.

Rogers knew the story of his father's first ranching venture, before the Civil War; he knew of his service as a Confederate officer; he knew of his recouping of fortune after the war, first by hauling freight and then by a return to ranching and farming. About the whole saga of the rise was the aura of the self-made man—the same honesty, grit, brains, and inspiration that found an epitome in the story of the great cattle drive in 1855 to St. Louis. Young Rogers knew, too, that his father was a big man among the Cherokees, for many of them came to him for advice as a former judge and frequent senator of the Cherokee Council. In the future, the boy would watch his father seek to serve Cherokee interests by assisting the Dawes Commission in its study of Cherokee holdings; he would see him as a successful banker in Claremore; he would see him become a delegate to the constitutional convention for Oklahoma.

Meanwhile, however, during the eighties, scenes passed before the boy's eyes that dramatized the energy and success of the strong, often silent man on horseback who was Clem Rogers. Work went on for seven days of the week on the ranch; the elder Rogers could still take a direct hand, but his maze of affairs often took him away from home. As his son watched, the operation on the ranch grew, together with the amount of cattle, cowboys, and cropland. The place must have seemed a small empire to the youngster. It would be a reminder to him for the rest of his life of the success that had been his father's.

Sometimes Rogers would hear his mother discussing her

dreams for him with his father. Young Rogers had become even more precious to the mother after the death of the last brother, Robert. Looking at her only son, she may have felt like the mother of the prophet Samuel: She wanted to dedicate her only son to God—she wanted him to be a Methodist minister. Clem Rogers would not argue; he would simply comment, reports Homer Croy, that there was not much money in preaching. The gospel for the father was hard work and he set an example of driving ambition and labor that may have seemed impossible of emulation to the son. Young Rogers' wife recounts a story that may be symbolic of the relationship between father and son:

> "Riding along with papa," Will told me, "I never could keep up with him. Papa could ride all day long and his horse would never be out of a little fast walk or dogtrot. We'd start out in the morning side by side, but my horse was soon lagging way behind and I'd have to kick him in the sides to catch up. At the end of the day I was plumb played out and my horse was in a lather, but papa wasn't tired and his horse never turned a hair."[15]

Rogers may well have despaired of succeeding in the way his father had. By the nineties, it became increasingly clear that eventually the big spreads utilizing the open range would be carved up and fenced off. Besides, with a father of such physical and mental prowess, how could he equal him? Too, the boy seemed to be more of his mother's temperament than of his father's—gay spirited, loving of jokes, folks, and singing.

The father, though, did his best to guide the boy toward a successful career. In Rogers' boyhood, his father had given him a herd of orphan or "dogie" calves and allowed him his own "dogiron" brand. After the son had left his last school and had done a stint of cowpunching in the Texas Panhandle, the elder Rogers offered him either the ranch heartland, or a place in the bank of Claremore. But for young Rogers to accept the boost and its lifetime of respectability would have been harder, perhaps, than to strike out alone in a new territory—his success would not have been his own. What Will Rogers probably received from his father's influence was the desire to excell and succeed, for Clem

Rogers was a man whose rise placed a burden of success upon the son. Precisely for that reason, the son—perhaps both attracted and repelled by the father's accomplishments—had to find a way to succeed on his own.

In a geography book at one of his numerous schools, reports Day, Rogers had seen a picture of verdant grazing land in Argentina. Didn't that "new" country offer possibilities for the son of a well-off man to be a self-made man himself? So, as a young man, he went to Argentina. Whatever other reasons the youth from Oologah may have had for going, his letters to his father show that he was interested in success, that he wanted to please his father, and that he cared what neighbors thought about his career. In one of his earliest letters he wrote, "I have been out into the interior and have seen a little of the country, which looks like a good cattle and farming country, but it's no place to make money unless you have at least $10,000 to invest."

Later, when he was ready to quit the country after a try at cowpunching, he sent a revealing letter to his father. It began with immediate plans and with a concern for worldly success.

> I will write you again, as I guess I will get away from
> this country about the third of August, or four more days.
> I have given this place a trial and I know that it is no
> better or, for that matter, any other place any better than
> the U.S. for a man with a small capital, or none at all.

There followed a rationalized disclaimer of an interest in money, and then he showed a concern for his reputation, lest the shirtsleeves myth be attached to him:

> All that worries me is people there all say—"Oh, he is
> no account, he blows in all his father's money," and all
> that kind of stuff, which is not so. I am more willing to
> admit that you have done everything in the world for me
> and tried to make something more than I am out of me
> (which is not your fault) but as to our financial dealings,
> I think I paid you all up and everyone else.
>
> I only write these things so we may understand each
> other. I cannot help it because my nature is not like
> other people, and I don't want you all to think I am no
> good because I don't keep my money. . . . I have always
> dealt honestly with everyone and think the world and all

of you and all the folks, and will be among you all soon
as happy as any one in the world, as then I can work and
show the people that I am only spending what I make.[16]

The year was 1902; Rogers did not go directly home. Instead, he worked his way to South Africa aboard a freighter
carrying a cargo of cattle, mules, and horses for an English
rancher. Later, a chance meeting with the American pro-
prietor of Texas Jack's Wild West Show won for him a place
as a fancy roper and rider. It was not the type of "sound
business success" that his father had achieved, but it was
done by "riding his own horse." And in another letter home
he showed that his rise in show business could be marked
by the same kind of moral purity as that possessed by
Ragged Dick, "It isn't a wild mob like them at home, for
Jack don't drink a drop or smoke or gamble, and likes his
men to be the same," Rogers wrote, as if seeking parental
approval. He admitted that it was not "the best business,"
but felt that as long as it had "good money in it" and was
honest, there was "no objection to it." He added a line that
fitted him for the role of those practicing virtue in the success quest: "I still keep sober and don't gamble, and Jack
thinks a lot of me."

Perhaps more important than Jack's moral influence,
cash pay, and good opinion was that he gave Rogers the
feeling of success. Croy reports that "Will was so pleased
with his rise in the world that he had a professional card
printed."[17] Rogers' identification with the Cherokees persisted as he billed himself on the card as "The Cherokee
Kid." Later, Texas Jack made the success role fit Rogers
explicitly when he wrote a letter of recommendation on the
occasion of the Cherokee Kid's departure for what both
hoped might be fairer fields:

I have the very great pleasure of recommending Mr. W.
P. Rogers to circus proprietors. He has performed with
me during my present South African tour and I consider
him to be the champion trick rough rider and lasso
thrower of the world. He is sober, industrious, hard
working at all times and is always to be relied upon. I
shall be pleased to give him an engagement at any time
should he wish to return.[18]

Thus Texas Jack confirmed that Rogers had the qualities so important to success. He was sober, hard-working, reliable; he had found a place where people did not accuse him of wasting his father's money.

After completing a round-the-world odyssey by doing stints with wild West shows in Australia and New Zealand, Rogers returned to Claremore with his way to success in clearer perspective.

By the time the wife whom he took in 1908 had the opportunity to observe him closely, Rogers exhibited all the marks of Ragged Dick's winning ways with employers. The Cherokee Kid had become an established performer, and Betty Rogers traced his success:

> From the beginning Will was ambitious. On tour during the old vaudeville years, our little hotel room was always littered with ropes. He practised roping day in and day out, creating new tricks or perfecting the old ones. Later, when talking became part of his act, Will exercised the same thoroughness in keeping himself posted on what was going on. He strove for perfection in whatever he tried; he was restless and impatient when he felt he had fallen into a rut and that he wasn't going ahead fast enough. And he was keenly alert when a new opportunity presented itself (pages 23-24).

Perhaps it was easier to exercise a father-given ambition along lines not athwart those of the father's accomplishment; perhaps it was simply more fun to work hard in show business. But such stories were to make it clear that to his public he was following the success formula of hard work and taking advantage of opportunities. Such approved habits, together with the fact of Rogers' success in an unorthodox undertaking for the self-made man, gave him identification as both devotee and debunker of the traditional success vision. If this stand was ambivalent and at times ambiguous, it was appropriate to the decade of the twenties and to the first half of the thirties.

MANY Americans in the twenties probably remembered well the prewar years and the anxieties they brought relating to hopes of success. The early years of the century, believes Lynn, were "bewildering and confusing times," as a result of changes effected by industrialism, urbanization, and immigration. But a special burden of insecurity lay upon what supposedly was the most stable segment of American society—the middle class. For these Americans, disillusionment with the promise of success lurked in its definition for their generation: Success meant having to outdo one's successful parents.[19] Too, in those prewar years, the growth of trusts as well as of corporations dwarfed the efforts of the individual to achieve a do-it-yourself success; because of the business colossus, light from the apparently receding dream fell less and less upon the would-be entrepreneur and more and more upon the rising class of managers. Yet, in an earlier day, the myth had said that the fellow who stayed with the boss and did not strike out on his own was marked for respectable failure. It was all rather confusing and discouraging. No wonder Americans in 1916 were still wanting to hear Russell Conwell reassure them that diamonds awaited in the backyard, if only they would open their eyes and see them. Meanwhile, business and government seemed to be struggling for supremacy, one in the name of success and the other in the name of freedom. The result for Americans who could remember such years is summarized by Wyllie: "On the eve of the first World War men could still make money, but only under handicaps. . . . One fact stood out: the American self-help tradition had fallen upon evil days" (page 167).

These memories, like a ghost that wouldn't down, may have troubled many Americans, even though the war and its easy profits rekindled the success dream and raised—as James Truslow Adams has phrased it—"small town Chamber of Commerce shouts for 'Coolidge prosperity,'" which supplanted the "battle cries of Roosevelt and Wilson in the struggle to realize the American dream."[20] Thus, in the twenties, the success dream became equated with the larger vision. If government were scandal-ridden, that condition may have seemed an undesirable but inevitable by-product of the national need to make money; besides, the national conscience could be eased by finding a national leader who symbolized the old virtues. If Henry Ford needed what one day would become the Tennessee Valley

Authority, perhaps the government ought to help him get it, as its part in providing the opportunity to rise. If people didn't know of the widening gaps in wealth in the country, they may not have been concerned for the good state of the dream; but if they did know, they may have felt encouraged to "get theirs while the getting was good." An epitome of such efforts on the national scale may be the story of the great Florida land bubble, as described by Hicks:

> According to one estimate the number of lots platted and offered for sale reached 20 million. Prices, once low, rose to fantastic heights. A New Yorker who had bought a stretch of land in West Palm Beach for a reasonable price before the craze struck sold it in 1923 for $800,000. It was then turned into city lots which sold for $1.5 million. By 1925 it was valued at $4 million. Lots fronting on the sea were most in demand and might bring as much as $15,000 to $25,000 each. Prices grew more moderate farther inland, as well they might, for sometimes the plats extended into swamps and thickets, ten, twenty, or even thirty miles from the shore. Throughout most of 1925 the boom continued unabated, but by January, 1926, it was apparent that something had gone wrong; the visitors were not coming in the numbers expected, installment collections were beginning to fall off, new purchasers grew harder and harder to find. It was all over before nature took a hand, but a vicious hurricane that struck the state on September 18, 1926, and turned the jerry-built developments into ruins, sobered up even the most ardent enthusiasts.[21]

How many Americans knew that the practice during the twenties of constant mergers, stock splitting, and creating holding companies was the wind that stood to reap the whirlwind? Some surely knew, including Bernard Baruch. But more likely, the impression created by such headline news as the Florida boom was that the old-fashioned success formula of work and thrift and honest character was obsolete. In January of 1929, the self-made man from Claremore wrote, tongue-in-cheek, "We are loaning Europe two financiers to show 'em how to pay each other off without any money, by just reorganizing and issuing more stock like we do." If, occasionally, events such as hurricanes hastened punishment for speculation, they may not have seemed the rule; or they may have been accepted as part of the risk in playing the new game of success. Had that prophet of the old game, Henry Ward Beecher, been on the scene, he might have been aghast at the change in the success dream in favor of speculation. It was a time when Will Rogers, the country boy, could stand before glittering "uptown" banquet audiences and be laughingly accepted when he would say, "Loan sharks, and interest hounds: I have addressed every form of organized graft in the United States, excepting Congress, so it is naturally a pleasure to me to appear before the biggest."[22]

Other changes in the success dream were manifest. Because the day may have seemed past when an aspirant could go it on his own and because some tip or break might be needed to "get in on the ground floor" on some new project, emphasis upon personality replaced some of the other virtues. It was a time for the smart man (as apart from genius), one who was shrewd and educated. These really smart men were the managers of the great industrial machines, not—usually—entrepreneurs. Too, the country boy was no longer the favorite candidate. Finally, as John Blum has explained, in some cases the steps to success were overleaped for purposes of consuming success, itself: "The neat progression from work and thrift to riches and social status faced a powerful challenge during the 1920's. Americans were then shown a shortcut to esteem—a shortcut that reckoned thrift a vice. . . . Most of all advertising sold success" (page 129). The decade was heavily influenced by the success dream, but it was a different dream from that of earlier times.

Possibly, the popular heroes of the success worshippers reflected in their symbolic qualities some of the same state of flux. On the one hand, Henry Ford kept for admirers the old, comfortable, and familiar qualities of country origins, honest work, concern for his workers' well-being, and love of simple pleasures and the old fashion. Joining him in the practice of the old self-help doctrine was, almost certainly, Calvin Coolidge, whose role as the American Adam has already been noted. Besides his Adamic simplicity and seeming lack of artifice, "Silent Cal" also "incarnated thrift, self-denial, . . . [and] straightforward, hard-headed honesty," concludes Gamaliel Bradford. The ambivalence with which the average American may have viewed the dream and the reassurance that he found in the symbolic figure of Coolidge also appeared to be clear to Bradford. The average American, remembering the virtues that were supposed to have made men and the nation great, "saw with a sigh that even when he practiced them himself, he had little taste for them, and that his children had much less taste than he; but there was all the more reason why he should turn to a President who embodied them completely."[23] Coolidge's New England origins and his well-known dedication to work gave him the cast of the old Puritan whose busy-ness could set him in the presence of kings. In all this, he lent an air of stability and continuity between the old time and the dynamism of the twenties.

On the other hand, Al Capone was not only—as mentioned earlier—an anti-Adam for Americans during Prohibition, but he also played Mr. Hyde to Coolidge's Dr. Jekyll in the success drama of the time. Was not Scarface Al an entrepreneur? He even expressed a sense of community responsibility, in the tradition of the success vision. "Public service is my motto," Fishwick (pages 197-98) quotes him as saying. "Ninety-nine percent of the people in Chicago drink. I've tried to serve them decent liquor and square games." An unmistakable sign of Capone's role as a distorted hero of the success dream was the publication in 1930 of a full-length biography with the title, *Al Capone: The Biography of a Self-Made Man.*

Between these two extremes, another hero of folk legend nature exhibited a transition from the old version of the success dream to the newer one. Paul Bunyan, moving from folk into popular literature during the twenties, exhibited a certain nostalgia for a lost, golden, preindustrial age, but his image shaped by those who adapted him for popular literature was also that of the shrewd manager.[24] Finally, publications such as *American Magazine* and *The Saturday Evening Post* kept the doorknob to success polished with their updated versions of the rise of self-made men.

Fictional heroes had for many years struck a dissonant note to that sounded by Ragged Dick. Before the twenties, Jack London's Martin Eden had appeared, a success by material standards but a failure in the pursuit of happiness. Theodore Dreiser, steeped in Nietzsche and Darwin, transformed the success dream with the creation of Frank Cowperwood in 1912. This success figure was an Alger hero, all right, but Lynn (page 51) shows he was also "a 'rebellious Lucifer . . . glorious in his sombre conception of the value of power,' " Nietzchean, and full of "chemisms" that gave him personal magnetism together with powers of thought transference. Other writers, such as Frank Norris, Stephen Crane, Hamlin Garland, David Graham Phillips, and Robert Herrick, either had championed pessimism regarding the success myth or were searching for alternatives to the dominant values of their society. Then, in the twenties, came the defeat not only of Dreiser's success aspirant in *An American Tragedy* but also of F. Scott Fitzgerald's heroes. Perhaps most prominent in the minds of Americans, however, was the portrayal of the illusions of the success dream in the life of another fictional hero, by Sinclair Lewis. Robert E. Spiller writes:

> His portrait of *Babbitt* added a new word to the
> American dictionary because it created a symbol of the
> little man caught up in the success-worship, the
> materialism, of a city world in an industrial society.
> Compassion mingled with scorn to reveal the lost
> humanity in this pathetic victim of the illusions with
> which he was surrounded.[25]

Dream became nightmare for those who met Babbitt, whose humanly ambiguous figure, for once, may have provided a meeting ground for imaginations of Americans of all intellectual habits.

The dream became nightmare, too, after the autumn of 1929. At first the yawning cracks and chasms seemed far off. Through the worst five days of the panic of October, 1929, thousands of investors lost fortunes overnight. For the month taken together, Hicks reports that stock values declined an average of over 35 per cent. Millions of Americans paused in their daily rounds, wondered what such events could do to them, and stirred uneasily. The answer was not many months in coming. By 1930, unemployment reached five million persons; it would stand at thirteen million in 1932. Hicks has pictured vividly the effects:

The horrors of these troubled times, unknown to later generations, were terribly real to those who lived through them. Savings disappeared; purchases made on installments had to be returned; substantial citizens lost their homes on mortgages; insurance companies had difficulty in meeting their obligations; stores closed for lack of customers; vandals or pranksters broke out the windows of vacant factory buildings; theatres went dark; university enrollments dropped abysmally, and faculty members lost their jobs or had their salaries cut; hospitals were short of patients; soup kitchens opened; bread lines began to form; local relief systems broke down; panhandlers roamed the streets; philanthropy dried up to a trickle; the jobless slept on park benches, in the doorways of public buildings, or on the ground; uncounted numbers knew the meaning of hunger and cold and fear (page 229).

Depending upon the general attitude of the publisher or writer, the extremes of America's "fundamental soundness" would be presented: *The New York Times* rotogravure section could picture one of the specially-decorated roadsters being purchased by a rich debutante as gifts for friends in a patriotic effort to keep money in circulation; Edmund Wilson could write about the garbage eaters.

"Passed the Potter's Field yesterday," Rogers noted in a daily wire. "They was burying two stanch [*sic*] old Republicans, both of whom died of starvation, and the man in charge told me their last words were, 'I still think America fundamentally sound.' "26

The words of Roger Babson may have sounded a bit thin to Americans as they read his predictions for the year 1932. "Hard work, hard thinking, efficiency and integrity are coming back into vogue. The surest signal of business recovery is the recovery that is already taking place in our ideals." Actually, the depression was dulling the American sense of enterprise and tarnishing the success dream that had invited worship in the preceding decade.27

What was wanted, then, in heroes symbolic of the American dream of success during these years was reassuring signs that the old idea of country origins, hard work, honesty, social integrity, and responsibility still operated toward success, while successes that did not follow the formula were also accepted. Rogers filled both roles in the publicity he received and in his own words.

IN 1926, for instance, the real-estate bubble in Florida broke, and a disastrous hurricane struck. Readers of *The New York Times* could see the heart-warming story of how the generous passengers aboard the *Leviathan* had subscribed over $40,000 for Florida disaster victims, with gifts ranging from $8,000 to the 25¢ contributed by an immigrant on the way to win his fortune in America. In the second paragraph of this paean to American idealism appeared the following tribute to the man from Oologah: "The raising of this large sum was mainly due to the zeal, energy, humor and personal magnetism of Will Rogers, American comedian and international story teller."[28] Besides the fact that Rogers was given such names of success qualities as "zeal," "energy," and "personal magnetism," the story also cast him as the good steward of wealth. For, in addition to getting Charles Evans Hughes to tell jokes and thus provide a strong attraction, Rogers had contributed $1,000 himself. With such press notices, such distinguished company, and such a generous purse, Rogers would not long need an identifying phrase after his name. His public status as humanity's benefactor fitted him to identify with the dream of success in the same way as had philanthropist Andrew Carnegie—rich, famous, and generous.

In the spring of 1927, the mighty Mississippi went out of its banks and flooded its bordering southern states, ruining farms, homes, and means of livelihood for many thousands of Americans by engulfing an estimated 10,000 square miles. The Red Cross went to work immediately, but additional funds were needed. Rogers, on the lecture circuit, went to New York for a one-night stand with the tenor John McCormack as a means of raising funds for flood relief. As a result, a news story in *The New York Times* reported that the Red Cross would receive nearly $18,000 from the benefit and also listed among the donors of gifts of over $1,000 the name of Will Rogers. In a flood so devastating that President Coolidge would issue a call for an emergency Red

Cross fund of $5,000,000, much remained to be done. Rogers went to New Orleans for another flood benefit. "The town was Will's from the minute he arrived this morning," announced a special dispatch to *The New York Times.*[29] The Claremore Sage had actually been sworn in as mayor pro tempore of New Orleans in gratitude for all that he had done for flood sufferers, including the show in New Orleans, with top seat prices of $500. The story made clear, however, that Rogers was not going to stop his efforts in behalf of the sufferers. "Tomorrow the cowboy humorist will make a tour of the flooded sections of Louisiana and Mississippi, probably by airplane." The trip was not mere sightseeing. "He wants to get plenty of material, so he'll know what he's talking about when he asks people for relief fund contributions, he says." Those who did not read the story in the newspapers were to have a chance to see him as the benefactor on the rest of his lecture tour. Because of his experience with the flood, he would later appear before a congressional committee to testify in behalf of proposed control measures by the federal government. For the time being, sufficiently gratifying to Rogers' public was the news story that revealed his selection for life membership in the Red Cross. In recognition of his services, John Barton Payne, Red Cross chairman, wrote in a letter made public, "You are unanimously elected a life member of the American Red Cross. . . . I want you to know how grateful we all are for your splendid service in connection with the Mississippi flood disaster."[30]

Rogers' national audience was also aware of his helpful presence on the scene of another disaster that received national attention. In the spring of 1931, Texas, Oklahoma, Arkansas, and other states were parched from a long, dusty drouth, as well as starved by the depression. A short time before, hundreds of desperate farmers had converged on the town of England, Arkansas, to take by force the supplies they and their families required for survival. Newspapers announced on January 14 that Rogers would make a two-to-three-week tour of three of the stricken states, that all proceeds would go toward drouth relief, and that he would fly with Captain Frank Hawks in order to increase the number of appearances by traveling fast. A little over a week later, news stories revealed that the trip had begun, with Rogers and Hawks arriving in Arkansas; also newsworthy was the fact that Rogers would appear on a coast-to-coast broadcast with such notables as Al Smith and Calvin Coolidge. For the next seventeen days, papers in the region would report the comings and goings of the flying cowboy as he covered an estimated 15,000 miles and gave an exhausting total of fifty-two benefit performances, netting almost a quarter of a million dollars for relief. Here was the success hero combined with the cowboy of legend who took direct action to set affairs right.

By the time of the catastrophic earthquake in Nicaragua later in that same year of 1931, the statement that "Will Rogers is coming" meant that more than a good time was in the offing. By this time, no doubt existed that Will Rogers' disaster doings were national news. An Associated Press dispatch told the public of its hero's actions:

> Will Rogers came to desolate Managua today and his coming, acted as a tonic of cheer to a stricken people.
>
> He arrived by Pan-American Airways plane from San Salvador to be met by an excited crowd of United States Marines and Nicaraguans. He was taken to the temporary quarters of the United States Legation and there was greeted by Minister Matthew Hanna and Marine Corps officers.
>
> Starting on a tour of the ruins from earthquake and fire, he made himself popular at once by his searching questions on the disaster and his humorous remarks. News of his presence spread like wildfire and he became the centre of a smiling crowd.
>
> Foreign Minister Irias, who was introduced to Mr. Rogers, said of him:
>
> "I know of him from two angles—that he is a famous humorist and a writer of philosophy as pleasing as an old shoe and that his presence on this earth has been beneficial to mankind."[31]

Americans agreed.

Such were some of the nationally-prominent causes in which Rogers enlisted his talent. His philanthropies, of course, did not begin and end with such headline material. While it is reasonably certain that his national audience was aware of his role in such causes, one cannot be so sure of public knowledge of other donations of his time and money. If his philanthropies seemed less calculated to encourage young men to self-help than had those of Rockefeller or Carnegie, that may have helped him appeal to those who were doubtful of the efficacy of the traditional self-help doctrine.

In other ways, the Will Rogers portrayed in publicity was the typical Horatio Alger hero, a self-made man. Implicit in the story of his wanderings and development in show business was, of course, the story of the rise. It became explicit when a writer would do a piece for a publication that treated the rags-to-riches theme as one of its dominant ones. The dollar signs in the following quotation are clear clues to the success slant given to the outlined version, appearing in *American Magazine* in 1930, of Rogers' career:

> Had a fortune teller predicted then [during courtship days] that Will Rogers, a Cherokee Indian, would become one of the highest-paid actors in motion pictures, he would have grunted and said to Betty, "See? What'd I tell you? They're nothing but fakes. Who'd pay money to see a Cherokee cowhand?"
>
> Even the most farseeing astrologer, palm reader, or clairvoyant would not have been so daring as to suggest that a few years would bring into every home a magic contraption called radio and that this Cherokee cow-hand would be paid $12,500 to talk into a funny little dingus for fifteen minutes. Nor that magazines and newspapers would pay thousands of dollars for the privilege of printing sly comments such as he was delivering then of evenings around the stove in the Oologah general store just for the fun of it.[32]

If any element of the old success dream depicted in Rogers' rise was missing, it was the "work and win" idea; this omission, however, may not have seemed serious at the time, when good "breaks" rather than strong backs may have seemed primary determinants of success.

An earlier feature writer had not overlooked Rogers' industry. "Mr. Rogers is a tireless worker and is not content to rest on his laurels already acquired," a reporter had written for *The New York Times* in the summer of 1917. A 1934 feature also vividly pictured Rogers' dedication to work and his activism:

> Mr. Rogers, one of the busiest men in pictures, is also one of the busiest men in the world. During filming of the "Judge Priest" picture he managed to portray the leading role in the stage production of "Ah, Wilderness" at the El Capitan Theatre, get out a daily syndicated newspaper column, crowd in a few radio broadcasts and attend innumerable banquets wherever a Senator, Congressman, statesman or film executive appeared. During his leisure hours he personally supervised the renovation of his Beverly Hills home.[33]

That kind of busy-ness should have satisfied even those who felt that the unorthodox way to success by entertaining was not demanding enough of hard work.

Of the virtue needed to rise to success, little doubt is possible that Rogers' public image was replete with it. It remained, however, for his observers to give it the almost deific quality so important to the success dream. Three days after Will Rogers' death, Ted Malone was extolling on radio the qualities of character that had made the man from Oologah rich; he was also stating the theology of success:

> Yesterday the papers carried a story that was a most interesting epilogue. It was an estimation of what we may call the worldly accumulations of a life of this philosophy. The estimate was five or six million dollars. That is a lot of money, and in this day of competitive business, we have been taught to believe that it requires close trading, sharp bargains, shrewd deals, cold-blooded decisions, hard-boiled business, to climb to the top. But strangely enough none of these characteristics were a part of this man's make-up. . . .
> Here is a man who loved all men and all men made him rich. Here is a man who has given to America a living proof that a man can make good without making enemies. Here is challenge to the cut-throat competition of world business today. . . . This man's life proved that one can be a man—a Man's Man—can live the philosophy of Christianity, can make it a part of his every-day life, his every-day work, and the world will shower him with its love and its wealth.[34]

As it was pictured in the publicity accorded him during his career, Will Rogers' success was above reproach either by the Babsons or the Menckens. In his own words relating to the vision of success, Rogers managed to merge himself with the dream as both a devotee and a debunker of some aspects. ("He was a debunker, but he was a *kindly* debunker," one admirer of Rogers once told me.)

Because the success dream was shot through with such themes of the other visions as the powers, goodness, and self-fulfillment of the common man—as well as freedom and equality—what Rogers said was often relevant not only to them but also to the hope of success as well. For instance, when he wrote of the powers of the "old broad minded man of the world of experience," he was not only speaking as the American Adam searching after wisdom for the sake of self-fulfillment, but he was also identifying himself with the dogma of the success dream that dictated against the college-educated man, since that individual seemed to some to threaten the self-made part of the dream. As long as an everyday man had the possibility of success, the dream of his powers seemed valid. Again, when Rogers reported one day that the most "human" thing he had seen in the papers was the return of successful, honest businessmen to their reform school alma mater, he was not only testifying to his belief in the essential goodness of mankind but also was relating himself to the view of success as virtue rewarded. Relevant not only to the dream of social equality but also to the success vision's principle of virtue rewarded was Rogers' annoyance with the Social Register over what he understood to be its admission by inheritance of members whose "morals or personal behaviour" had nothing to do with their acceptance, together with its denial of Henry Ford, king of all self-made men. When Rogers entered the lists in favor of a meaningful inheritance tax for sons of rich men, he was not only speaking to the dream of economic equality but also to the shirtsleeves tradition of the success vision. He would see to it that rich men who endangered their descendants' virtue by leaving fortunes intact would have their "error" corrected by legislation, if need be. Because, in such fashion, Rogers' identifications with the dreams of freedom, equality, and the worth of the individual were also relevant to the success vision, he could appear, and be accepted, as a devotee of the success tradition. Combined with what he said, which related simultaneously to success and other categories of the great dream, Will Rogers acquired the face of success mainly in two modes. Since the essence and substance of the success dream were virtually the same, Rogers could illumine the principles of success in the actions of success heroes (many of whom he counted as his friends). Too, in his own behavior he took the role of the successful man. In both of these modes, his tone was sometimes admiring and sometimes bantering, so that every kind of success dreamer could find something for himself.

The creator of Ragged Dick has become synonymous with the legend of success, even though he is famous for writing novels rather than success manuals. Neither did Will Rogers write any success guide, but he did use the mass media of radio and widely-circulated newspapers and magazines in order to share with his audience the living, rhetorical examples provided by American success heroes. "America is a land of opportunity and don't ever forget it," the nation's beloved self-made man told his national newspaper audience in 1931.

As though to prove it, the erstwhile cowboy would tell of his friends and acquaintances who had become self-made men. In a predepression piece for *American,* he made clear his intention—at the same time adopting a tone that would appeal to iconoclasts:

> Ever since I been trying to write (to keep from manual labor) I always did want to write one of those "success" Articles. They have always appealed to me as being the most interesting reading, for we all want to know just how our rich and our well-known people got that way. . . .
> I wanted to just be one of these fellows that wrote about some man that had got somewhere by "hard work, perseverance, and taking advantage of his opportunities."[35]

Bantering as his tone in opening may have been, Rogers was serious in his praise of the feats of the hero of his article, an Oklahoma farm boy who had won a coast-to-coast foot race. The significant ingredient in the boy's success had been his spartan origins—in a tradition true to the success dream.

> Do you want to know the real reson [*sic*] he won? Well, they are one of the only families that dident own a automobile. He used to run to school. So the moral of the story is, Dont own a car. If each one of our Athaletes [*sic*] in the races that went to the Olympics had never owned a car, we would have won every race there.[36]

The rural origins and habits of frugality and industry that the success legend extolled played a significant part in the character of another farm boy who made good, Calvin Coolidge. Writing in a "success" magazine in the summer of 1929, Will Rogers told of the reasons purportedly given for Coolidge's success by a mutual friend, financier Dwight Morrow:

> Now, you take the way he has been raised. His great-grandfather had a Farm, and skimped and saved, and after a life-time of work left it unencumbered, and a little nest egg of a couple of thousand dollars. Then his son took it, and worked and saved and left Coolidge's father perhaps eight or ten thousand. Then he works hard, saves and adds to that, and leaves Coolidge perhaps twenty-five or thirty thousand in addition to the farm. Now, that was progressive success. Each one took what he had, added to it, and left more than he started with.

Thus Rogers used his rhetorical example to make the point that success came partly as a result of rural or small-town beginnings. "Take every small-town-raised big man out of business and you would have nobody left running it but vice presidents," the small-town boy from Oologah commented on one occasion.[37] In other success stories, Rogers amplified other aspects of the doctrine of success.

In his feature on Sir Thomas Lipton, for instance, Rogers dwelt upon the theme of the rise to eminence—even to the point of entertaining royalty—of the poor, half-orphaned, mother-loving, industrious lad of all trades who remained virtuously modest after his great rise. He allowed Sir Thomas to speak directly in the article appearing in the September, 1930, issue of *American,* and managed—before proceeding to exemplify the success formula—to give America a share of the tea magnate's success.

> Did you know [Sir Thomas said] that I landed at Castle Garden as a boy, an immigrant, right here in your own country? Oh, I know your country better than you know it.
> I worked at everything under the sun, all over this great Country of yours. I was down in Virginia, around Charleston, into Tennessee a great deal; then to New Orleans.

Sir Thomas' devotion to his mother had been like the faithfulness of Ragged Dick.

> I used to bring me Mother home the half Crown and tell her some day I will have more horses and carriages for you to use than you will know what to do with, and she lived to have 'em too, plenty of 'em. . . .
> And at my big celebration at Glasgow for me, I told 'em that any Boy could get up in the World if he only used his Mother as his guiding spirit. She has been my inspiration all my life, and there has never been a night that I layed down that you wont find the picture of her the nearest thing to my pillow.

This once-poor boy had entertained, later, every king and queen and "high potentate" of his time; he had received the keys to more cities than any other human; he had retained his modesty, in the best manner of the success dream. " 'Famous Lipton'—I am an immigrant and will always be an immigrant. 'Famous' me eye," Will Rogers reported him as saying. Then Rogers drove home the point of his example. "He is a great old man; he should be a lesson to the World. Here is a man that does business in every corner of the World, and they all love him and he gets along with all of them."[38]

(Earlier in the article, Rogers had told of his years of acquaintance with Lipton and had described the setting of their latest meeting. "I had a whole evening with him not long ago . . ."; it had been "a lovely dinner and we just sit there and made a whole evening of it, as Sir Thomas was going great." Rogers appeared to his audience "to be going great," too. He was closely associated with a great success hero and with the dream that made him a hero. It was reassuring to believers in success; unbelievers may have had some difficulty in quarreling with the accomplished fact.)

The success demigod with whom the cowboy philosopher was most clearly identified, however, was the king of them all, Henry Ford. Rogers was to picture him as the good liege lord and the giver of honest value, and he had spoken on "Uncle Henry" even during the days of his banquet speeches in the early 1920's in New York City. He told, of course, his share of the famous Ford jokes that did so much to create the "Henry B" discerned by Marshall Fishwick. On several occasions, he was Ford's guest.

Over the years of his public ascendancy, Rogers spoke and wrote words that portrayed Ford as the ideal success figure. "Folks, I hate to brag," Rogers wrote in the lead paragraph of a story on Ford for a mass circulation magazine. "But it just looks like I have scored what Newspaper men call a 'Beat' on all these other folks that make a success writing about people that have made a success." Rogers had found the "champion" of them all: Ford was the self-made man who made his money by giving value received, not by speculation on Wall Street.

> Measured by the ordinary financial standards, he is not much shakes. I doubt if he knows what hour Wall Street opens, or closes. He thinks Margins are the things you leave around the edge of anything. He knows what calling Hogs is; but Call Money would be Greek to him. He never did merge two or more companies together and sell stock. He has had to make what little he has out of just what little he had to work with.

(Not only did Ford give full value in order to make his success, but he was also the ideal success hero in being the common man who exercised his powers of judgment. In a radio speech, Rogers gave a version of a statement he would repeat in his columns: "Ford's success," he drawled, "is due to the fact that he uses common sense in his business instead of a board of directors.")[39]

Further, in Rogers' statements, Ford was the conscientious liege lord with his employees. When coal miners were struggling to win a living wage in 1928, Rogers visited Pittsburgh and reported, "Henry Ford is paying $8 a day and having no trouble in his mines. Ain't it funny," he asked readers of his daily wire, "when it looks like a business can't be run right, he bobs up and shows that it can." Earlier, Rogers had developed the same theme of Ford's good stewardship with his men and had mixed in an element of the folk humor that surrounded the genial "Henry B." In a weekly syndicated article in 1925, the cowboy philosopher of success talked about Ford's operation of a railroad:

> He has only had the railroad a short time and the workmen are allowed to buy stock in it, and the stock is paying them 15 per cent already, and he won't let the thing run on Sunday. On Saturday night at 12 o'clock, no matter where a train is, they stop, the passengers get off go and hunt up a farmer's house and take out board and lodging for the rest of the weekend. On Sunday night exactly at twelve, the Engineer blows his whistle and they come running in and all get on and go till the next Saturday night catches them. . . .
>
> His men work only eight hours. But he goes on the rule that means do something that eight hours. It's rather an unusual rule in modern industry when an Engineer and Conductor and all the crew stop, they are supposed to start doing something, generally rubbing and polishing. You can tell a railroad man that works for Mr. Ford. He carries a piece of this cleaning in his hand instead of a Cigarette. While the Passengers are getting on the Engineer is scrubbing the wheels of the Engine, and while the train is going the Conductor is washing the windows and the Brakeman is painting the inside of the cars. Even running, there is no wasted energy. The throttle is in one hand and a dust rag in the other.[40]

Henry thus not only was the good steward over his hirelings by providing them with the satisfaction and human dignity of being miniature capitalists, but he was also doing his best to give them the industry of character so necessary for success. By contributing to the legend of Ford, Will Rogers was identifying himself with the success dream, too: He was one of those "folks that make a success writing about people that have made a success."

Another article in the success disciple's credo was his

Will Rogers

finding self-fulfillment through wise use of his wealth. He articulated the principle as part of an article on Henry Ford:

> A rich man has either got to make his name on what he did with his money or what he did for people in the way he was making it. If they feel he give 'em a run for their money, and really helped out his fellow man while alive, and tried to do something to make life a little more easy for him, why, then he is readily distinguishable from the herd.

On other occasions, Rogers was more pointed in his expression of the need for philanthropical stewardship on the part of self-made men. "All of our disgustingly rich men are at a loss to know what to do with their money," he wrote during prosperous years. "Funny none of them ever thought of giving it back to the people they got it from."[41]

When wearers of the silk-hat crown of success did use their wealth in enlightened philanthropy, Rogers was prompt to praise them. For instance, regarding a banker who in late 1927 had announced that his institution was for the benefit of borrowers rather than for his own personal fortune, Rogers went right down to see "how he would help other people." The test was crucial: "I put in a bid for a loan, to try and do all I could to make him die poor, and the funny part about it is that this fellow is on the level with it, he really is practicing it." In such predepression days, the wise innocent as self-made man could high-spiritedly conclude, "I got the loan; so hurry up and get in, everybody, before he turns banker." Other good stewards of wealth received kind words from Rogers, but the rich benefactor who attracted his highest accolades was John D. Rockefeller, Sr. Rockefeller, faithful to the success dream's dictum that the rich man practice discerning philanthropy, provided aid aimed at self-help. Writing just a few months before the great crash, Rogers saw Rockefeller as a model for wealthy men:

> The best news in the paper today was no joke. The Rockefeller foundation, for the health and betterment of people of all parts of the world, spent $22,000,000 last year and $144,000,000 since its organization in 1913. And

196

it's been worth $1,000,000 as an inspiration to other
tremendous rich men to do fine things.

The whole viewpoint of the people in regard to our rich
men has been changed in the last few years. Now we
judge a man's greatness on how he has spent his money.
. . . Just to be rich and nothing else, is practically a
disgrace nowadays.

(From time to time, the cowboy philosopher of success repeated his praise of Rockefeller's stewardship of wealth
and clarified his own association with the Standard Oil
magnate. Telling of meeting Rockefeller in Florida during
his three solo tours, Rogers wrote, "I always had a few local
jokes about him, and would go down off the 'Rostrum' and
shake hands with him and he would quietly ask me to come
to his home on the following morning and have breakfast
with him, at eight o'clock."[42] Dining and exchanging dimes
with the elder Rockefeller, Rogers not only appeared to his
public as the American democrat hobnobbing with all
classes of men, but he also identified himself with a success
figure who had survived the muckraking period. Through
Rockefeller, Rogers became consubstantial with the dream
of success, as he had done by his messages on other success
heroes of his acquaintance, such as Coolidge, Lipton, and
Ford.)

To conclude, with such men as illustrations, he managed
to vivify the ideas that success awaited the man who disci-
plined himself through obscure beginnings, who formed his
character under the inspiration of a saintly mother, and
who worked hard and won success by giving honest value
for wealth received. Satisfaction with life and self-fulfillment awaited the rich man as benefactor who provided
well for his underlings and who practiced philanthropy. By
embodying such rules in those features, Rogers produced a
success manual in somewhat the same way that Alger had
done with his novels starring Ragged Dick. Thus, Rogers
managed one mode of his material identification with the
way of success that led to the Paradise to be regained. At the
same time, he could put tongue-in-cheek or have "a few
local jokes" with success heroes and thus remain something of the "kindly debunker."

In the second mode of identification, however, Rogers was

himself the success hero. Significant were the titles he gave to his odysseys into foreign affairs for *The Saturday Evening Post:* He was the "Self-Made Diplomat" who wrote to President Coolidge and to Senator Borah. Appearing in a magazine that under the editorship of George Horace Lorimer became a leading success organ, Rogers had an audience ready-made for an identification as a self-made man. In other ways perhaps equally significant, he projected the picture of himself as a successful man to his newspaper readers and radio listeners.

Rogers never let his national audience forget his rural origins. "I am just an old country boy," he would write. "I have been eating pretty regular and the reason I have is, I have stayed an old country boy." He attributed his sense of humor to his mother, whom he revered, and referring to his formal education he quipped: "In 1898 Kemper Military School was not being run in accordance with the standards that I thought befitting a growing intellect. So I not only left them flat during a dark night, but quit the entire school business for life."[43]

He reviewed his career for his readers from time to time, telling of his humble beginnings. "The limit of my 'Pay Dirt' was I think 30 dollars a month," he wrote of his first cow-punching job. Another time, in a way appropriate to the theme of busy-ness in success, he might summarize his first trip around the world:

> You know I never did do much along that line for just
> pleasure. I was always pretty busy. Done a lot of
> traveling but it was always working my way. In the early
> days it was working my way on a boat to try and get
> home.[44]

In his weekly columns, he would tell of his early days in the wild West shows, of his experiences in vaudeville, the Ziegfeld Follies, and the early movie years; as an established star of the new medium of talking pictures, he would also on occasion give a behind-the-scenes look at the glamorous business of movie making. Coupled with his stories of mingling with the powerful and the rich, such articles made Rogers' rise to riches and success clear.

Luck, he said, had been on his side. For instance, when he

wrote in 1925 of his thrill at the reception the "home folks" at Tulsa had given him on his solo tour, he actually went so far as to deny the old success formula.

> I am no believer in this "hard work, perseverance, and taking advantage of your opportunities" that these magazines are so fond of writing some fellow up in. The successful don't work any harder than the failures. They get what is called in baseball the breaks.[45]

Even in the face of such a denial of the success formula, Will Rogers' own rise was clear and satisfying to his audience: To those who accepted the work-and-win formula, he was simply being modest; to those who rejected the success rule, he was a debunker. Many members of his public so identified him with the paradigm of success, wrote Betty Rogers, that they believed him to have struggled to riches from Oklahoma rags, when in fact he had been denied almost nothing.

Rogers was a success because as the American Adam he found self-fulfillment. "All there is to success is satisfaction," he wrote on one occasion. His own life was full of friends, fun, travel, and earthly rewards.[46] He may have also included in his definition of "satisfaction" the self-fulfillment that comes from the successful man's benefactions. Certainly, his message in behalf of good causes provided for his public the "good steward" dimension that completed the image of the idealized self-made man.

Through the years, Rogers used his channels in mass media to support causes as various as year-round Christmas charities, the March of Dimes, Helen Keller's work for the blind, and hurricane relief for Puerto Rico. His public character as benefactor, however, probably developed most clearly for his audience at those moments of acute, widespread crisis, when he often was on the scene of trouble and backed up his appeals for help with his own ready purse. Such actions permitted him to retain for his public the best of the dream of success, the altruistic practice of *noblesse oblige.*

When, for instance, the muddy waters of the 1927 Mississippi flood left more than a half-million people homeless, the man from the banks of the Verdigris spoke and wrote words for weeks, requesting help for the sufferers; he printed jokes about sending out society levees in New York to help with broken levees on the Mississippi; he asked Americans on Mother's Day to show their mother-taught virtue by sending dollars to the Red Cross. He exhorted, praised, cajoled, and resorted to irony: "Come on, let's help them, even if they are not Armenians. They can't help it because of their nationality." When the goal of $5,000,000 may have begun to look big to donors, Rogers "visualized the idea" of distributing the millions to show the paltriness of the sum. Figuring that twenty million Americans were either children or "conscientiously too small to give," he still had a theoretical base of 100 million who could be expected to contribute; twenty cents from each would produce twenty-million dollars instead of the asked-for five.

> Now, if we sorter feel they dident get hardly wet enough for a couple of thin dimes per head, why let's kinder spread our generosity a little anyway and give a dime each and that will give them ten million. That's about ten dollars a head for the ones that suffered loss. Now you will hear lots of people say, "What do they do with all this money? Here people are giving millions!"
>
> Well, take for instance ten dollars a head in case my suggestion is acted on and everyone of the 100 million will give 10 cents. That will give the sufferers $10 a head. Now I know that is a pretty lump sum to go and squander on a fellow that hasn't lost anything but his house and barn and stock and all his seed that he had planted already. It is liable to bring on an era of squandering.[47]

Through the end of April, all of May, and halfway into June, Rogers wrote appeals for help. He was the successful man because he was being the good steward with his time, talent, and money. That he didn't utilize the success dream's formula for philanthropy aimed at self-improvement may have mattered little to his public.

He did, however, make use of an audience's value of self-help in his messages on behalf of drouth and depression relief during his famous tour of Arkansas, Texas, and Oklahoma early in 1931. The march of hungry farmers on England, Arkansas, in order to take by force needed food, had aroused the attention of the nation and of Rogers. "Paul Revere just woke up Concord. These birds woke up America," he wrote in a daily wire labeling hunger, rather than balanced budgets, as the real national problem. A couple of weeks later, Rogers was on the scene, making a flying drouth relief tour with the famous Frank Hawks as his pilot. Rogers' daily dispatches kept the nation informed and utilized the persuasive appeal of needy people trying to help themselves. In Arkansas, he wrote, "Here is the great thing about this State where they have been hit hardest. They are going to make their Red Cross quota, and help to help themselves. If they can do it, no other State or city can possibly have an alibi." Self-help, he apparently believed, was not only part of the American tradition but was also a practical necessity. "Congress may help us," he said in a nationwide broadcast from Arkansas, "but you won't live long enough to see it."[48]

Rogers went on to do more than fifty benefit performances in little more than two weeks. It was an exhausting schedule, but in his daily telegrams that dealt with the tour, the aura of the eternal boy shone, together with the spirit of survival that permeated the drouth philanthropy.

> These people in the drouth stricken country ain't waiting for the government to relieve 'em. Their well to do are helping their less fortunate than themselves. At a matinee today in Wichita Falls, we played to $9,100. At Fort Worth tonight, the cowman's paradise, we played to $18,000, at my breakfast matinee yesterday morning at Abilene at 10 o'clock, got $6,500, and every cent of that is net.
>
> People in America have got the money and will give if they know the need is there, and these people know it.

He did three shows a day in three different cities, day after day. But his wires to his public showed no flagging of interest or energy. Again, he tasted the sweetness of being the prophet accepted in his own country at Tulsa:

> Say, that Tulsa is a bear! We played there last night to exactly $30,000 at one single performance, making $100,000 the State of Oklahoma paid in one week.
>
> It wasn't the attraction, it was the cause. These people down in these States know that there is folks that are

hungry and they are going to feed 'em as long as they are able.

And, say, they got a great gag down here. They don't just open up a soup kitchen and feed a lot of professional bums. They make 'em work, and then give 'em the money to buy some food.[49]

It "wasn't the attraction" that had drawn the crowd, the Oologah success hero wrote. His modesty was becoming.

On other occasions, he reinforced the benefactor's aspect of his image. Many of his words on the depression, for instance, did so. In a statement not only supporting the economic underdog but also bearing upon his role as the socially-responsible success hero, he supported the 1931 Community Chest drive by saying, "Now a miracle can't happen and all these people get a job overnight, it's going to take time, so they must be fed and cared for perhaps all winter." One reason was clear: "There is not an unemployed man in the country that hasn't contributed to the wealth of every millionaire in America." During the spring of 1932, Rogers kept up his idea of helping people to help themselves, championing the plan of "block aid," whereby the unemployed received help from the employed in the same city block: "This is a time when, I don't care where you live, you can't throw a rock without hitting somebody that needs help worse than you do. Here is a scheme where charity begins at home."[50] He was still concerned with depression relief in 1935, advocating a "pay-as-you-go" idea.

Because Rogers' words gave him the character of the benefactor, he could be accepted as a self-made man. Thus, he could be the success hero and still say, as he did in 1934, "By the way, this depression and the fall of the big man has kinder knocked the props out of all those success storys we used to get fed up on." He concluded, "This is just an age of being a good Democrat and holding an office. Thats all there is to success now."[51] Even while debunking the dream, Rogers still shone as an untarnished hero of the legend. His affirmation of it by his benefactions had provided a mode of identification acceptable to a national audience unprepared to hear preached the old doctrine of "hard work, perseverance, and taking advantage of opportunity."

Thus, by earlier illustrating the strategy and principles of the success dream in the lives of self-made men whom he knew personally, and by revealing himself as a country boy who rose to fame and later became an openhanded benefactor, Will Rogers played his part as success hero attendantly with other roles that made him an icon of the dreams of freedom, equality, and the worth of the individual.

The new Adam, by virtue of his experiential self-fulfillment, was a self-made man. Accordingly, the Adamic sense of newness and wise innocence conveyed by Rogers' use of word bending, slang, and his "wiser-than-I-look" facial expression were appropriate also to the look of the self-made man who rises to the ranks of the new rich by practicing the wise innocence of being intelligently good. Accordingly, as the American democrat demonstrating his freedom by unconventional platform behavior, Rogers the democrat coalesced with Rogers the self-made man. His loose, relaxed posture, together with his habits of leaning and sitting and gum chewing, were appropriate not only to the intuitive Adam and the free democrat but also to the appearance of a man who was self-taught and self-made in the art of speaking. In other respects, Will Rogers had more particularly the form or the "look" of the self-made man.

In the first place, and perhaps most obviously, his standard form of stage dress after his vaudeville and Follies years was the business suit. So fixed was this habit of dress during the years of his greatest prominence that the only concession he made to formal occasions was to wear a navy blue business suit with a bow tie. He succeeded, however, in keeping some visual reminder to his public of his country origins, which were so germane not only to agrarian freedom but also to the nineteenth-century success vision. Without resorting to chewing a cud of tobacco or gnawing on a haystraw, he avoided formal identification with the "city slicker" who wore his hair in a Valentino style. Rogers simply combed his forelock over his forehead and let his hat rest far enough back to show the hair. Between the uptown look of the double-breasted business suit and the country look of his hair, he had the appearance of the success hero, new or old, whether from the country or the big town.

In a more metaphorical sense, his use of language aided his self-made man image. Through his ungrammatical approach to language and his unadorned prose, he gave the senses not only of the intuitive Adam and the free democrat remaining "just plain folks," but also of the success hero risen to eminence without advantages of birth or cultural breeding.

Given the dais of his newspaper columns, magazine space, or radio microphone, Rogers clearly had the aura of success that accompanied "breaking into print" or being the popular voice on the radio. At times, he made his formal identification by use of redundancy, such as his description of Hoover's own Ragged-Dick childhood: "Mr. Hoover, he was left an orphan when he was a little boy, at a very early age, and he went to live for a while with an uncle." Occasionally, he used the sentence fragment, as when he theorized that contributions for an eastern flood would come in faster than for a Mississippi flood: "Makes a lot of difference where a thing happens." From drouth-stricken Arkansas, he told readers of his own impending inspection tour: "Going out among it tomorrow." A related form was the run-on sentence. Urging a plan for self-help relief units of a city block each, he wrote, "That's one trouble with our charities, we are always saving somebody away off, when the fellow next to us aint eating." He used "ain't" so frequently that Carl Sandburg once remarked that Rogers almost made the word respectable. He gave a light dash of misspelling to his writing: Reason might become "reson"; athletes, "athaletes"; kind of, "kinder"; most frequent, perhaps, was his misspelling of contracted verbs: "Wouldent," "dident," and "couldent" were common.

The heart of the sentence, the predicate, most often got Rogers' ungrammatical treatment. Besides misspelling, he frequently omitted auxiliary forms or used the wrong number or tense of the verb. Examples occurred in his sentences on the success of Woolworth: "Now he has a tower in New York where for twenty-five cents you can go and see what he done for a dime." Woolworth was "a Guy that was smart enough in his youth to see that just about everybody he come in contact with just had a nickle or a dime." Perhaps Rogers established some kind of record when he used the wrong number of verb three times in only twenty words after commenting on Ford's success: "I attribute his success to selling motor cars exclusively and not selling stock. He don't dread inflation and he don't fear it if it comes. In fact, he don't seem to fear anything." Such rough-and-ready use of verbs appears to constitute most of Rogers' assault on grammar. (His niece has testified that he knew much better English usage than he practiced.)[52]

In another way, Rogers used language to identify formally with the dream of success. His paucity of adjectives and adverbs was true to the principle of simplification that H. L. Mencken found in the practice of the American language. Adamic in its effect, this vigorous, plain language was also appropriate to the no-nonsense quality of the self-made man.

> Well, here we are at Managua. They tell you pictures don't lie, but the ones you saw of this earthquake did, for they didn't tell that eight days after it happened there is from one to three hundred bodies still under the ruins.
>
> Sitting here in a marine tent writing this and am going to sleep here. The doctor is coming around to shoot me for typhoid and then I am going to learn to cuss and will be a real marine.
>
> Naturally what they need is money. The government, or the people, haven't got a cent. The Red Cross, combined with the relief organization here, has done great work as usual and still is doing it. They are feeding about 8,000.
>
> . . . If through the Red Cross and public donations from up home they could get $250,000 it would relieve the situation as to food and get some roofs to cover these people.
>
> Now, what they are afraid of is the rainy season which starts in just a few weeks. Lord help you, if you have no cover when it starts.
>
> Goodness knows, you generous folks have been asked till you are ragged, but honest if you saw it you would dig again. I have finally found somebody poorer than a Southern cotton renter farmer. . . .
>
> If you saw, as I did this morning, 2,500 mothers with babies in their arms go by and get their ration of milk you would say there was some poor devil that needed it worse than you do.[53]

Thus, the plain prose written at moments of high drama was fitting for the persona of the self-made man; whether enlisted in the aid of flood victims or survivors of a mine-disaster, it helped provide Rogers the role of benefactor.

THUS, through the formal devices of his appearance, his violation of grammar rules, and his unadorned prose, Rogers identified with the success vision. Together with his material identification with the rags-to-riches myth, he remained an embodiment of the best of the success dream in a time when it had too often become a nightmare. He was good company for Americans in years when they needed it. He could be believed when, at the end of 1933, he put out his own prediction for 1934:

> Taking the year all the way through, you can mighty easy report "Progress." This depression was deep, and you dont climb out of anything as quick as you fall in. Its certainly been a year of excitement; not a dull moment. I think we can kinder get time to relax in '34, and give some of these plans a chance to jell. So, '33, you are liable in some future World's Almanac to be pointed out as the turning point.[54]

Even though he was not uttering Babsonian sentiments on the recovery of American business by the retrieval of the old success attributes, Rogers was an emblem of success. He was a hero of progress, too.

Will Rogers, American Prometheus

Americans of the mid-twentieth century received greet-
ings sent more than two hundred years ago from Nathaniel
Ames, physician, innkeeper, essayist, publisher, and
dreamer of progress: "O! Ye unborn Inhabitants of America!
Should this Page escape its destin'd Conflagration at the
Year's End, and these Alphabetical Letters remain legible,
—when your Eyes behold the Sun after he has rolled the
Seasons round for two or three Centuries more, you will
know that in Anno Domini 1758, we dream'd of your Times."
The forward-looking Ames envisioned the "Progress of Humane Literature" from the East to the West, and had anticipated the dissipation of "Heathenish Darkness" by the
"Coelestial Light of the Gospel"; but the greatest space of
his dream for this century he gave to material advancement:

> Huge Mountains of Iron Ore are already discovered; and
> vast Stores are reserved for future Generations: This
> Metal more useful than Gold and Silver, will imploy
> Millions of Hands, not only to form the martial Sword,
> and peaceful Share, alternately; but an Infinity of
> Utensils improved in the Exercise of Art, and Handicraft
> amongst Men. Nature thro' all her Works has stamp'd
> Authority on this Law, namely, "That all fit Matter shall
> be improved to its best Purposes."[1]

This gazer into the future, linking our own time with his,
had probably been bequeathed the dream of progress by
those, in turn, who had lived before him. The rise in western
civilization of commerce, invention, and natural science
had carried with it—in the words of Charles Beard—the
prospect of "an immense future for mortal mankind, of the
conquest of the material world in human interest, [and] of
providing the conditions for a good life on this planet without reference to any possible hereafter." The bringer of this
good life and teacher of the useful arts would be a hero of
progress, a modern Prometheus. In America, progress
seemed possible and plausible to the rising Buckskin on the

frontier, to the Puritan dreaming of the approaching millennium, and to the common-sense revolutionary advancing toward the goal of popular sovereignty. Because, therefore, the hope of progress has thus intertwined with other categories of the great American dream, it can serve as counterpoint to them. In the second place, just as Ames attached the valuative dimension of the "best Purposes" to the improvement of matter, most Americans have found moral progress in material advancement as a strategy for re-creation of a paradise.* Both strands in the progress dream are important.

Dreamers of other aspects of the American dream also envisioned an ideal of linear advancement of humanity: For them, progress was counterpoint. The Constitution itself, designed to implement the dream of freedom and equality that was articulated by the Declaration of Independence, had the idea of progress written into it in the form of its avowed purpose "to form a more perfect union." Further, with its built-in provisions for change, the Constitution stands as an open-ended instrument always adaptable to the end of producing a more perfect union. Progress was the natural accompaniment of Jefferson's vision of the effects of universal education, of his hopes for religious liberty, and of his beliefs that government existed to serve the welfare of the governed and that it could effect the better future. Jackson and his followers, dedicated to rule of the masses, not only fostered American hopes for equality and freedom, but they also committed themselves to the idea of inevitable progress on the part of the American people. Jacksonians interfused progress and democracy, believes Francis Graham Wilson, because "the potentialities of the democratic system indicate a better future."[2]

The prophets of the dream of the dignity and worth of the individual also had their versions of progress. Emerson, after a period of questioning the progress doctrine, returned at the end to a measure of the optimism he had felt as a

*Beard's comment occurs in the introduction to J. B. Bury, *The Idea of Progress,* xi; to Charles L. Sanford, *The Quest for Paradise: Europe and the American Moral Imagination,* 266, I am indebted for the idea of the commingling of material and moral progress. I take responsibility for the application made here.

youth. On the deepest level, progress for Emerson was dependent on the progress of the individual.

> And if one shall read the future of the race hinted in the organic effort of nature to mount and meliorate, and the corresponding impulse to the Better in the human being, we shall dare affirm that there is nothing he will not overcome and convert, until at last culture shall absorb the chaos and gehenna. He will convert the Furies into Muses, and the hells into benefit.[3]

The individual, relying on the divine self within him, would advance; others would see his actions and be inspired to move forward, too. "Since Providence out of our evil not only seeks to bring forth good but succeeds in doing so," concludes Mildred Silver regarding Emerson's belief, "in the course of time there will be progress for the race."[4] Whitman, for his part, dreamed of common man's highest fulfillment by progressing to a universal brotherhood. In his "Passage to India," he returned to a theme that Henry Nash Smith says he once stated had lurked underneath every page and every line he had written. In the poem, he pictures the sons and daughters of Adam and Eve questing, baffled, for a return to happiness and fulfillment. At last, with the completion of the Suez Canal, the laying of an Atlantic cable, and the finishing of transcontinental railways, the purpose of God—and the condition for which Adam's children quested—came clear.

> The earth to be spann'd, connected by network,
> The races, neighbors, to marry and be given in marriage,
> The oceans to be cross'd, the distant brought near,
> The lands to be welded together.

To such an end Whitman placed all his hope for the common man—his power, his virtue, and his self-fulfillment. Possibly Americans who dreamed of the goodness of the average man viewed the idea of brotherhood as a natural consequence, an advancement to be sought for humanity.

The success dream carried a countertheme of progress, too. It contained, as did the myth of the garden, a vision of gigantic economic development—even though the one was agrarian and the other commercial and industrial. Success and material progress were often signs of one another.

Emerson, sure as he apparently was that progress ultimately depended upon the individual, nevertheless could praise material improvement. In his Phi Beta Kappa lecture in Cambridge, July 18, 1867, when his optimism might have been on an upswing, he asked "Who would live in the stone age, or the bronze, or the iron, or the lacustrine? Who does not prefer the age of steel, of gold, of coal, petroleum, cotton, steam, electricity, and the spectroscope?" Whitman, having accepted a material kind of success in his "Democratic Vistas," and having at the same time been aware of the shallowness and crassness too often associated with it, kept the success dream as the foundation stone for progress:

> I perceive clearly that the extreme business energy, and this almost maniacal appetite for wealth prevalent in the United States, are parts of amelioration and progress, indispensably needed to prepare the very results I demand. My theory includes riches, and the getting of riches, and the amplest products, power, activity, inventions, movements, etc. Upon them, as upon sub-strata, I raise the edifice design'd in these Vistas.[5]

Indeed, the counterpoint of progress to success may have been the most nearly universal definition of advancement in America. So strong was the connection between success and material progress that the latter became not only the foundation for moral progress (as it was for Whitman) but also the approximation of moral progress. Even when self-made man Andrew Carnegie espoused social Darwinism in the competitive struggle, he envisioned a result consonant with what Russel Nye calls "Christian duty and progress."[6]

From the time, of course, that the Puritans taught that success was virtue rewarded, the material progress resulting from success constituted a moral rise. In more comprehensive fashion, however, Americans associated material and moral progress. The pairing of ideas took place to a lesser or greater degree, as will be shown, in all the activities ranging from Chamber of Commerce promotions, to the writing of Utopian novels, to the growth of the social gospel, to the spiraling of technology. The grand idea was the mastery of man over his environment.

One way to control environment—at least in a continent empty except for a few hapless red men—was to populate it as thickly as possible and share the task of founding a civilization. The idea of "bigger and better" was the sloganized Chamber of Commerce version, and to a point it was correct. "In the frontier stage," writes James Truslow Adams, "size, as also the material development of houses and farms and roads and stores, did mean the scaffolding on which a civilized life had to rest; and numerous frontiers burned that thought deep into the developing American soul." Instead, however, of progress in stages from "bigness" to "betterness," a commingling of the phases occurred: ". . . it was much easier, in a land of unlimited opportunity, to make things bigger than to make them better, and in working for bigness first we came to a great extent to forget the ultimate purpose of humane value," continued Adams. The result was that Americans transferred "ultimate value to the scaffolding instead of the civilization."[7] Thus, the tub-thumping of promotional schemes to turn villages into towns, and towns into cities, became identified with moral advancement. The material advances implied in "bigger" merged with valuative or moral progress implied in "better." Such promoting, of course, had other origins than the frontier: Hamilton had linked expanding industrial wealth and orderly society for the benefit of all; further, the Jacksonians and Emersonians saw in science and technology, says Nye, strong allies "for the improvement, not only of material life, but of the intellect and spirit as well" (page 12).

Boyd C. Shafer has remarked that the most numerous and significant post-1865 American writings dealing with the future were those on the subject of economic life. The laissez-faire, individualistic dreamers found expression in the plethora of success manuals. Another significant opinion in America, however, offered visions of group advancement rather than of individual material progress: The dreamers were, Shafer says, in general, "those who wanted to widen equality and increase productivity by governmental action."[8] A favorite, but not quite universal, manner of expression came to be the Utopian novel.

Henry George, although not a novelist, may have exerted

Will Rogers

influence upon writers of Utopian fiction. George disagreed with classical economists who held that wages are drawn from capital and that poverty is the natural accompaniment of population increase. He held that wages came directly from social effort through the work of hands, and that poverty resulted from ever-rising rents on land, with the rents—ironically—being based upon land value increased *because* of social effort. Thus, the increase of wealth became an unearned increment for the landowner and a deprivation to the worker. George examined other advanced societies of the past, concluded that the paradox of the increase of wealth accompanied by the increase of poverty had in each case eventually caused a reversion to primitive conditions, and believed that if such cycles were to become linear progress, strong governmental action was necessary. In a statement of a plan for material progress, his blending it with moral advancement was clear. "What I ... propose, as the simple yet sovereign remedy, which will raise wages, increase the earnings of capital, extirpate pauperism, abolish poverty, give remunerative employment to whoever wishes it, afford free scope to human powers, lessen crime, elevate morals, and taste, and intelligence, purify government and carry civilization to yet nobler heights, is—*to appropriate rent by taxation.*"[9]

Among the Utopian novels, possibly none more than Edward Bellamy's *Looking Backward* spoke the progress dream of Americans. "The book appealed to the middle class, who are usually the last to realize the need for an alteration of the existing economic scheme," writes the younger Parrington.[10] The hero of the novel, after being put into a condition resembling suspended animation, awakes over a century later to discover the perfect society that had evolved by the year 2000. Produced by a supermonopoly vested in the state, the world of 2000 had as its cornerstone the correct distribution of wealth and labor; given these material advances, the machine was a blessing rather than a curse, according to Bellamy. "His was a materialistic and technological society," concludes Francis Graham Wilson (page 297), "but one in which the human spirit blossomed." That Bellamy approximated material and moral progress is evident.

214

Allies and antagonists of Bellamy followed him into print, producing radical and conservative Utopias. Perhaps significant to our concern with the American identification of material with moral improvement is that Bellamy's socialized capitalism apparently drew attacks not on the ground that material advancement was irrelevant to moral improvement, but rather that *equality* of material progress produced spiritual decay. Thus, opposition to Bellamy's dream could range from urging a return to government by an intellectual aristocracy in George Sanders' *Reality* to mend-and-repair proposals like those of Richard Michaelis and J. W. Roberts. The objections to Bellamy were similar within this range of opposition, however; with equal material rewards, spiritual progress (as evidenced in the desire for excellence) declined.

Before and after Bellamy, other nineteenth-century Utopians concerned themselves with material paradises produced by cooperation, moral uplift, and governmental reform. Education generally received emphasis, with a great variety of dreamed-of curricula and methods of financing. Equal or greater emphasis occurred on schemes for material improvement: model housing, better diets, revamped financial methods, reformed taxes, improved use of fertilizers with irrigation, weather and crop control, progressive roads, stores, and streets. The visions of Utopian novelists, various as they were, exhibited an "intensely, almost mystically serious" purpose, writes Parrington (page 177) of their prevailing tone, perhaps indicating the moral nature of the writers having such concern with the material. Then, after the turn of the century, the muckrakers focused hopes for material advancement on the path of governmental reform and action; novels like *The Jungle* portrayed the dehumanizing of men denied material goods and the chance of self-progress. All this culminated, perhaps, in the Utopian novel by Edward M. House entitled, *Philip Dru, Ambassador.* House's hero sought a paradise through governmental economic reform: big taxes on big incomes, shares for government and labor in the profits of corporations, nationalization of public utilities, provision of easy credit, among others.

Thus, almost to the eve of World War I, Utopians wrote of

a bigger and better America. Drawing most of their ideas from contemporary sources, the Utopian vision was an index to ideas that were in the air; that some of the suggestions have been acted upon is further testimony to the living quality of the ideas in the minds of their dreamers.[11]

If the connection between material progress and moral advancement is clear in the Utopian novels, it becomes so intimate in the social gospel movement, broadly considered, as to make the two forms of progress confluent. Wasn't the Christian to feed the hungry, clothe the naked, heal the sick, visit the criminal? Would not the elimination of such material evils be at once the fruit and seed of moral advancement?

As early as 1845, well before the social gospel had the name, Sylvester Judd pictured in *Margaret* a community that through the application of Christian ethics achieved a model town, free not only from crime but also from such evils as women's unwise expenditure of money. By 1888, Christian dreamers of progress were approaching the interests central to the social gospel movement; Edward Everett Hale's *How They Lived in Hampton* showed how the application of Christian ethics in a textile town produced desirable working and living conditions. Charles M. Sheldon, with his *In His Steps* (1896), reflected the move of institutionalized Christianity away from nineteenth-century pietism to social concerns.[12] The gradual emergence of a Christian ideal of material progress is evident in such novels.

Such an ideal naturally involved figures other than novelists. In 1886 Cardinal Gibbons kept the Knights of Labor from coming under papal condemnation; social concern of Christians also appeared with the publication during the nineties of such titles as Washington Gladden's *Tools and the Man: Property and Industry under the Christian Law.* Walter Rauschenbusch, writing mainly in the first two decades of the twentieth century, insisted that the message of the Bible was clearly on the side of social justice and that economic exploitation in industry was unjust. Moreover, such injustice was subject to remedy. Rauschenbusch and other prophets of the social gospel, says Boyd Shafer, "usually felt that progress was divine, that the Kingdom of

Heaven was possible on this earth, and that men through their own will could mould such a society" (page 440). Standing in a direct line of descent from the millennial dream of the Puritans, the social gospel nevertheless exhibited a distinctive turn in its move away from pietism to a concern with the physical well-being of the American Adam and his progeny. Physical progress was moral progress.

The dream of material progress through a spiraling technology is harder to document, for as Shafer has commented, technologists simply have said and written less about their visions. Americans, however, from mechanics to Henry Adams (doubtful as he was of improvement) were aware that the dynamo intensified the technical revolution and hastened material change. Dr. Oliver Wendell Holmes, moving in the regions of science and technology as well as in the world of literature, took time in one of his "medicated" novels to give the Promethean cast to science: "The attitude of modern science is erect, her aspect serene, her determination inflexible, her onward movement unflinching; because she believes in herself, in the order of providence, the true successor of the men of old who brought down the light of heaven to men."[13] To Holmes, the technological revolution was unwaveringly forward. Rather than being cyclical, this change was linear. Thus, technology offered no closed system.

How does this view of scientific and technological progress become identified with moral and spiritual advancement? Is this not completely counter to the dream of the new Adam in a new Eden? In *The Machine in the Garden,* Leo Marx concludes that American writers, aware of the intrusion of the symbolic locomotive into "Sleepy Hollow," have been unable to find a substitute for that pastoral garden or "middle landscape." But he also shows how such Americans as Tench Coxe and Timothy Walker, in the first half-century of our national existence, harmonized technology and the garden both by identifying machine power with the forces of nature in American topography and by assigning it the tasks of freeing the human intellect, easing human labor, and providing material abundance. Further, Charles L. Sanford believes that the horn of plenty pro-

duced by science and technology is in itself seen as an outward sign of Edenic virtue. To Americans, as part of Western civilization,

> The lost state of innocence to be regained is associated
> with or interpreted as a paradise of material bliss. This
> association rests upon a primitivistic assumption
> somewhat similar to what is discovered in Augustine—
> that things in their natural abundance as originally
> created by God retain the innocence of God.[14]

Thus, the dream of progress is at once open-ended and a
means of closure in the great American dream. Dynamic by
its nature, material progress seemed limitless; bountiful in
its harvest, it seemed to promise the "enamel'd fruits" of a
paradise—thus linking with the cluster of associations contained in the images of the new Adam and the myth of the
garden. Technology promised a form of the wise innocence.

Like the other major categories of the great American
dream, the vision of progress carried with it ideals of behavior for the American Adam, in his character as the American Prometheus.

As an accompaniment of all the other categories of the
dream, the hope of progress included in its strategy many
of the tactics already mentioned. It was not difficult to
recognize as a representation of progress the American
whose behavior marked him as being on the way to realizing his potential powers and virtue in a free and equal society that rewarded those qualities with material prosperity.

The American Adam was to reject the stifling traditions
of the past in order to prepare himself for highest self-
fulfillment. Correspondingly, as Adam-become-Prometheus, he was to look to the future, where a richer and better
way of life awaited. "The belief," writes Henry Bamford
Parkes, "that America has a peculiar mission to establish a
new and higher way of life has, in fact, become a part of the
American character, even though few Americans have
been prepared to interpret it in any very radical fashion."[15]
This sense of mission probably contributed heavily to the
trait perceived by James Truslow Adams in Americans
after 1830: The builder of the future had a primary responsi-

bility to "boost" the growth of his society; so strong was the compulsion to "boost" that any criticism could be taken for "kicking." If the forward-looking American ever faced the East from whence he had come, it was only to salute the rising sun and turn with its rays to a beckoning West.

The new Adam seeking to perfect his virtues in freedom and equality had to go forth on a quest. The quest meant an openness to nature, comprehensively considered. There was the face of the earth to learn to know, and there were the faces of people to be known and accepted in brotherhood. The quest also meant an activism—a scrambling after the material "good things of life" as a test of the perfection of virtues and powers; it was a quest that called for a happy reliance upon intuition. And all the time that the American Adam did so quest, he exhibited the signs of being Promethean. For all these reasons, as Leland Baldwin has pointed out, rootlessness has been a marked trait of the American character. The quester might digress or move sideways for a time, but his general movement was forward; or if he did move in a cycle, it was so large that it was man's return to perfection. In "Facing West from California's Shores," Whitman expressed, perhaps, the spirit of the search of Adam's children:

> Inquiring, tireless, seeking what is yet unfound,
> I, a child, very old, over waves, towards the house of
>   maternity, the land of migrations, look afar,
> Look off the shores of my Western sea,
>   the circle almost circled;
> . . . .
> Now I face home again, very pleas'd and joyous,
> (But where is what I started for, so long ago?
> And why is it yet unfound?)

Americans have had a fever in the blood, an itch in the foot, and a constant look in the eye toward the horizon; even if they moved for such mundane reasons as economic depression or worn-out, exploited land, the change was potentially for the better. The wanderlust and its associated searching were integral to the American Prometheus.

The ideal American thus achieved progress in his quest for self-realization. In addition, however, as Adam-become-Prometheus, he sought to keep the door always open to further vistas that might lie before him. Thus he sought to learn to live with insecurity; he accepted his responsibilities in order to preserve his freedom; he cultivated an open nature that practiced brotherhood and fair play. He remained, like the dream of progress, an open-ended system. Appropriately, he developed and exhibited buoyancy, optimism, and a spirit of boundlessness. James Muirhead, a British observer during the last years of the nineteenth century, was able to draw the following conclusions, among others, about the ideal American behavior:

> The American note includes a sense of illimitable expansion and possibility, an almost childlike confidence in human ability and fearlessness of both the present and the future, a wider realization of brotherhood than has yet existed, a greater theoretical willingness to judge by the individual than by the class, a breezy indifference to authority and a positive predilection for innovation, a marked alertness of mind, and a manifold variety of interest—above all, an inextinguishable hopefulness and courage.[16]

Americans felt free to innovate, believes Nye (page 186), because they were "not bound to the past." Too, they were perhaps Adamically optimistic because of what Boorstin, studying the national experience, has discovered about the peopling of the West: "They lived on a little-known continent, but they did not know how little they knew. Yet if they had known more they might have dared less," he believes. "Their enterprises were stirred by misinformation, fable, wild hopes, and unjustified certainties."[17] This was another form of the American innocence. Looking to the future, roaming and questing, living in hopefulness, the American Adam—with his "positive predilection for innovation"—was also the American Prometheus, culture-hero of the progress dream.

LIKEWISE, in some respects, heroes of other categories of the great American dream became identified with that of progress. The wandering, restless spirits of Leatherstocking, of the cowboy, and of Huck Finn symbolized the quest as well as freedom. Particularly suitable for progress was Daniel Boone, rejector of Atlantic seaboard culture, lone wanderer of the forest, optimistic dreamer of new empire in old "Kaintuck," and leader of the people to a new and better life in a new Eden. Moreover, wasn't Old Hickory also raising man to new heights of influence, affluence, and aspiration? Certainly, the Horatio Alger hero on his journey to success traveled a way that formed a junction with the route to progress.

Thus, Henry Ford's legend fitted him for a double title in the American peerage of heroes. A mechanical genius whose restless rejection of the horse and buggy brought a billion dollars to his own treasury, he was also the Promethean bringer of fire on wheels to the people. The jokes that pictured the lovable man as the good liege lord of success also stressed Ford's inventiveness. "After-dinner speakers told about the old lady who sent her tomato cans, or the farmer his tin roof, to Detroit, and got a Ford car back by return mail," relates Marshall Fishwick. "Neither Jove nor Charlemagne nor Beowulf had done anything more remarkable than Henry Ford, who turned bits of tin into automobiles."[18] Thus, in a country where progress and technological advance were almost synonymous, Henry Ford stood as a Promethean provider of mechanical largesse that in turn promised a measure of the material bliss expected from the new Eden.

Ford had a fellow demigod in the realm of progress, one who perhaps even better symbolized that dream. He was Thomas Edison, self-made man. With sayings like "Genius is ninety-nine per cent perspiration and one per cent inspiration," he at once kept the "common touch" and affirmed the gospel of success as two strands of his appeal to mass worship detected by Matthew Josephson. Mistrustful of college-trained thinkers, making a gospel of work, he typified the self-made man. When he traveled to Dearborn in 1929 for the "Golden Jubilee," his re-enactment on the train of his old candy selling was, says Josephson, "sheer symbolic drama, the American dream reenacted before the world's newspapers and movie cameras."[19]

But it was as inventor that Edison captured the American fancy. Improving telegraphy, developing stock tickers, working in telephone research, inventing the phonograph, and wizarding innumerable gadgets, he identified most clearly with the dream of progress by his invention of the incandescent light. By the time of the World's Fair at St. Louis in 1904, Edison was pictured in most Americans' minds as the modern giver of light—a Prometheus in spirit, if one unnamed. "Edison symbolized electricity—thoughts and words soaring across great distances; energy freed from the engine and belt by smokeless motors; cities wreathed in light," concludes Josephson (page 433).

That Edison's technological progress was fulfilling the American dream was obvious to at least one of his admirers. Henry Ford was to remark in 1930, "Our prosperity leads the world, due to the fact that we have an Edison. His inventions created millions of new jobs. . . Edison has done more toward abolishing poverty than all the reformers" (Josephson, 464). Perhaps most Americans agreed with Ford. For whatever they are worth, public opinion surveys in newspapers and magazines between 1904 and 1924 consistently indicated that the American people regarded Edison as America's "greatest" or "most useful" citizen (page 434).

The titanic stature of this hero of the dream of progress is indicated in a newspaper reporter's paraphrase of Pope, reported by Dixon Wecter: "God said, Let Edison be! And there was Light."[20] The connection between America's technological paradise and God's original Eden was explicit.

(In December of 1886, Henry W. Grady—apostle of industrialization of the South—told a New York audience of "The New South," "enamored of her new work," one whose spirit "stirred with the breath of new life." For the South was "thrilling with the consciousness of growing power and prosperity." The speech was immensely successful, partly because it was in tune with the national song of progress. "Bigger and better!" might also have been in that year the slogan at the Rogers Ranch, Indian Territory.)

IN THE span of his lifetime, Will Rogers saw big changes in the patterns of living in America. In his own pasture of the Southwest, he saw the free range give way to homesteaders. He was eleven years old when the 1890 census declared that the frontier, in the sense of a continuous line of new settlement, was ended. He was forty-one when the 1920 census confirmed (what was already self-evident) that America was an industrial society: It was the first census that reported that over half of the population lived in cities. He saw the horse give way to the automobile and the airplane; he saw the kerosene lamp replaced by the incandescent light, the telegraph supplemented by the radio, vaudeville outmoded by movies, silents by talkies—many of the circlings of the technological spiral. Too, he saw much of the change from a laissez-faire capitalism to a mixed economy; besides the changes in women's hemlines, the higher status of the woman in political endeavor came about during his lifetime. He witnessed the ascent of the labor union to a position of both political and economic power. Like millions of other Americans, he saw attempts to epitomize the change by means of expositions, such as that one in 1904 where Rogers and Betty Blake had met again, as in the song, in St. Louis. "Nineteen hundred and four was a wonderful year," she was to write later, in Rogers' story; "Theodore Roosevelt was President; there was general prosperity; and to youngsters of my generation the World's Fair in St. Louis was the last word in progress."[21]

Whether the changes Rogers saw in American society constituted progress to him remains a question. It may have been easier, however, for him to accept them as such because of his having shared the experience of many others of those frontiersmen described by Adams as having found in the "bigger" of American life the "better." As a boy and young man, Rogers loved to go to the big cities; he liked the lights, clothes, and songs he saw, bought, and heard in such places as Kansas City, St. Louis, and Chicago. To return to the wide-open spaces of his home territory and see the rise of towns and hear talk of more growth and of coming statehood could possibly have said to the boy from Oologah that as Claremore and Tulsa got bigger, progress would occur. This change from frontier to city was the experience that may have most set Rogers apart from other Americans of his time, who also had seen many of the changes mentioned earlier.

Will Rogers

Nevertheless, Will Rogers would—in the good company of Emerson—maintain some doubt about the real progress of the people, while at the same time accepting with a kind of joyous skepticism the mechanical innovations of the period. In so doing, he was in harmony with "Thoreau's 'Adam' [who] did not seek to regain his paradise at Walden by rejecting all mechanical means."²²

Mechanical gadgets offered Rogers a way to satisfy the restlessness that was apparently so much a part of his nature. From the time that he had dreamed of being a cowboy, with new sights anticipated beyond the next rise, Rogers had experienced the American itch of the wandering foot. To add the dimension of quest to this wanderlust, however, another event in the boy's life may have been significant. Rogers lost his mother to typhoid fever when he was ten years old, himself too ill to go to the funeral. The loss of his mother finished the destruction of the warm and secure household that the boy had known in his first decade: His sister Sallie was married and gone, May and Maude were gone to school, and the elder Rogers at times was gone on business and official trips. The loss of the mother was to remain poignant for the rest of her son's life. Betty Rogers, perhaps her husband's only real confidante, would recall it thus:

Will never quite got over his mother's death. He cried when he told me about it many years later. It left in him a lonely, lost feeling that persisted long after he was successful and famous. "My mother's name was Mary," he wrote, "and if your mother's name was Mary and she was an old-fashioned woman, you don't have to say much for her. Everybody knows already" (page 47).

Possibly an Adamic, symbolic search for the old, lost "home" partly motivated Will Rogers' lifelong questing.

The marvel of physics and mechanics Will Rogers was most to appreciate was the airplane. His first experience of rapid ascent and descent may have been at that American showbook of material progress, the Chicago World's Fair of the nineties. There the original Ferris wheel, reaching almost three hundred feet into the air and carrying more than two thousand people at a time, could have carried the boy from Oologah to its height. Then would come the day in 1915 when Rogers would swallow his fear and allow himself to be carried out by a wading porter to a Glenn Curtiss flying boat at Atlantic City and a five-dollar ride. "When he landed," wrote the waiting Betty Rogers, "he was still scared, but vastly excited, and so pleased that he had a picture made of himself in the plane and took delight in exhibiting it" (page 200). Thus began the romance between the Adam from the West and the gleaming product of the technological revolution. Later, he would become strongly associated with the progress promised by the airplane, so great was his love for it. The airplane would satisfy his need to see the new country just over the rise; its soaring wings would give his lifelong quest a Promethean cast to a people whose nostalgia for the days of normalcy would blend with their zest for a gleaming mechanized future. He would be equally welcome to a public shaken in its faith in progress by the Great Depression. He was suited to embody progress in a time of need.

No BETTER indication, perhaps, of the mass American attitude toward progress in the twenties exists than that provided by the adulation of Lindbergh; his feat brought not only parades, but also a flood of editorials, magazine articles, and other commentary that John Ward has utilized to extrapolate the nation's interpretation of the meaning of the flight. On the one hand, as already noted, metaphors recurred that named Lindbergh a pioneer of the frontier, a self-sufficient, Adamic hero at the center of the American world. "The mood was nostalgic and American history was read as a decline, a decline measured in terms of America's advance into an urban, institutionalized way of life which made solitary achievement increasingly beyond the reach of ninety-nine per cent of the people," concluded Ward of this half of the Lindbergh worship. On the other hand, Lindbergh emerged as something of an American Prometheus, bringer of light and teacher of useful arts. For paired in conflicting fashion with the Adamic Lindbergh riding alone on a new frontier was the Lindbergh as harbinger of the future. This aspect found expression in the public's celebration of "the machine and the highly organized society of which it was a product," says Ward.[23] This aspect of the flight celebrated the future, which most Americans probably regarded with hope in the decade of the twenties.

If Herbert Croly was correct in his assessment near the end of the first decade of this century that Americans—in spite of "a more friendly acquaintance with all sorts of obstacles and pitfalls"—nevertheless believed that "somehow and sometime something better will happen to good Americans than has happened to men in any other country" (page 5); even World War I may not have been sufficient to do anything more to the average man's dream than to make it somewhat more conservative in its vision of the good future.

Readers of mass-circulation magazines such as *Popular Mechanics* could, for example, see in its pages pictorial proof of a paradise via technology. There, a housewife might be pictured standing beside a machine, tall as she, and designed to be wheeled to the table to receive the dirty dishes and to be returned to the kitchen, there to wash and scald the eating implements, thus allowing the housewife time to enjoy being a lady. Such innovations as electric pressure cookers, radio-equipped delivery trucks, and even television could be seen in photographs during the twenties. Occupying significant space, of course, were exploits of fliers, whose marvelous aircraft carried them into space with speeds never before known, so that something like the Renaissance excitement about the New World may have appropriately clung to their exploits in the new world of space. Present in the pages of *Popular Mechanics* were the Army fliers who had opened new possibilities for air travel with their flight around the earth in 1924; pictured, too, was Lindbergh in the cockpit of the *Spirit of St. Louis,* with glimpses into the future of long-distance flight over oceans.

Actually present for many Americans was the radio, which advanced from local to network broadcasts in 1926. *The Jazz Singer,* with Al Jolson, proved the attractiveness of sound movies; such technical marvels provided a bit of the future in the American present. As Americans perused their newspapers between attendance at movies and listening to radio programs, they probably saw announcements of plans for the tallest building in the world, to consist of eighty stories, to climb over one thousand feet into space, and to be called the Empire State Building. Airplanes, by the end of the decade, flew with the pilot "blind" except for his instruments, which told him his exact location. Sound and pictures from greater distances than man had heard or seen before; aircraft that propelled man, himself, at speeds and heights never known before: All these promises and realities probably conditioned Americans to expect and welcome technical change in the name of progress. The heavier-than-air flying machine, being used to carry the mail, transport passengers, fight insects, and sink battleships, may have been the most wondrous of all in the American imagination.

True, among thinkers, the doctrine of inevitable progress was falling into some disrepute. But Oswald Spengler's *Decline of the West*, which would have a large audience, did not come to America in translation until 1926. An early American critic noted with no surprise the cyclical theory of history that Spengler proposed, and spent most of his time assailing the German's lack of philosophical and historical knowledge as well as his morphological method. The critic apparently remained unperturbed by the picture of Western civilization on the decline. Frederick Jackson Turner, it was true, found it increasingly difficult to bring what Henry Nash Smith calls his "original theoretical weapons" to bear upon the problems of the postwar world, so that much of the agrarian synthesis may have receded to mere vapor. Hart Crane, after having confidently begun to celebrate the great dream of progress through spiritualization of material gains in America, admitted failure and believed in 1926 that the nation no longer had the possibilities that Whitman had earlier glimpsed.[24] The uncertainty of progress was perhaps, as Nye has indicated, only underlined by the continued faith in it of writers like Will Durant and Charles Beard.

Most Americans did not make themselves keenly aware of such questions about the promise of progress. True, their

zeal for reform of the Roosevelt years and through the first
Wilson Administration had cooled; their attempt to make
the world safe for democracy had ended in their turning
away from the League of Nations. Nevertheless, writes
Hicks, "Although the prevailing mood was conservative,
this did not mean that the people had lost faith in the idea
of progress."[25]

After 1929, however, instead of simply welcoming the
symbolic figure who could blend the individualistic past
with the technological future, Americans found themselves
questioning the reality of the American promise of a better
future for all.

To begin with, the Great Depression forced upon even the
average man a cyclical interpretation of history. While the
youth of America, especially the unemployed and students,
were moving toward a disenchantment with all sets of values, oldsters who had lived through post-Civil War panics
found themselves in the worst state ever. One octogenerian
described by Wecter was to recall that the panic of 1873 had
left him unemployed and that he had drifted west to work
as a railroad section hand and eventually had become a
modestly successful grocer. When the panic of 1893 had
stripped him again, he had migrated to California, bor-
rowed a stake, and had become a successful rancher; now,
he had once more lost everything. He told why this was the
worst blow:

> There isn't an acre of decent land to be had for
> homesteading. There isn't a railroad to be built
> anywhere. Years ago Horace Greeley made a statement,
> "Young man, go West and grow up with the country."
> Were he living today, he would make the statement, "Go
> West, young man, and drown yourself in the Pacific
> Ocean, like the lemmings do in Norway."[26]

Cycles in the business world had certainly been apparent
before the depression; what made this cycle destructive of
progress, however, was that it marked the end of the
dreams of a garden in the West where the unemployed
could start anew, and of the magical economic development through railroad building. Where lay the American El

Dorado? If the panics thus kept getting worse, what they may have presaged was decline instead of progress. Instead of "bigger and better," the depressions were getting "bigger and worse."

Conditions seemed to worsen steadily in spite of unprecedented efforts on the part of the national government to ameliorate the suffering and effect recovery. Working to relieve and revive industry through the Reconstruction Finance Corporation, attempting to resuscitate agriculture through the Federal Farm Board, and making available to the Red Cross vast stores of government commodities, the Hoover Administration still failed, partly and simply because of the magnitude of the task. So far from recovery was industry in the summer of 1932 that blue chip stocks such as American Telephone and Telegraph stood at 72, after a predepression high of 304; General Motors was down from 73 to 8; United States Steel was at 22 after a high of 262; since 1929, market value of all stocks had dropped from nearly $90,000,000,000 to about $15,500,000,000. Thirteen million in the laboring force were idle. On the farms, capital value had declined from $79,000,000,000 in 1919, to $58,000,000,000 in 1929, to $38,000,000,000 in 1932; Department of Agriculture estimates set the average annual net income per farmer at $230.

The result of all of it was that relief, much less recovery, seemed impossible. Although the Red Cross was in the process of distributing 85,000,000 bushels of wheat and 844,000 bales of cotton held by the Federal Farm Board, the hungry and naked suffered. The American Association of Social Workers reported that the situation had passed beyond local experience and, therefore, local control. New York City families on relief were receiving an average of $2.39 per week; one-third of Pennsylvania's population was on relief; 40 per cent of Chicago's work force was idle; and in Houston, Texas, destitute Mexican and Negro applicants for aid were being told to shift for themselves. "Too much wheat, too much corn, too much cotton, too much beef, too much production of everything," wrote Will Rogers. "So we are going through a unique experience. We are the first nation to starve to death in a storehouse that's overfilled with everything we want."[27]

Faith, then, in the ability of the big men in finance and industry was destroyed. Cries of America's "fundamental soundness" would fall increasingly upon unbelieving ears. By the time of the fourth winter, writes Schlesinger, "The mighty had fallen." He recalls the conclusion of George Sokolsky: "Confidence in the erstwhile leadership of this country is gone. . . . No banker, no great industrialist, no college president commands the respect of the American people." So also said Walter Lippmann: "The industrial and financial leaders of America have fallen from one of the highest positions of influence and power that they have ever occupied in our history to one of the lowest." Will Rogers had his own word: "The case has got too big for the doctors, but the doctors haven't got big enough to admit it."[28]

In their place, as the sudden popularity of "Technocracy" would signify, masses of Americans were ready to substitute the man of science who could engineer progress. As early as 1930, inventors, scientists, and engineers, including Elmer Sperry, Lee de Forest, Michael Pupin, and Lillian Gilbreth had responded to attacks on the dehumanizing effects of science by arguing that the material advance of science could provide moral progress. Summarizing their views, Charles Beard wrote:

It is difficult to discover any value ardently desired by the critics of machine civilization which these engineers and scientists do not likewise desire. Is it leisure? They propose to make it universal. Is it the good life? They will provide the necessary material conditions to make it more abundant. Is it beauty? They insist upon fostering the love of it and incorporating it into the daily lives of millions. Is it truth? They propose to pursue it, not merely within the confines of historical categories, but wherever it may lead in this mysterious world of substance and power. Is it anything covered by the term humanity—fair dealing, toleration, freedom from pain and suffering, relief of misery, succor for them that are hungry and athirst, aid for the weak and afflicted, guidance for the stumbling? They propose to use the engines of science and invention to fortify, speed up, and multiply the agencies of humanity.[29]

Notwithstanding that as early as 1932 labor leaders and others argued with scientists over whether technological unemployment was a curse greater than any blessings from the machine, by the summer and winter of 1932, the people were ready for a technological religion. Of the new faith in "Technocracy" Will Rogers, skeptical as he himself was, observed, "We don't know if it's a disease or a theory. It may go out as fast as Eskimo pies or miniature golf courses. But people right now are in a mood to grab at anything."[30]

One claiming to be a new messiah of the faith came in the person of Howard Scott, who—influenced by Veblen—had been nursing for years a scheme to engineer a society of plenty. Scott had concluded that an obsolete price system caused the imbalance of consumption and production and planned to substitute for it a price system and currency based upon the amount of energy required of the worker to produce the objects to be consumed. Theoretically, since the available currency would match exactly the total productive output of the nation, consumption would catch up with production; the depression cycle would be broken and a paradise would be possible again. But Scott was never able to produce the energy surveys needed; nor was he ever able to account very satisfactorily for the amount of energy spent not in production of goods, but rather in services.[31] His movement became unrespectable, and Americans instead looked with hope to Roosevelt, a politician, whose "Brain Trust" might be expected to engineer progress out of the depression.

By the time of the Chicago exposition, unemployment was down several million from the high of thirteen million. The name of the fair was "The Century of Progress," and Americans could, for a time, turn away from unemployment figures, high murder rates, farm surpluses, and starvation in the cities, to find on the four-hundred acres of the exhibition the promise of the future. They could see race drivers test new autos on special courses; inside exhibit buildings erected in ultra-modern style, they could see automobile assembly lines, hear talking robots, view advances of modern medicine, and see television (which may have been—as one visiting Professor from Yale said—"more imagination than vision").[32] They could see, too, the newest aircraft and hear talks on their speed and safety. The fair was a niche full of the technological paradise. If visitors felt some cultural shock at reading in newspapers later of a dysentery outbreak in the city of progress or of an airplane crash fatal to twenty people, they may not have felt that progress was impossible, though the thoughtful among them may have condemned it as a myth.

Meanwhile, readers of *Popular Mechanics* could console themselves with do-it-yourself methods: Emblems for the times were money-saving products like new shoe soles costing less than a nickel apiece. Too, Americans could vicariously journey into space with an old friend who was realizing the better future in his own life via the airplane. He was the "Lay Lindbergh," Will Rogers.

IN HIS roles as the optimistic Adam, as the American democrat, and as alleviator of suffering, Rogers stood out as a progress figure. In addition, the well-known story of his frontiersman's amiable accommodation of twentieth-century marvels such as radio and "talkie" pictures probably conveyed a sense of progress to many Americans. His close association with the airplane, however, became the chief mode for his identification through publicity with the dream of progress. The adulation given to Lindbergh had in a large part been related to the great machine that had bridged continents. Moreover, just as Lindbergh's worship stemmed also from a folk-picture of him as a frontiersman, Rogers' own well-known westernness, coupled with the appeal of a machine that freed earth-bound man to soar, made him an ideal symbol of progress for a nation undergoing "the big change." If Lindbergh was the number one pilot, Rogers was the number one air passenger.

Many news stories told Americans of Rogers' air journeys over the years of his public prominence. He was flying over the Mississippi flood area for inspection purposes; he was flying to Nicaragua to help in earthquake relief. After a 1934 newspaper interview on a recent around-the-world trip, writers told of Rogers' flying experiences across China and the Middle East, and newsreel cameras recorded the talk, making recollections of his odyssey available to millions of moviegoers. In 1929, a clear identification of Will Rogers with the progress dream took place in the widely-circulated popular bible of technical advance, *Scientific American.* His status as the number one passenger was clear in the article.

> Mr. Rogers' enthusiasm for aviation was born during his very first flight. This was made in an army plane in Washington in 1925 [*sic*]. Since then he has flown nearly twenty-five thousand miles in a network of lecture tour and journalistic hops over practically every state in the Union and across a dozen countries in Europe. He has ridden in planes and airships of every size and variety and nationality. Now, like Colonel Lindbergh, he never travels by train or motor-car if it is possible to get to his destination by air.[33]

Not only was Rogers' name mentioned in the same breath as Lindbergh's, but the Oklahoman also had performed an air "first" of his own. The magazine related that in 1927,

> Mr. Rogers unwittingly established a new record by making the first round-trip passenger flight in regular mail-planes from Los Angeles to New York and back within four days. This was not a stunt flight. Will had to go to New York on business and he wanted to be back as soon as possible.
>
> Although his air-tickets cost him eight hundred dollars, or twice the train and Pullman fare, the air route saved him a full week's time, and so more than justified its cost (page 284).

Such a feat was what could be expected from a traveler of such personal daring. Just as a broncobuster would get up off "terra firma" and climb back on the mustang that had pitched him off, the Oklahoma cowboy would come back for more—only to go the "hoss-breaker" one better, as the magazine writer made clear.

> Not until . . . June 1928 did he ever experience a "mishap." Everything had gone smoothly until the mail plane in which he was traveling was about to land at Las Vegas, New Mexico, for a new supply of gasoline. Here, upon hitting the surface of the landing field, the plane's

right wheel crushed and the machine turned a somersault and landed flat on its back with its pilot and passenger upside down. No one was injured, however. . . .

That seemed to be Will's unlucky day, for at Cherokee, Wyoming, late in the afternoon, a section of the landing gear of another plane collapsed and spilled him out on his ear. After the second crash, Will remarked: "Once in a while I've had a horse throw me where I've been underneath him and him topmost, but I've never been thrown like I was today. They're getting easier, however. The first spill wasn't so bad, and the second was almost a pleasure" (page 284).

Rogers finished the trip by air and became the cowboy hero who had traded his saddle horse for a mechanical Pegasus. He also was the American Prometheus, teacher of the useful arts; for in the same magazine feature he emerged as a crusader for airmindedness and air progress. He had done a good deal of flying in Europe in the summer of 1926, and he had been impressed:

> While in Europe, Mr. Rogers saw so many fine municipal airports and rode over such a large number of scheduled airlines that he decided, upon his return to the United States, to tour the country on a lecture crusade to awaken Americans to their backwardness in commercial aviation. On this tour he ended the fears of local reception committees, after the last train had pulled in without bringing him with it, by a last minute arrival by plane (page 284).

While the actual motivation for the lecture tour may have been to continue profits such as those enjoyed during the previous season, to readers of that magazine article Will Rogers was inspired by a desire to lead Americans to a better future. He was going to continue to "boost" air travel, the feature writer announced; new projects under way included promotion of more municipal airports and more landing fields, particularly on golf courses. "Will's enthusiasm increases with the years," began the final paragraph of the story. "He declares he is going to keep on flying until his beard gets caught in the propeller" (page 286).

Will Rogers' life, as it was portrayed in the mass media and as its events circulated by word of mouth, became identified with all the major categories of the great American dream. Because he seemed to be a composite of Americans' hopes, he gained from his audience a trust and confidence that gave him the entree to high government and social circles. He simply had too many "votes" to be ignored. In addition, his power begat power: Evidences of his growing influence in high places sifted back to his admirers and added to his status as a shaper of America. As Americans read of his life and of his comings and goings, he became to them in the picture painted by publicity more than a crackerbox philosopher, a cowboy, a comedian, a benefactor, a journalist, a world traveler, an aviation pioneer, a lover of humanity, and an apostle of equality. He was all of these, and the sum of the whole was greater than the parts.

As is the case with other major categories of the American dream, Rogers' own words and the way he said them also provided for his audience the character of the American Prometheus to complement those of Adam, democrat, and self-made man.

Like Emerson, however, Rogers at times expressed doubt about whether mankind's changes were really advances. He revealed his doubts, for example, when he wrote in the tradition of Rousseau: "Civilization hasent done much but make you wash your teeth, and in those days eating and gnawing on bones and meat made tooth paste unnecessary." On other occasions, the doubt of progress implicit in the dream of man's goodness in his natural state came out directly, as when Rogers wrote, while answering in an open letter Will Durant's inquiry regarding Rogers' philosophy: "Any man that thinks Civilization has advanced is an egotist." In 1926, he wondered whether the "progress" brought by the automobile was worth the many thousands of deaths it caused each year. A few years later, in the context of a deepening economic crisis, he expressed doubt that technological change was progress. "Well, we been twenty years honoring and celebrating the inventor who could save a dollar by knocking somebody out of work, now we are paying for it."[34]

Yet, like Emerson, Rogers also identified with the ideal of progress. As late as 1933, after remarking that society had changed from destroying its cripples to rehabilitating

235

them, he wrote that "even though we don't think so sometimes, civilization has advanced."[35]

Not only did he thus merge himself with the dream of
progress, but he also did so in conjunction with comments
on other facets of the great dream. On one occasion, when
as the natural man he extolled the goodness of life, he
wrote, "Happiness and contentment is progress. In fact,
that's all progress is." Several avenues existed for arriving
at that happiness and contentment. When Rogers stated a
belief that all Americans, of whatever "breed or color," had
a right to belong to the "club" set up by the Declaration of
Independence and the Constitution, he was not only addressing himself to the dream of freedom and equality, but
was also identifying with the ideal of progress toward a
more perfect union. The same was true for his idea that
government should serve the good of all, rather than the
interests of any privileged group. Progress also was interfused with the doctrine of the self-made man's rise from
rags to riches, as when Rogers told of the successes of
figures like Lipton and Ford. Moreover, the dream of
change for the better was tied to the success dictum that the
steward of wealth should practice discerning philanthropy
for what Rogers called the "betterment of people."

When Rogers offered plans for relief or recovery during
the depression, he not only spoke to the dream of equal
economic opportunity, but he also fitted himself into the
procession of those who had earlier written novels and
books picturing progress through governmental reform.
Rogers' persona, however, was never that of the impracti-
cal visionary; he often had fun with those advocating plans.
"Now everybody has got a scheme to relieve unemployment
—there is just one way to do it and that's for everybody to
go to work. Where?" he asked, getting ready to offer only a
half-serious solution. "Why right where you are—look
around, you will see a lot of things to do—weeds to cut,
fences to be fixed, lawns to be mowed, filling stations to be
robbed, gangsters to be catered to." With his wise innocence
established by such sallies, Rogers could propose his own
paths to progress in the depression without being condemned as "visionary." When Roosevelt the candidate was
still being tutored in the economics of relief and recovery

by Tugwell and Moley, Rogers gave readers of his weekly article, in 1931, a plan based on the assumption that the United States was becoming "the richest, and the poorest Country in the world," because "of an unequal distribution of the money." Rogers would effect reform "by putting a higher surtax on large incomes, and that money goes to provide some public work, at a livable wage." The jobs would not compete in attractiveness with those in private industry, for they would be only half-time. But the wages in hope for the future would be significant: "There is nothing that makes a man feel better than to know that no matter how bad things break he has something to fall back on, that he can make a living out of." Always careful to remain a Prometheus rather than become a messiah, Rogers concluded, "It might not be a great plan, but it will DAM sure beat the one we got now."[36]

Thus, at times when he addressed himself to other aspects of the American dream, Will Rogers concomitantly spoke to features of the progress vision. He merged himself with the American hope for a better future, too, when he dealt with America's spiraling technology. For him, apparently, the material dimension of "bigger" could carry with it the moral dimension of "better." At times, Rogers seemed to say just that. In 1934, with the hope of the great dream still dimmed by the depression, he wrote, "We are so big, and move along with such momentium [sic], that we are able to live through everything. As cockeyed as we are, we are better than all the rest put together."

The chief way in which Rogers related material and moral progress was his wholehearted approval of certain aspects of technology. In his notion that bigger mechanical and technical improvements produced a better way of life, he identified with the prime doctrine of the dream of progress in America. He made the statement explicitly when he wrote, "What a godsend the plane and radio is to out-of-the-way places!" In more detail, he praised modern, rapid systems of communication and advances in aviation.[37]

To Will Rogers—the busy self-made man, the cowboy free in space, and the American Adam seeking a breadth of direct experience—modern systems of instantaneous communication were welcome miracles. He praised the convenience of transoceanic telephone calls and of "progress in a regular passenger plane" that was equipped with radio. During a radio broadcast, he called the wireless "the greatest invention of our lifetime." In a daily telegram, he elaborated and kept his role of the wise innocent. To him, radio was "our greatest invention, far greater than the automobile, for it don't kill anybody. It don't cost us millions for roads," he explained; further, "when we are too lazy, or too old to do anything else, we can listen in."[38]

Technological refinements in aviation attracted Rogers' praise as well as did rapid communication. "Aviation is the greatest advancement in our times," he might say, unperturbed by the fact that he had said the same of the radio. For years the real and the possible developments in aircraft had appealed to Rogers. In 1927, before Lindbergh's flight, an aircraft stayed aloft for over two days, proving the dependability of aeronautical machinery. Rogers' hat went sailing into the air in praise, "Hurrah for our aviators that broke the continuous flight record. Fifty-one hours!" Then he explained the significance of the flight by comparing it to another endurance contest: "That breaks the Arizona Senator's continuous air record in the last Senate filibuster. That was not [sic] contribution to science like this was." Then came the stinger: "Theirs was just a tribute to poor Senate rules." Later in the same year, Rogers gave his audience startling glimpses into the future of aviation by reporting an interview with Henry Ford, hero of progress as well as of success. The topic had turned to airplanes:

> He is all wrapped up in their progress. . . . He thinks the future will see a plane that will have 10 or 20 engines and carry 100 people strong enough to buck all the winds and storms. I went back to Chicago the next day in one of his three-motored ships. Thirteen of us made the trip.[39]

Thus, Rogers' comments on the advancement of aviation were generally of two types: He praised technological developments that at first glance may have seemed only curiosities (as in the case of the endurance fliers) and he reported actual or future improvements in commercial aviation (as in the storm-safe plane in Ford's future).

Rogers was quick to point out the possible importance of scientific breakthroughs in aviation. Appearing to be the messenger from the fire-bringers, for example, he commented to his national audience on the implications of an announced air development:

> Next to the discovery of a cancer cure there couldn't possibly be anything of any more value than the claim in the papers today that Mr. John Hays Hammond Jr, had discovered television that would penetrate fog, and that an aeroplane pilot could look at his television and see exactly what was through the fog.
>
> If they got that, why that's all they been needing— finding a way to eliminate fog. The next big discovery is to find a way to get prohibition out of politics.[40]

With the rest of the country, Rogers joined in the jubilation over Lindbergh's triumph; later, when the nation seemed less aware of the implications of the Post-Gatty flight around the world in only eight days, he gave the journey's significance in a homely simile, "No news today as big as this Post and Gatty that are making this world of ours look like the size of a watermelon." A few years later, from California, Rogers informed the nation of the world's first attempt to utilize the thin atmosphere of the stratosphere for speedier air travel, a flight that was not only to be "the most hazardous" one yet, but also "the most beneficial to aviation of any since Lindbergh's."

> [Wiley Post] is pioneering a new world, flying a long course at 35,000 feet. Never attempted before. Eight hours on oxygen is new. He drops his landing gear on leaving. He has to come in on (pardon the expression, but it's all he has to land on) his "belly." . . .
>
> It's a real scientific flight. If it works everybody will fly up there. It's an old-style ship, five years old. He has flown it around the world twice.
>
> So a prayer, or at least a good wish, for Wiley.[41]

In such comments, Rogers mirrored the implications of technical change and thus merged himself with the vision of progress.

When he reported actual or future improvements in aviation, he also made technical refinement synonymous with

progress. Followers of his career could find in his own messages progress from flight in mailplanes to new twin-
engined transports cruising at 180 miles per hour. "Now
this aviation is getting somewhere!" Rogers exulted. "You
see, all our advancement in speed has been made with
small single-motored ships. But now they are all out to cut
down the flying time at least a third." Another time, Rogers
might quote the opinion of Frank Hawks, the great speed
flier, on future improvement of commercial travel. As was
a fairly common practice with him, he quoted Hawks in the
first person:

> You can't get any worse hurt flying at two or three
> hundred miles an hour than you can flying at ninety, so
> what we have to do is develop planes that will fly at
> what we now call a tremendous rate of speed. I see the
> day coming in the not far distant [sic] when you will
> leave New York at noon, fly across the country at the
> rate of a thousand miles an hour, and reach Los Angeles
> at noon.

Even when the improvement in flying was as down to earth
as providing planes with reclining seats for sleeping,
Rogers saw progress. "There is your success of passenger
aviation. Fix it so everybody can lay down and have a good
sleep. The air is much better at night."[42] During the years
of his greatest popularity, Will Rogers often aligned himself with progress in a direct material way by picturing
technological refinements as changes for the better. Their
material improvement was moral advancement: the bigger
and the faster, the better.

Thus, to read or hear Will Rogers on the progressive
achievements in technology such as those in communication and transportation may have been like a visit to a progress fair. He seemed to be the messenger from the priests
of progress. When he identified with the dream of betterment by performing its action corollaries, he seemed more
Promethean, himself. Like the demigod of foresight, he
looked to the future with optimism. Too, he boosted for the
bigger and better; in such a role he was the teacher of useful
arts. Finally, he quested for the good life. In all these ways
he fitted himself in an indirect material way with the

dream of progress, and through it, to the dream of Paradise to be regained.

"If every history or books on old things was thrown in the river," Rogers had once begun as the past-rejecting American Adam; he concluded as the forward-looking Prometheus, "and, if everybody had nothing to do but study the future, we would be about 200 years ahead of what we are now." Rogers did look forward more than backward; his comments on future technological developments have illustrated that stance. Moreover, he seemed to agree with the progress dreamer's dedication to the future. "What spoiled China," he remarked in a "letter" to Senator Borah (and to the American people), "was somebody saving their history." Starting from this Adamic premise, the forward-looking Rogers explained the difference between East and West by telling how the Chinese viewed the world: "They are standing still, looking backwards." Americans would "be more lost" than the Orientals if they, too, looked back, for "we can't see nothing but our shadow when we look back." Thus, the "biggest difference between the two races" was that "we are a foresight people, and they are a hindsight people."[43]

Rogers' optimistic tone was clear in regard to the future in a 1930 prediction about Lindbergh:

Round June 22, 1950, here is what will be headlined in the Planet Mars morning papers:

"A young man from a place called Earth flew in here yesterday. He had been in the air continuously for two months. He had some letters of introduction from the Chamber of Commerce in a place called Englewood, New Jersey. He asked to have his ship refueled as he is taking off for Venus in the morning."[44]

The cost of such an effort in space either did not occur to him, or he did not worry about it. In either case, for Rogers, no problems marred the approach of the space age.

Given everything else that lent trustworthiness to his character as national commentator, Rogers' expressions of optimism were a welcome note in the long slump that followed the 1929 crash. With Americans still "hearing things go bump" in the darkness, the cowboy philosopher forecast

that when economists began writing history, they would
record 1933 as the year of the turning from worse to better.
"So, so long '33!" he typed optimistically. "Panics come every twenty years, so we will be seeing you in '53." By mid-
1935, he could report the encouraging results of his own
private poll:

> From what I can gather from everyone I talk with, things
> are definitely picking up. If they just get more folks to
> working which they are doing now too, there is no way of
> stopping this Country. Just quit listening to the
> politicians. They have to make a noise the nearer it
> comes to next year. . . . The Constitution will remain as
> is. The Russians are not going to take us. Everywhere I
> have been on this trip there is a fine feeling. Let folks
> quit argueing [sic] over who did it, or dident do it. Just
> join in it.

When he visited San Francisco for the last time, Rogers
reported a substantial increase in bridge building as a sign
of better times. San Franciscans didn't dare leave a bucket
or two of water out overnight, he happily exaggerated, or
else they would find a bridge over it the next morning.[45]
Rogers did not sound the note of optimism so often that it
grew thin; but during the time of his national prominence,
he appeared as the forward-looking American Prometheus.

Almost coalescent in the progress dream with the
strategy of hopefully looking to the future was the action
corollary of "boosting" improvements in order to propel the
future to fruition. On at least one occasion, he even gave
boosting a boost, in the form of an object lesson about a
place that had progressed from town to city. The promoters
had "dug deep" to charter a train and load the baggage car
with samples of crops and products to be shown to prospective residents and businessmen along the line:

> Well, it was a joke—a hundred men getting off a train,
> marching with a Band, a boosting a place nobody had
> ever heard of. But business men in the places we paraded
> commenced to realize that there must be something in
> our Town or we couldn't do all this.
>
> Now, if you are anxious to know whatever became of
> this Tank town, it's Tulsa, Oklahoma, which would have
> been a real town, even if its people weren't greasy rich

with Oil, for it is founded on the spirit of its people. . . .
It's the Towns, big and small, that don't do or try to do
anything at all that are funny to me.[46]

Approving, as he seemed to, of helping the future come
true, Will Rogers boosted for bigger and better cities, for
more populous states, and for booming growth in aviation.

His "plugs" for American cities often succeeded without
Chamber of Commerce jargon. In 1932, from faraway
China, came another tribute to Tulsa. That city was "aged
now, kinder like Peking. But when she was new and had no
Tradition, she was a hummer." This was a boost with a
difference: It had the aura of the wisely-innocent American
Adam about it, so that superlatives may have been unnecessary. At times, Rogers was irreverent, as with the "tire capital": "This town of Akron is responsible for the most ag-
gravating invention that ever was let loose on modern civilization," he averred. "There is 110,000 people in some part
of the world every minute of every day just fixing punctures
in Akron tires, part of 'em rubber." Or he could conjure the
aura of the American frontier, as he did with another town
he had always wanted to see—South Bend. "I was born in a
Studebaker wagon, awakened every morning by a Big Ben
clock, grew up walking between the handles of an Oliver
chilled plow, wore home made shirts made by Singer sew-
ing machines and read all my life of Notre Dame, whose
scholastic standing is one touchdown and a field goal higher
than any other modern educational hindrance." A few
months later, after an ambitious, up-and-coming community had utilized the promotional talents of one of its residents by making him mayor, that dignitary addressed his
national constituency in behalf of Beverly Hills. "Boy, we
got a town! We are putting an immigration quota on millionaires now, they [*sic*] getting too thick." Claremore often
was "the town that you take those wonderful baths that
cure you of everything but being a Democrat." By mixing in
the character of the wise innocent, by avoiding colorless
Chamber of Commerce superlatives, by sometimes seeming irreverent, by showing a frontiersman's optimistic exaggeration, Will Rogers offered boosts to up-and-coming cities. He was still at it near the end of his life: At the opening
of Chicago's "Century of Progress," even in spite of long-

winded preachers and shortsighted policemen, he could write, "It's a great fair, don't miss it."[47] He was boosting Americans toward a bigger and better life.

That dream was clear, also, in the praise Rogers gave to states. Over the years, he ranged from West to East telling his national audience of the roads to paradise. In a dispatch from California, the "plug" took the form of allusion to an old paradise and reference to a new one by means of man's ingenuity; the Imperial Valley was the subject:

> It's below sea level and the most fertile spot outside the
> Valley of the Nile, and that's only good for burial
> purposes. But this raises real alfalfa and cotton and
> grape fruit. No time to monkey with old King Tut here.

In early 1935, Rogers found many things in a southwestern state worthy of praise:

> Texas is having a big centennial next year and while
> you are sorter planning your vacation ahead, you want to
> come to our biggest State.
> You ought to read a list of what this State produces,
> and her modern up-to-date cities, and size and distances.
> Plenty of ranches here as big as Germany or France.
> Horse pastures as big as England. Your Belgiums or
> Switzerlands would get lost in some farmer's cotton
> patch in Texas. And oil! They are the only State that can
> serve you oil hot or cold.

If readers had not seen Rogers' boosts of other states, they might have concluded that everything in "Big T" was bigger and better than anywhere else. He was no more restrained, no less Crockettlike in his accolades for his native state, however. "If Oklahoma does in the next twenty-two years what we have in the last, why New York will be our parking space, Chicago our arsenal, New Orleans our amusement centre and Los Angeles segregated for Elk and Shrine conventions."[48] The man from Oklahoma could well have been an adopted son of nearly all the states. Their natives could be expected to feel warmly toward one who praised their industries, their energy, and their geography. Americans outside those environs may have approved of Rogers' boosting, simply because he was performing an action corollary of the progress dream.

Thus by spreading the news of cities and states that were advancing, Rogers projected the impression of a teacher of useful arts. That aspect of his public character was clearest, perhaps, in his continual efforts to further the cause of aviation. A persuasive teacher is the doer, and Rogers taught the values of aviation by flying and then sharing his experiences with his readers. One of his lessons came to the readers of his weekly syndicate in the days when the flying cowboy was doing one-night stands all over the country:

> Well, all I know is just what I read in the papers and what I see as I soar over these old United States. . . .
> We laugh our heads off at some old joke about seeing people living down in Arkansas that never rode on a train in their lives. Why havent they been on one? It's because they havent seen them. But here is the whole of America bigger Rubes than they are, for all of you have seen planes, see 'em every day and read every day of the wonderful trips and feats they do but the furtherest they can get you off the ground is on some summer roof garden, and you won't venture up there till the orchestra is playing.

Then the cowboy philosopher told of the joys of his new-found Pegasus as he covered the open spaces of Montana, "third in size."

> Would stay all night in the town I had just played, have a nice breakfast and then we could leave just whenever we wanted to. . . . Fly over the beautiful mountain tops, and in two or three hours catch up with the train that had left the night before.

The view from the plane was just of the sort from New York City's tallest building—"only better for you are not standing looking at the same thing all the time."[49]

Rogers presented himself as the living example of one who had benefited from the speed, safety, and pleasures of flying. Possibly the clearest transmission of this message occurred in the autumn of 1927, when the flying cowboy set a record of only four days' time, coast-to-coast, in regularly-scheduled mailplanes, while on a business trip to New York City. At least part of his first wire was written in the open cockpit with the mail packed around him. Speed? "We are

coming into Salt Lake. Only been six hours from Los Angeles." Safety? "They have flown 650,000 miles, with only
four forced landings and no one hurt." Joy? "Brigham
Young might have seen more women than I have, but I have
seen more of Utah today than he ever saw. Who said this
country was all settled up?" Next day, the dateline was
Lewiston, Pennsylvania: "Breakfast at home in Beverly yesterday (Tuesday) and dinner in New York tonight (Wednesday). Only one bad feature on whole trip. Got lost in pistol
smoke over Chicago."[50] Other telegrams stressed the efficiency of air travel and its importance to the man whose
time was valuable.

A few months later, Rogers told his story through the
mass medium of a national magazine, rehearsing again the
theme of his own experience with the speed, safety, and
economy of riding the mailplanes. His closing paragraphs
of the two-article series made clear his own identification
with air travel as progress. On the final leg of the trip, so
went the story, Rogers and his pilot had overtaken a train
that had departed much sooner from the East than had
Rogers:

> The train was just at that time passing an old wagon
> that some old mover was going from one part of the
> Country to another in. It was covered.
> Now I got pretty good hearing when the wind is
> blowing right. There was a bunch of fellows sitting out
> on the Observation, fanning themselves and wiping the
> cinders to keep cool while they were crossing the desert.
> As they passed the old fellow in a Wagon, they all looked
> at him. One spoke. But they all had the same thought,
> even if he hadent spoke it for them:
> "Well, that's a pretty tough way to travel. Just think
> how the old-timers had to get from one place to another,
> and to think that poor devil is doing it still."
> "Well, it's his own fault. Why don't he sell that old
> outfit and get on a train? It's his own fault."
> "Well, some people just don't take to progress even
> when it's brought right to em," said another of the group.
> "Just think, that fellow mebbe left Salt Lake before we
> left New York City, and this is all the further he is."
> Another spoke up: "Well, the only way you can account

for it is that he just don't know any better. It's people
like him that can't see things that's holding this country
out here back. They need some Eastern Pep and life and
Go-getem, and wake-up-and-move-around spirit out
here."[51]

Will Rogers made his appeal for progress effective not only
by using a symbolic narrative and casting the characters in
the dramatic irony resulting from their own ignorance, but
also by speaking from firsthand experience as a doer of the
dream of progress. During the years of his greatest prominence, he continued his teaching in behalf of air travel so
that he was dubbed "Aviation's Patron Saint." Rogers himself exemplified part of what "progressing aviation" meant;
to read of his flights into the new world above the earth may
have given to his comfortable earthiness a touch of the
empyrean so important to an American Prometheus.

In writing of his doings, he often told of encounters with
other American heroes. When they were icons of progress,
he added—through association—to his own stature as a
demigod of progress. Such was the case with Lindbergh,
with whom Rogers flew on more than one occasion. Such,
too, was the case with Edison, when that most highly regarded of all Promethean heroes re-enacted a drama symbolic of the American dream. Rogers had been among the
party that had journeyed to Dearborn in those waning days
of predepression prosperity. Edison, of course, was the star
of the show:

> Well, he even as a young boy was of an inventive mind.
> He used to keep his junk in the baggage car, and along
> with it a lot of chemicals and tools that he would
> experiment with. Well one of the first things he invented
> was setting a train on fire from the baggage car while it
> was in motion. . . .
>
> Well, Sir, do you know this man Ford had reproduced
> that whole thing, the train, the little depot where he was
> fired. They put on everything but the fire and would have
> done that if Mr. Edison had just had some matches. Mr.
> Hoover and Party were on the train. Mr. Edison was in
> his old role of Candy Butch. He went through the cars
> crying his wares.[52]

Thus, not only was Rogers a progress hero, but he also became associated with others on the slopes of the American
Olympus and thus added to his own stature. As he looked
optimistically to the future and boosted improvements, he
merged himself with the vision of progress.

The crowning mode of Rogers' indirect material identification with progress was his questing, which he shared
with his audience via the mass media at his disposal. In a
sense, he came full circle from Prometheus to Adam: The
man of "experience," seeking self-fulfillment by saturating
himself with living, was also on a quest. Therefore, when
Rogers, as the American Adam, told his readers of the paradise within the borders of all "those old states," he was
writing not only about what the hero of individualism
would do, but also about what a figure symbolic of progress
would do.

By the time, however, that Rogers gained prominence, the
westering spirit of a restless people had come up against
the Pacific Ocean and the reality that denied the dream of
the garden and its safety-valve theory. Perhaps one reason
for Americans' fascination with Rogers was his ability to
overleap the boundaries of the old dream and go forth to
quest for God's country all over the world. Periodically he
launched forth on odysseys to Latin America, to the Orient,
or around the world. "Just flew over and looked right down
in crater of Popocaterpillar," he might write from Mexico,
happy in his misspelling. "It's easier to fly over than it is to
pronounce." He shared with his readers his low-level, all-
morning flight over the "beautiful coral island" of the San
Blas Indians. With a joke about the foresightedness of the
chief in not allowing visitors to remain overnight, and thus
keeping the inhabitants as "the only 100 per cent Indians,"
Rogers looked ahead: "The coast to Columbia is beautiful.
I am nearing Venezuela. Will stop for the night at
Maracaibo."[53] Faraway places and exotic-sounding names
constituted but another kind of paradise.

On a trip so far west that he would meet the East, Rogers
might call the Hawaiian Islands "the Garden of Eden" and
tell of his own idea of a cowman's paradise. "There are
marvelous cattle ranches on these islands, and these native
cowboys are plenty salty with those rawhide riatas," wrote

the flying cowboy in a letter home to his "folks," the American people. On the ranch of over a half-million acres were thirty thousand Herefords; perhaps of more interest, the ranch had "the best horses I ever saw on any ranch anywhere, and over six hundred here just in the saddle horse string." The same journey would carry him to the Orient, through Japan, Korea, and across the breadth of Manchuria on the Chinese Eastern Railway. In Siberia—possibly contrary to the common stereotype—he found an Eden that deserved his descriptive attention. "This is the heart of Eastern Siberia. All a beautiful prairie, not a tree, just grass up to your stirrups." On an earlier quest, he had described the Edenic qualities of western Russia:

> It's a beautiful country to look at. And grass? Oh, Boy, I
> just thought if some of my old ranchmen could see all
> that big fine grass going to waste—millions of acres and
> very little stock on it, with plenty of water.[54]

On to Finland, Sweden, and then to Norway, where he explored fjords for hours in a small seaplane and chased herds of reindeer, Rogers was the embodiment of the questing hero.

And on one occasion, of which Rogers told his audience more than once, the Adamic Prometheus came full circle to the general area of the original "home." In the short, dark days of early January, 1932, Americans read their daily personal note from their traveling friend. "You Bible students, stockmen and hunters better note this: Flew low all morning between the Euphrates and the Tigris." Then came the Edenic promise: "It's all level prairie and uncultivated. Most animals I ever saw were there, thousands of cattle, donkeys, camels, water buffalo, deer and wild boar." A few years later, he expanded his description and made the object of the quest explicit:

> Was in a very big long valley, hundreds of miles, and I
> thought looking down on it from the plane coming from
> China to Europe that I had found me a real new cow
> country, and I thought, my goodness, why dont folks
> settle here. I bet they dont know where it is. . . .
> I said to the pilot, a Holland Dutchman, too bad people
> dont know about this place, it sure looks fertile. Pretty

soon he circles the plane, and pointed down and said,
"There is the Garden of Eden."[55]

The heavier-than-air aircraft, Promethean marvel of ingenuity, had carried man forward by returning him to the scene of his state of perfection.

As an American Prometheus, Rogers identified materially with the vision of progress by extolling significant features of America's spiraling technology, by looking to the future resolutely and optimistically, by boosting improvements and growth, and by questing—via a product of technology—for Eden, itself. In the way in which he used language, too, he formally associated himself with the progress dream.

Among other qualities of the typical American already noted by James Muirhead were those that accorded with the dream of progress. "The American note includes a sense of illimitable expansion and possibility, an almost childlike confidence in human ability and fearlessness of both the present and the future, . . . and a positive predilection for innovation." Just as he had used word bending and slang in giving the aura of Adamic newness, Rogers used the formal resources of language to give the sense of Promethean forward-looking and questing.

Not only did the formal appeal of hyperbole suggest the equalizing of disparities by means of the heightening or lowering inherent within it, but that figure of speech also served Rogers in producing the breezy optimism so important to the dream of progress. Hyperbole, for instance, provided the mode for a boost of Florida's climate, where the "mule-slipper heaver can do more with a horseshoe than a manicurist can with a drunk." When the subject was the technological revolution, Rogers might write, "Well sir, there is not a man, woman, or Golf Player in the World that hasn't seen a Ford Car, no matter what country it is in." When writing of a hero of that technological revolution, he exaggerated joyously: ". . . well, this Gatty, just give him a compass and one peek at the Giant Dipper and he can tell you where you are even if you ain't there." His optimism for the future, too, seemed joyous and unlimited in 1925, because of a simile partaking of exaggeration: "To stop this

Country now would be like Spitting on a railroad track to stop a train." When Rogers boosted his native state with hyperbole, he could sound almost like one of the old backwoods roarers, as well as a champion of progress.

> Corn? When you speak of corn you are talking right up our alley. Why, the way that Florida got that little patch that sold for $10,000,000 was by Oklahoma's corn growing so high that some of the stalks fell over into Florida. We gather our corn in airplanes. Why, our corn last year in Oklahoma ran over 200 gallons to the acre.[56]

Just as Rogers' quests had been prime means of merging himself with the dream of progress, the shape of his sentences could reinforce the sense of the search. Frequently, he rambled in his sentences just as he rambled in his physical travels. When he told his readers of the flight over Eden, he used a long compound-complex sentence: "Was in a very big long valley, hundreds of miles, and I thought looking down on it from the plane coming from China to Europe that I had found me a real new cow country, and I thought, my goodness, why dont folks settle here." In a radio broadcast describing his plans for the summer of 1934, Rogers announced, "Reason I'm goin' to travel so much in Russia and try to go all over Russia, down the Black Sea and all around, see those big experimental farms that the farmers are supposed to be workin' on over there and all that—the reason I'm—you know, Russia today is—they're supposed to have the greatest experiment in the world—outside of us."[57] Skeptical of that experiment as he was and as he remained, Rogers as the American Prometheus had to see for himself. By such rambling sentence structure, he formally strengthened his persona as a quester.

In addition to appropriately shaped sentences, Rogers' communications also paralleled the quest in their form-in-the-large. Just as the search for the Holy Grail provided all kinds of side excursions, digressions, and adventures, the topics contained in a longer Rogers message often wandered along in free-associational unity at best. In the weekly article in which he told of his flight over Eden, the topics receiving attention were the following: (1) the plea-

sure cruise of Mrs. Rogers and daughter, Mary; (2) Rogers'
early travels, in which he left home going first class and
came back riding third; (3) his flight over Eden and the
Middle East; (4) meeting with Fred Stone, Broadway musical star, and driving over Arizona; (5) the West's need for
cars with more road clearance, rather than smooth boulevards to nowhere; (6) recent guests at the Rogers place in
Santa Monica, including humorist Irvin S. Cobb and actor
Leo Carillo. Such rambling main topics gave Rogers' works
a strong resemblance to the quest itself. A weekly article
illustrates the rambling, loose sentence effect:

> Well, all I know is just what I read in the papers and
> what I see here and yonder. Do you like to just be in a
> car prowling around? I know you do, everybody does. I
> would much rather be in a plane, but if you havent got
> one, and I havent, more folks ask me about my plane.
> They think because I do a lot of traveling that way I
> must have my own plane. Why I havent got any more
> plane than Alabama has Republicans. I have always just
> used a regular organized line, walk up and pay your fare
> get in and go where you want to. . . . But all this has
> nothing to do with planes. I am the greatest guy to start
> in on telling something and then switch over to
> something that has nothing to do with it at all. I get that
> from working in the movies. You notice it in our movie
> stories.
>
> Well, I was up in a town called Bishop making a movie,
> and we got through with our outdoor shots. . . . So I
> jumped in my car that very evening and went over a
> range of Mountains about 130 miles to Tonopah, Nevada,
> that's the old silver town. It's not a ghost town by any
> means because it has a couple or three thousand people
> living there yet and is a very interesting town. Used to be
> along in 1907 and 8 a big rushing thriving place of
> perhaps 10 thousand or more. . . .
>
> Well up early the next morning and down to Goldfield.
> Now dont that name and place bring back memories. One
> of the well advertised towns of the West. In 1906 on
> Labor Day, was the biggest and best advertised and best
> prize fight ever held. That was the famous Gans-Nelson
> fight of 43 rounds that was promoted by the famous Tex
> Rickard. It was the first big purse at that time $30,000.
> . . . It was just exactly 26 years to a day when I was there.

I had known two of three principals, Nelson and
Rickard. . . .
It's Gold town, and they are working some of the mines
by small leases. The Government is investigating it as
they think there is big pay stuff there yet. Now here was
an experience. The papers had been full of a new strike
at a place called Clarkdale, for a fellow named Clark
found it. So off I went to it, a newspaper man and mining
man went with me, and sure enough away out there in
the hills on those desert flats was dozens of camps all
around a hole in the ground. Lots of 'em had leased from
the original striker, and the others had staked near
around there. Well they say there was some real gold
there . . . .
Nevada is a great old State to prowl around in . . . .
Just get in your car and drive around some time no
matter where you live, you will be surprised the old
interesting things there is to visit. But don't miss
Nevada.[58]

This was not the quest for the Holy Grail but the search for
the golden El Dorado of the past as well as of the future.
This image provided a well-traveled road from which
Rogers could talk about the value of air travel, the thrill of
a flight of long-ago, the joys of rambling, and other matters.
On many occasions, he used his rambling form, as well as
hyperbole, to identify with the quest and with the dream of
progress toward the greatest bonanza of all, the Paradise to
be regained.

BY THE early thirties, the magic mirror of public reactions
to him had given Will Rogers the role of commentator. He
spoke, reports Homer Croy, of "influencing thought in
America." In 1932, he outlined a scenario to James M. Cox,
the plot of which is suggestive of the role Rogers accepted
in relation to American society:

It was based upon an old country philosopher who had
enough mind and assertion to pretty much run his whole
part of the country. He became famous statewide. And
then, as the fiction unfolded, he found himself by his
quaint philosophy to be known in every household in the
nation.

> The public opinion of the country became very
> turbulent and out of it came his election to the
> Presidency.[59]

Though Rogers' good sense dictated that the country philosopher would produce grotesque effects in Washington, the plot for the movie also indicated his awareness of his power with the public. By August of 1935, his national image as an embodiment of the great American dream was complete. Through his words he had traced every line of his public portrait until he was at once the American Adam, standing for the dream of the dignity and worth of the individual; the American democrat and "Mr. Cowboy," symbolizing the dream of equality and freedom; the self-made man, who, by his rise from rags to riches, personified the dream of success; and the American Prometheus, who, with his looking forward and teaching of the useful arts, was the icon of the progress dream. Rogers was a god-of-many-faces.

One quest remained. On June 9, he had ended his radio series, telling his audience that he would see them in the fall. Newspaper stories told of his starting on a long journey with the great air pioneer, Wiley Post. The hearts of many Americans went with them to Alaska, the last frontier and the most recent of all the American El Dorados.

On August 8, the hundreds of papers in the syndicate carried a dispatch from Juneau:

> Well, that was some trip. Thousand-mile hop from
> Seattle to Juneau. Was going to stop at Ketchikan for
> lunch, but mist and rain came up and we just breezed
> through, never over 100 feet off the water.
> And talk about navigating. There is millions of
> channels and islands and bays and all look alike (to me)
> but this old boy Wiley Post turns up the right alley all the
> time.
> Nothing that I have ever seen is more beautiful than
> this inland passage, by either boat or plane, to Alaska.
> You know, I just been thinking about things at home. You
> know who I bet would like to be on this trip, Mr.
> Roosevelt.

The next day, the telegram hitched the trip to the pioneers: "We are going to Skagway now and see the famous Chilkoot Pass. We will do it in ten minutes and it took the pioneers two and three months." And so it went, day after day, the telegrams coming from that distant place with unreal qualities. "Old Wiley had to duck his head to keep from bumping it as we flew under the Arctic Circle. What, no night? It's all day up here." On that final August 15 appeared the account of a flight almost symbolic: "In a Lockheed Electra we scaled Mount McKinley, the highest one on the American Continent. Bright, sunny day, and the most beautiful sight I ever saw."[60]

Even, perhaps, as some reader went over the message, the red monoplane's engine stalled, the craft went out of control, and the two questers plunged into the shallow water from which they had just taken off. Then there was silence, except for wavelets lapping against the hull of the airplane and for shouts of an Eskimo who had seen the crash.

When the news reached the "lower forty-eight" by Army radio, a nation mourned: In the Senate and House, debate stopped and eulogies began; from their camps, the hobos of America declared a thirty-day mourning period; in homes, restaurants, and stores, Americans in the "big, Normal Majority" waited for more news after the first shock. From foreign newspapers came comments on the national loss. American papers gave the story top prominence for days, until at last the funeral ended, with squadrons of government planes flying over the chapel as a last salute to Will Rogers, the American Prometheus felled by the technological miracle he had so strongly advocated.

A nation mourned. The voice of the American dream was silent; the man who had made the quest for paradise a believable reality was gone.

Perspectives

If Americans become heroes to the extent that they are
identified in the public mind with the categories of the
great dream, then the more completely a figure satisfied the
definitions, the wider would be his appeal. In the instance
of Abraham Lincoln is evidence to support the idea that our
supreme heroes fit several categories of the American
dream. Roy P. Basler, winnowing the fact from the legend
about Lincoln, nevertheless does not lose sight of the importance of both in producing Lincoln's attraction for the
American imagination. "It was the clustering of signifi-
cances about his figure that made him immortally *the*
American. He was the self-made man, the type of honesty,
perseverance and grit, the intrepid Indian fighter, etc."[1]
Emerson, addressing his Concord townsmen on April 19,
1865, had found Adamic qualities in Lincoln, "a quite native, aboriginal man, as an acorn from the oak," who had
been a "middle-class president . . . in manners and sympa-
thies, but not in powers, for his powers were superior." Poets of the time found in Lincoln, Basler points out, the
savior of a race, the embodiment of conscience and right,
the smiter of chains, the husbandman of brotherhood.
"Such is the legend of the Emancipator who, with the stroke
of a pen, shattered the manacles of four millions of human
souls in a state of servitude," concludes Basler (page 219),
pointing out that others had labored longer and harder to
bring about a sane view on the evil of slavery. Thus, in
Lincoln as the hero of freedom and equality was a "mag-
netic symbol around which all the ideal attributes, hopes,
prayers, and achievements of a horde of crusading prede-
cessors are clustered" (page 219). Biographers such as William M. Thayer wrote rags-to-riches stories of Lincoln that
treated the Illinoisian as a prototype of the poor but honest,
industrious lad who rises by virtue of hard work and taking
advantage of his opportunities. Lincoln as the hero of progress emerges most clearly, perhaps, in the often recalled
passage from his second inaugural:

> With malice towards none; with charity for all; with
> firmness in the right, as God gives us to see the right, let
> us strive on to finish the work we are in; to bind up the
> nation's wounds; to care for him who shall have borne
> the battle, and for his widow, and his orphan—to do all
> which may achieve and cherish a just and lasting peace
> among our selves, and with all nations.

These are, says Basler, "the words which are most com-
monly cited as indicative of his character and associated
with his name" (page 164). They are words hopeful of the
future, filled with dramatic irony in the light of what happened a month later. Within a decade and a half after Lincoln's death, another American was growing up to become
an embodiment of the American dream, although not in the
role of martyr nor statesman: He was Will Rogers.

BY THAT June day in 1939 when the Rogers family, their
friends, and high government officials gathered in the Capitol Rotunda to place Rogers' statue with those of others in
the national Hall of Fame, diviners of Rogers' meaning for
the American people were speaking.*

Oklahoma Governor, Leon C. Phillips, saw in Will Rogers
the embodiment of the dream of the dignity and worth of
the individual:

> Will Rogers was born with the elements of greatness in
> him. He is one more irrefutable example of the fact to
> which we as citizens of a democracy unwaveringly
> adhere, that out of the humblest heritage and the
> simplest circumstances can come great characters who
> will revive our faith, enlighten our thinking, and fire our
> souls to action.

Not only was the man from Oologah proof of the innate and
unlimited powers of the individual, but—in the words of
Phillips—he was "typical also of that belief in individual
worth, that tolerance and sympathy that has marked the
American character from the days of the colonial frontier."[2]

*I am indebted to Basler for the term "diviner."

Perspectives

Other speakers remarked upon other dimensions of the demigod of the great American dream. Luther Harrison, asserting that Will Rogers joined George Washington in being a unanimous choice of all America for membership in the Hall of Fame, saw in the Oklahoman the embodiment of the dream of freedom and equality:

> He was the true democrat also. He stood in the presence of kings, on terms of perfect equality, because he knew that to be an American is to be the equal of a king.[3]

Senator Alben Barkley amplified this line of thought. Speaking of Rogers, he said:

> Not only was he an intimate and a confidant of Kings and of Presidents and of Governors and of Senators and of Members of the House of Representatives, members of the legislatures; not only was he the friend and the confidant of the rich and the powerful and the mighty, but greater than all of these, he was the friend and confidant of the humbler men and women, not only of our own country but of the world.[4]

A few years earlier, Josh Lee, a congressman from Oklahoma, had seen another appealing facet of Will Rogers' public portrait. At the Oklahoma memorial services in August of 1935, Lee had told of his own hero worship:

> Will Rogers was my hero. He was the big brother of the world, whose wholesome humor always boosted the fellow who needed a lift.
> He was a self-made man. He blazed his own trail over the mountain to fame. He never waited for opportunities; he made them. While others slept, he was poring over the daily news, digging the fun out of it.[5]

Will "of the people" had risen by himself to fame, and in the tradition of the success dream, had been a "brother" to the world.

In the remarks of Senator Barkley, spoken while officially accepting the statue, Rogers was also a hero of the dream of progress. "He gave of his wealth, he gave of his time, he gave of his talents, he gave of his great heart to make America a better place in which to live,"[6] the Kentuckian said. Thus, to Rogers' roles as the American Adam, the American

261

democrat, and the self-made man was added that of the American Prometheus.

The comments of such interpreters and shapers of public opinion undoubtedly have had their part in moulding the latter-day image of Will Rogers. But first, of course, had been the words of the cowboy philosopher, himself. How had his expression of the dream been appropriate and effective? Where does he stand now, more than a quarter of a century since entering the national Hall of Fame?

In order to be appropriate and effective, Will Rogers had to manage throughout his ascendancy to affirm the great dream in a way that would be acceptable in the circumstances of a nation that during the twenties both looked nostalgically for normalcy and faced optimistically to the future—and that during the thirties underwent a time of bewildering change, often seemingly for the worst. Obviously, his commentary had to be fitting to himself. Further, his articulation of the great vision had to be appropriate to his audience. He succeeded on both counts. For Rogers, apparently, the roles as Adam, democrat, self-made man, and Prometheus were easy. To a large extent, he seems actually to have possessed the qualities he projected. He truly was a man of the American West, that historical, psychological entity that stripped men of the encumbrances of tradition and at the same time gave them an elemental rusticity so important in appealing to audiences of a complex twentieth century. He seems actually to have possessed an endless zest for living, being boyishly joyous in the simple, rural pleasures of riding, roping, and "just visiting." Such qualities, coupled with apparent genuineness, intuition, and trueness to friends, gave him the total character of the "natural" man. Moreover, Rogers seemingly did trust in the goodness of the average man; he seemed always ready to believe the best about most people.

He loved to mingle with people—in groups of all kinds and station. He seemingly could be as impressed by the character of a lowly commoner as well as by that of a royal blue blood. Himself a member of a persecuted minority, he possibly had a broad sympathy for other minority groups and was dedicated to the proposition of their equality with other Americans and to their freedom for the pursuit of happiness. Congruent with his nature as an equalitarian was the fact that he actually was one among those free knights of the range, the American cowboys. Even though it may be true that he enjoyed the thrills of rodeo work more than the everyday exercise of cowboy skills on a ranch, Rogers was a practicing cowboy before the turn of the century. Perhaps more importantly, he seems to have adopted the cowboy's code of judging a man by what he does, of doing one's best—as a responsibly free man—to set affairs right, and of combining courage, ideals, and sentiment as motivation for such deeds.

Probably, too, a fire of activism burned within him, spurring him to a variety and intensity of enterprising pursuits. If his combination of acting, broadcasting, journalizing, and traveling is any indication, he was dedicated to the gospel of hard work. His private fires may have been stoked by the "work and win" doctrine of the success dream. He apparently did have the urge to upward mobility so necessary to the visioned rise to riches. Moreover, he probably was as virtuous and as generous as the success dream and his own legend required him to be.

Little doubt can exist that he was driven to a lifelong search, of sorts, all over the face of the globe. That drive, coupled with ambivalent love and fear of the aircraft that deified Lindbergh, probably produced in him the forward-looking thrust of the devotee of progress. Finally, in coming full circle to the boyish delight of the natural man, he found thrills in man's ingenious devices that conquered time and space—such as the radio, the telephone, and the promise of television.

All this, of course, is only speculation as to the real nature of the man. The reader of Rogers' biographies is impressed by the outside-in point of view they adopt. The reader sees an anecdotal record of events that prepared the boy for his later success and recorded that rise, keeping the boyishness and generous nature intact. Homer Croy writes of a great unseen side of Rogers' nature; Betty Rogers writes of a husband who had perhaps only herself as a confidante; Donald Day likewise limits his own interpretations about the inner motivation of Will Rogers. The result for the student of the cowboy philosopher is that he sees specific bits of behavior in his subject and is left to supply his own systematic interpretation of them. Two bases for the lack of an inside-out approach to Rogers' character are clear: Apparently he left little in the way of private letters or diaries in which he expressed his own private thoughts, and most of his known attitudes and beliefs are framed in his public utterance—in which the desire to adjust his ideas to people must necessarily be considered a kind of refracting variable.

One can be certain that Will Rogers had a public mask. Homer Croy, who knew him both as working associate and friend, noticed the change in Rogers from private to public relationships. "You see," Rogers explained in a 1926 *Saturday Evening Post* article, "everyone of us in the world have our audience to play to; we study them and we try and do it so it will appeal to what we think is the great majority."[7] Rogers, therefore, had a form of rhetoric. How can judgments of his motives be based upon his public statements, and how can biographers affirm that he succeeded in public simply by being himself? The answer seems to be simply that what everyone knew (and still knows) of Rogers' private nature fitted rather well with his roles assumed in public. His messages were appropriate to him; they were also suitable for his national constituency.

In two chief ways, Will Rogers' comments were fitting for his audience, which in a time of accelerated change needed an affirmation of the old values in a new dress. By means of his rural, sturdy-yeoman flavor, his remarks shone with the mellow light of the agrarian past, even as the application of his ideals to significant current events gave his words an appealing immediacy. Perhaps more importantly, his was a strategy of wise innocence in making identification with the values of the great dream.

To invoke Rogers' appeal to "the good old days," one has but to recall his rhapsodies on country eating, his admiration of the "old rubes" that did their own thinking, his faith in the country people, his constant references to beauties of farm and ranch, his talk of horses, his memories of ranch life, and his use of "folks," "ain't," and "doggone." At times he reminded his audience that he was just "an old country boy," and when he reported big doings in social circles at Washington or when he told of long talks with a future king of England, he always made sure to present a country boy image. Cumulatively, the effect was to render nostalgically rural the once flashy dresser who had loved to visit Kansas City and bring back all the latest "uptown" songs. The same person, on the other hand, chose to assert the values of the great American dream not in the abstract, but as related to current news events attracting national attention. Rogers spoke of the "fundamentally generous" nature of the common man while millions listened to him and Herbert Hoover on a broadcast that was a major event; while the "Liberty League" was in the news, he defined liberty as an amount of freedom to be enjoyed to the degree that an equal amount was granted to others; he spoke for freedom of conscience and intellect at the moment that the Scopes trial occupied the nation's attention. Rogers also addressed himself to the dream of economic equality in a radio speech at the moment when the national government was marshalling its opinion leaders to win support for the NRA; he spoke for the success ideal of benefaction when the nation watched the devastation wrought by the great flood of 1927, the drouth disaster of 1931, the Nicaraguan earthquake later in the same year, and during the depression; he "plugged" for air progress when Post and Gatty made flying history with their record-breaking flight around the world. The result was that in such contexts, the values of the great dream had a timeliness that made them not only relevant, but that also gave the impression of being "modern as tomorrow." Will Rogers' rural flavor, coupled with the expedience of his identifications with values of the great dream, enabled him to be appropriate to an audience that for only one generation had not had an actual frontier to tame or to visit vicariously. At the same time, he was fitting his messages to a society so interested in the up to date that the adjective "modern" was applied to houses with running water and electricity.

Yet, Rogers' appropriateness would not have been complete without the wisely innocent approach he brought to his identification with the American dream. That strategy permitted him to appear as one who was both worldly and visionary, sly and open, sophisticated and simple. The method had several specific techniques.

In order to appear both worldly and visionary in his articulation of the great dream's values, Rogers often modified his affirmation with a bit of skepticism or shrewd calculation. Speaking for the goodness of the common man, he commented, "I don't know anything about America being fundamentally sound and all that after dinner 'Hooey,' but I do know that America is 'Fundamentally generous.' " Regarding the dream of freedom he preceded his ideal of liberty according to the Golden Rule with the shrewdly calculating statement, "So, the question arises 'how much liberty can I get and get away with it?' " When he committed himself to the belief that American clubwomen would not exercise racial discrimination against an American Indian aspirant for high office, he had his eyes open to other possibilities of human behavior. An affirmation of the dream of progress had its qualifier: "Even though we don't think so sometimes, civilization has advanced." Rogers' frequent use of his unique style of speaking permitted him to seem both realistic and idealistic, and appear to be the wise innocent.

Another technique of that strategy was his use of the ironist's mask, being so apparently open, naïve, or chauvinistic that the pose slyly condemned itself. Speaking of the goodness of the noble savage, he seemed to be saying the opposite when urging that "something ought to be done" about "primitive" people. Rogers "agreed" with the jailing of the nonviolent, liberty-seeking Gandhi, for "naturally a man that's holy couldn't run at large these days." He "felt sorry" for the sons of the rich who had to sell a yacht or even resign from a golf club in order to pay an inheritance tax intended to produce a degree of economic equality. He readily "admitted" that during the great war, Americans had been lax in deciding who were proper candidates to be accepted as Americans; that the "America Firsters" and their kind had saved the country when it was on the "brink" by showing that the plan for freedom and equality in the Declaration and the Constitution was "no good"; and he offered his own "improvement" in the form of his "America Only" society.

His ironic "improvement," of course, had the effect of rendering "America Only" absurd. Rogers often identified himself with the American dream by reducing opposing values to absurdity, a form of irony in the sense that his intent and statement differed only in degree rather than in kind. Newspapers, for instance, so violated the dignity of the individual and the right to privacy that they made suicides stand up, re-enact the "crime," pose for pictures, and promise not to repeat the act of killing themselves without calling the papers first. Boston book censors were at one point engaged in reading between the lines of *Pilgrim's Progress* to see if the book didn't have some "hidden meaning." In Alabama, after one of that state's national senators had delivered himself of an intolerant speech, Rogers reported that he was asking Alabama's citizens "to please not exterminate all Catholics, Republicans, Jews, Negroes, Jim Reed, Al Smith, Wadsworth, Mellon and Coolidge and the Pope." Through his use of irony in these and other situations, Will Rogers gave a double edge to his apparently frank and straightforward statements and, in that sense, was the wise innocent.

Rogers also managed to give the impression of being both simple and sophisticated in his voicing of the great dream. One technique was to pretend to an ignorance belied by his comments, giving the clear impression of being wiser than he seemed. "I have heard so much at this [national] convention about 'getting back to the old Jeffersonian principles' that being an amateur, I am in doubt as to why they *left them* in the first place." No reader, of course, would believe that Rogers was as much in doubt as he seemed about the relationship of political oratory to the values of the American dream. Again, when he was standing for freedom of small nations, he asked, "What was that slogan the whole country was shouting just exactly ten years ago today? Does this sound like it, 'Self determination of small nations.' " Probably the most consistent device, however, for posing as being ignorant consisted of his standard opening for the weekly articles. In a variety of ways he would say that all he knew was what he read in the papers. "Well, all I know is just what I see as I am combing this entire country in search of an honest politician," he wrote in 1925; he was still using the technique regularly in 1932: "All I know is just what I read in the papers or what I run into as I prowl like a coyote . . . looking back over my shoulders to see whats going on behind me."

Six days after his death a weekly article appeared that opened in the same general way: "Well, all I know is just what little I see behind the old Lockheed's wings." On other occasions, his pose of ignorance could produce both hilarity and the quality of a joyous spirit finding happiness in the vagaries of life—as in the case of his "not understanding" the necessity of a certificate to prove one's birth. His pretence of innocence of knowledge acted as a foil for his wisdom; he was sophisticatedly simple.

Rogers' practice of reducing complexities of the great dream to basic terms was also part of his wise-innocent strategy. By means of analogy or application of everyday or judgmental principles, he appeared to deal with matters directly and simply. The pursuit of happiness in some respects was analogous to keeping cattle satisfied on the range; free speech for Communists was as necessary for the country as exhaust for an automobile; international naval interference in the politics of one small country was like a public regatta—anyone could come in who had a boat. The National Recovery Act, ostensibly for the dream of economic equality, should have been written on a postcard, using rule of thumb to say that no man could be worked for a certain number of hours without overtime pay, that no pay be under a certain minimum, and that no children be hired. The question of social precedence at great dinners could be solved in a true spirit of equality by serving everybody "Los Angeles" style—giving everybody a plate and telling him to find the "grub." The complex matter of spiritual equality could be illuminated by the observation that water was as high on Negro flood victims as on whites and that the Lord so constituted everyone that all required about the same amount of nourishment. The secret of air progress was to "fix" it so that everybody could "lay down and have a good sleep." Differences between East and West boiled down to the one that the Chinese were a "hindsight" people and Americans were a "foresight" people.

By blending memories of America's rural past and the sparkle of timeliness in his affirmation of the American dream, Rogers achieved appropriateness. By using words

Perspectives

that allowed him to be both worldly and visionary, both sly and open, both sophisticated and simple, he exercised the strategy of being the wise innocent in his affirmation of the great dream.

In a real sense, of course, the appropriateness of Rogers' articulation of the dream was synonymous with the reasons for its potential effectiveness. In addition, other qualities of his identification with the great vision quite possibly could have added to the impact he had on his national audience.

Will Rogers seemed to offer something for everyone: Cowboys like Will James were admirers; magnates like Henry Ford and the elder John D. Rockefeller were more than acquaintances; Presidents made him their guest; airplane pilots considered him almost one of them; intellectuals like Reinhold Niebuhr respected his Adamic thrusts at sham; Rogers was fascinating for the "big Normal Majority." The catholicity of his appeal was related, perhaps, to the comprehensiveness of his identification with the American dream. That comprehensiveness, in turn, had at least three aspects: its breadth, in the sense that Rogers' identifications covered all four major categories of the great vision; its adhesiveness, in the sense that not uncommonly he related simultaneously to more than one aspect of the dream; and its depth, in the sense that the cowboy philosopher merged himself with more than one level of each category.

In considering possible reasons for the effectiveness of Rogers' expression of the dream of Paradise to be regained, one must not discount the obvious. Among all the heroes in the American gallery, only a few, perhaps—Lincoln, certainly—stood as icons of all the major categories of the American dream.

Among heroes contemporary with Rogers, Clarence Darrow, champion of the underdog, perhaps symbolized the dreams of individualism, freedom, and equality; Ford was the personification of success; Lindbergh and Edison, of progress. If these figures appear not to be retaining as much hero appeal as Rogers, a partial cause may be that they were heroes of the dream in a narrower sense than the man from Oklahoma.

Will Rogers, in his individual adaptation of the values of the great vision, joined himself with audience beliefs in the

powers, goodness, and potential, triumphant self-fulfillment of the common man through his trust in, and search
for, wisdom-giving experience. In addition, he coalesced in
his public portrait with that dream of freedom and equality
that pictured a government serving the good of all citizens,
that envisioned relative absence of restraint upon freedoms
of press, speech, and religion, and that included a society
where men were socially, politically, and economically
equal because they were spiritually equal. As Rogers rose
from wild West shows to radio appearances with Presidents, he aligned himself with the success dream, which
portrayed the rise from rural origins of the man with a
nonintellectual background, perseverance, industry, honor,
and good stewardship of ability and money. Finally, as he
promoted new technology, boosted continued economic
growth, and quested for Eden, he merged himself with the
progress dream.

Rogers fascinated Americans by the fact that he attached
himself to separate categories of the great vision that might
attract those chiefly interested in them. Additionally, for
those who saw him as the embodiment of more than one
category of the American dream, his identification with
each in turn was strengthened by appearing congruent with
the over-all vision. The principle is one that social psycholo-
gists have stated thus: "The properties of an item in a per-
ceptual structure are determined not only by the properties
it has when studied by itself but also by its relation to other
parts."[8] In other words, Will Rogers' alignment with the
dream of success could be made clearer and stronger because his alignments with other dreams in the over-all vision helped to draw the identifications into the paradigm of
the whole. The cumulative effect of the paradigm of the
great dream upon each category within it could have made
Rogers' total identification greater than the sum of his
separate identities.

Too, Rogers' identification with the dream was comprehensive in a second way: His statements not infrequently
were simultaneously relevant to more than one aspect of
the hopeful vision, thus providing adhesiveness to his identification. He was not only Adam, the hero of the individual's dream, but he was also the apostle of progress

when he simultaneously rejected the past and boosted the future in his rejection of Europe. "I say there is nothing new there; we got everything over home, only bigger and better." He tied the dream of self-fulfillment to that of progress when he wrote, "Happiness and contentment is progress. In fact, that's all progress is." When he expressed a belief that the real powers of the "big, Normal Majority" would pull us through even the "next war," he was also looking to the future optimistically as a devotee of the progress vision. His trust of the knowledge gained by the "old broadminded man of experience" was relevant not only to the powers of the common man but also to that part of the success dream that envisioned the rise of the nonacademic candidate. His apparent self-fulfillment through an expressed love of comrades was not only ancillary to the dream of man's goodness but was also part and parcel of the dream of brotherhood through equality.

When Rogers wrote that the government should be as interested in the health of children as in that of hogs, he served not only freedom's dream of a government for the good of all but also the principle that the individual is worthy. He combined his plea for free speech—even for Communists—with his trust in the powers of the average man to detect falsity of Communists' appeals. In all that he communicated on the relations of minority groups to other Americans, he implied the need to judge the individual by his own dignity and worth rather than by membership in a particular group. When he railed at what he considered to be "high" society's admission of members by birth only, pointing out the exclusion of self-made man Henry Ford, he combined not only the dreams of social equality and success but also that of the dignity and worth of the individual who, like Ford, could make good use of his own great powers. When the cowboy philosopher praised the benefactions of Rockefeller, he aligned himself with a significant feature of the success dream, and also underlined his identification with a belief in the goodness of people on the one hand and with the dream of the betterment of mankind's condition on the other. When he wrote of the joys of traveling through all "those great old States" of the Union, he not only was relevant to the dream of the individual's self-fulfillment through experience, but also to the vision of progress through his boosting of all the states of the forty-eight. By means of such interrelating of several facets, Will Rogers achieved comprehensiveness in paralleling the American dream.

This sort of adhesiveness applied also to his formal identification with the constellation of American values. His use of word bending and slang in giving the sense of the American Adam was appropriate to the aura of newness in the self-made man among the ranks of the newly rich. His rambling sentences and free form, which reflected the quest in the dream of progress, were suitable for giving the impression of freedom and, further, for fitting the nature of the experience-seeking Adam. His assault on grammatical convention not only fitted the persona of the self-made man, but accorded well also with the American Adam, freed from convention. When Rogers used his "wiser-than-I-look," sideways glance, when he chewed his gum, rammed his hands into his pockets, and combed his hair over his forehead, he was not only the free democrat or the self-made man, but he was also the wisely-innocent American Adam. The efficaciousness of such crossing of categories, both materially and formally, possibly lay in bringing the light from the great American dream into one focus. In that sense, Rogers was comprehensive in joining himself to the vision of Paradise to be regained.

His comprehensiveness was further enhanced by the depth of identification within each category of the American dream: He aligned himself on several levels within each division itself. The result was a kind of shotgun effect: If a statement at one level of the dream missed its mark, perhaps one on another level would reach it. For example, Rogers spoke on the direct material level of the dream of freedom and equality when he responded ironically to the activities of the America Firsters, and when he advocated freedom of press, speech, and religion. For whatever reason, some members of his audience may not have been attracted to such pronouncements. These same people, perhaps, could have been drawn to him by the language of his behavior that accorded with the vision of freedom and equality. He moved with aplomb among princes, heads of state, and celebrities; he also enjoyed meeting "the regular bird." He practiced an independence from blind party loyalty. His heart belonged to the underdog, and he practiced fair play in his columns and speeches. This kind of identification in depth provided "something-for-everybody" in another sense of the term. Rogers could thus be engaging for members in the audience who admired only segments of his identification within a category of the great dream; for those Americans who accepted all the levels of his alignment, he was irresistible. His "vertical" comprehensiveness complemented his "horizontal" inclusiveness in his embodiment of the American dream.

Because of the appropriateness and effectiveness of his expression of the great vision, Rogers achieved a deep sense of recognition in members of his audience. By the transmission of his message through the mass media, he was a daily, trusted companion. Americans may have felt that he, the most American of them all, had gone with them through all the sunlight and shadows of their private lives. He was a man for the times.

The sudden final breaking of the ties between Rogers and his Americans made clear to them the extent to which they had identified with the cowboy philosopher. Will Rogers, seven years before his last quest, had understood the effect of sudden partings of heroes from their worshippers. "This thing of being a hero, about the main thing to it is to know when to die. Prolonged life has ruined more men than it ever made."[9] He did not have to worry. He died a few months short of his fifty-sixth birthday, at the height of his popularity, and the image of the American dream shattered with him.

The image of the dream remains fragmented today, for no one else has appeared to combine all the appeals that Rogers made. Bits of that comprehensiveness appear in many figures. The late Herb Shriner, who nasally intoned wry, rural Indiana comments, and Pat Buttram, skinning city slickers, are perhaps the best representations of the wise innocent, although Red Skelton is in the mold of the Adam with irrepressibly high spirits. Danny Kaye bears the look of the versatile Jack-of-all-trades and lover of humanity. Jack Benny, with his standard routines based upon his miserliness, is a distorted image of the self-made man. Bob Hope, snapping the whip at political parties and traveling incessantly, has about him the cast of the individualistic quester. Above all the figures mentioned so far, perhaps Arthur Godfrey, during the middle fifties, came closest to approximating the posture of Will Rogers. Godfrey—with his "friends," his farm, his flying, his occasional comments on "the American Way," and his hobnobbing with high political and military men—had for a time some of the same believability about him that Will Rogers had possessed.

The image, however, remains shattered. What of Will Rogers and the American public since that day in 1939 when he entered the national Hall of Fame? Available indications are that he is holding up remarkably well as a national hero. A decade and a world war after the unveiling of Rogers' bronze image in Statuary Hall, a writer for a national magazine observed that the nation regarded the cowboy philosopher as almost a legend:

> William Penn Adair Rogers has been dead a short time as history goes, but already he is enshrined as one of the great folk heroes of the U.S. Three western states— Oklahoma, California, and Colorado—have elaborate Will Rogers memorials which register the names of one million visitors each year. Other Will Rogers monuments and statues are scattered across the continent from Point Barrow, Alaska to Fort Worth, Texas. . . .Nov. 4 is an official statewide holiday in Oklahoma, and last year the federal government joined the observance by issuing a Will Rogers 3¢ stamp—the first time that such an honor has been conferred on a comedian.[10]

At about the same time, an English student of the American scene took a measure of the hero worship of Will Rogers, bracketing him with two other American heroes of legendary stature:

> A national memorial week was lately proclaimed for a man whose plane crashed in Alaska fourteen years ago, but there's no doubt that if he'd lived, the 4th of November 1949 would have seen a national day of thanksgiving unlike anything that can be imagined outside the resurrection of Mark Twain or Abraham Lincoln. On the 4th of November, we should have had the seventieth birthday of possibly the most endearing American of his time: Will Rogers.[11]

Perspectives

The passage of more than another decade and a half since such observations has apparently little dimmed memories of Rogers. The early fifties saw the production of a successful motion picture of his life. He is the subject not only of biographies for adults but also for children, and he continues to be immortalized in television biographies. An hour-long presentation by the National Broadcasting Company appeared annually from 1961-1963. A half-hour version of Rogers' life and career in a syndicated television series called "Biography" places him in the company, among others, of Franklin D. Roosevelt, the Duke and Duchess of Windsor, Winston Churchill, and Babe Ruth. In recognition not only of his role as Mr. Cowboy but also of the conjuring power of his name, officials of the National Cowboy Hall of Fame picked Will Rogers' name first among those to be enshrined there, together with such historical, legendary figures as Theodore Roosevelt and Charles Goodnight. In 1965, plans were announced to name the last of this country's Polaris submarines the *Will Rogers.*

In 1955, Senator A. S. Monroney of Oklahoma, speaking as a former Oklahoma newspaper reporter, remarked, "Today after many years, the memory of Oklahomans of Will Rogers is as fresh and great as his was for them during his lifetime."[12] In 1969, the memory was apparently strong for many other Americans: To the Claremore Memorial alone, thousands of visitors from all states of the Union made their pilgrimage.

They continue to come to the shrine: Parents, who were themselves children or teen-agers when Rogers died, holding quiet their children; old people, who truly were contemporary with Rogers; and visitors from foreign lands. Into the curator's office they come to tell what Will Rogers means to them, and the comment often is, "If Will Rogers were here, he could help us. He could help us through this difficult period that our country seems to be going into." Visitors see his saddles, his famous ropes, the battered typewriter from the crash, a diorama of his career, and photographic slides of his life; they listen to recorded excerpts from his radio talks; soon they will see an exact replica of the study in the Santa Monica ranch house where Rogers wrote many of his columns and speeches.

On the south exterior of the building, facing the tomb,

ᅠ

Will Rogers

they read memorial plaques that tell of his place in the American dream. On the plaque dedicated by the Cherokee Nation, Will Rogers is remembered as the American Adam and democrat:

WE HONOR THE MEMORY OF OKLAHOMA'S BELOVED NATIVE SON. A MODEST, UNSPOILED CHILD OF THE PLAINS, COWBOY, ACTOR, HUMORIST AND WORLD TRAVELER WHOSE HOMELY PHILOSOPHY AND SUPERIOR GIFTS BROUGHT LAUGHTER AND TEARS TO PRINCE AND COMMONER ALIKE. HIS AVERSION TO SHAM AND DECEIT, HIS LOVE OF CANDOR AND SINCERITY, COUPLED WITH ABOUNDING WIT AND AFFABLE REPARTEE, WON FOR HIM UNIVERSAL HOMAGE AND AN APPROPRIATE TITLE, "AMBASSADOR OF GOOD WILL."

The memorial from Variety Clubs International, with representations of Rogers in wild West shows, vaudeville, and the Ziegfeld Follies, makes clear his success: It reads,

TO THE MEMORY OF
WILL ROGERS
THE WORLD'S MOST BELOVED SHOWMAN
A GREAT HUMANITARIAN

Almost in a due line with the tomb is the plaque placed by the Air Transport Association, representing the scheduled airlines of the United States. On it, Rogers is the American Prometheus:

TO THE MEMORY OF
WILL ROGERS

1879   1935

HE SAW IN AIR TRANSPORTATION A NEW PAGE IN THE CHAPTER OF ENDLESS POSSIBILITIES [.] THROUGH HIS VISION COURAGE AND PERSEVERANCE THE CAUSE OF AIR TRANSPORT RECEIVED PHYSICAL ENCOURAGEMENT, MORAL ASSISTANCE AND GUIDING GENIUS AT A TIME WHEN SUCH SUPPORT WAS MOST NEEDED.

At the end of *Huckleberry Finn,* that all-American boy is planning to flee to the open spaces of Indian territory. He entered, and came out as Will Rogers, the all-American

276

man, who disappeared into the wilderness of Alaska. He was, and is, an embodiment of the great American dream.

Yet, in this day of the dying of the old generation, there may be another national image of Will Rogers waiting to be discovered by another generation, for each has to find for itself its icons. Perhaps Alistair Cooke was divining this legend of Will Rogers for Americans when he said (page 179), "He opened up the grave beneath their feet. . . ."

But that is another story.

1. For these comments relating Rogers' role as truth-teller, see *NYT,* 28 August 1927, p. 22; 12 January 1928, p. 29; 31 October 1926, III, p. 2; 19 November 1928, p. 22.

2. For these tributes, see *NYT,* 17 August 1935, p. 1; *The Daily Oklahoman,* 17 August 1935, p. 10.

3. *NYT,* 28 November 1935, p. 29; 5 November 1938, p. 21; remarks of Hoover on NBC broadcast of November 19, 1935, text in the Will Rogers Memorial, Claremore, Oklahoma.

4. Part Two of "Biography in Sound."

5. *Ibid.*

6. *NYT,* 25 October 1929, p. 31; 26 October 1929, p. 19. (See also the issues of 6 May 1931, p. 27; 15 May 1931, p. 25; 22 December 1932, p. 19; and 8 February 1933, p. 21.) *NYT,* 16 February 1934, p. 21.

7. Homer Croy, *Our Will Rogers,* 325; Allen spoke on Part One of "Biography in Sound."

8. Donald Day, *The Autobiography of Will Rogers,* xv; *NYT,* 3 November 1935, VII, p. 4.

9. For examples of Rogers' advocacy of religious tolerance, see *NYT,* 19 April 1927, p. 29, and 26 November 1928, p. 31; the World's Fair quote is in *NYT,* 20 June 1935, p. 21; 13 July 1928, p. 19.

10. Constance Rourke, *American Humor: A Study of the National Character,* 99.

11. James Truslow Adams, *The Epic of America,* 36 and 31.

12. Henry Nash Smith, *Virgin Land: The American West as Symbol and Myth,* 138.

13. The life span of the millennial dream is estimated by Perry Miller, "The Shaping of the American Character," *New England Quarterly,* 28 (December, 1955), 445. See also Russel B. Nye, *This Almost Chosen People: Essays in the History of American Ideas,* 188-94.

14. Marshall W. Fishwick, *American Heroes: Myth and Reality,* 144.

15. See Wesley Frank Craven, *The Colonies in Transition: 1660-1713,* 28, for a balancing of some historians' views of the undemocratic Puritan society; see also Craven's *The Legend of the Founding Fathers,* 20-22, for a discussion of some influences leading to religious toleration among the Puritans.

16. Leland Dewitt Baldwin, *The Meaning of America: Essays toward an Understanding of the American Spirit,* 44.

17. Quoted in Rutherford E. Delmage, "The American Idea of Progress, 1750-1800," *Proceedings of the American Philosophical Society,* 91 (December, 1947), 312.

18. Bernard Bailyn, *The Ideological Origins of the American Revolution,* 34-35. Chapters I and II provide much of the information on the image of conspiracy against liberty.

19. Raymond G. Gettell, *History of American Political Thought,* 89-90.

20. Thomas Paine, "Common Sense," in *Life and Writings of Thomas Paine,* Daniel Edwin Wheeler, ed., II, 1-2.

21. See the reprinted portion of a King Features column by Runyan in *Folks Say of Will Rogers: A Memorial Anecdotage,* William Howard Payne and Jake G. Lyons, eds., 207.

1. *NYT,* 22 July 1923, VII, p. 2; 18 November 1923, IX, p. 2; 24 February 1924, VIII, p. 2; *TDW,* 21 December 1924, IV, p. 4; *NYT,* 29 October 1926, p. 25; 24 November 1926, p. 25; 18 January 1927, p. 27; *TDW,* 10 April 1927, V, p. 5; 17 July 1927, III, p. 4; *NYT,* 29 June 1928, p. 7; *TDW,* 11 November 1928, V, p. 4; *NYT,* 4 January 1929, p. 27; *TDW,* 13 January 1929, V, p. 2; 11 May 1930, V, p. 1; 1 June 1930, V, p. 1; *NYT,* 10 October 1930, p. 25; 27 June 1932, p. 11; *TDW,* 3 September 1933, IV, p. 4; 30 December 1934, IV, p. 6; *NYT,* 11 July 1934, p. 19; 13 August 1935, p. 19.

2. Henry Bamford Parkes, *The American Experience: An Interpretation of the History and Civilization of the American People,* 337.

3. Frederic I. Carpenter, *American Literature and the Dream,* 28.

4. Walt Whitman, "Preface" in *Leaves of Grass: Comprehensive Reader's Edition,* Harold W. Blodgett and Scully Bradley, eds., 710; "Democratic Vistas," in *Leaves of Grass and Selected Prose,* John Kouwenhoven, ed., 482.

5. Leslie A. Fiedler, *An End to Innocence: Essays on Culture and Politics,* 132.

6. James Truslow Adams, *The Epic of America,* 405.

7. Ralph Waldo Emerson, "Self-Reliance" and "Experience" in *The Complete Essays and Other Writings of Ralph Waldo Emerson,* Brooks Atkinson, ed., 144, 166, 350, 162.

8. Preface to *Leaves of Grass,* Kouwenhoven, ed., 446.

9. Perry Miller, "The Shaping of the American Character," *New England Quarterly,* 28 (December, 1955), 449-50.

10. Constance Rourke, *American Humor: A Study of the National Character,* 75 and 99.

11. Marshall W. Fishwick, *American Heroes: Myth and Reality,* 59-60.

12. Frederick Jackson Turner, "Contributions of the West to American Democracy," reprinted in *The Frontier in American History,* 267.

13. Quoted in Henry Nash Smith, *Virgin Land: The American West as Symbol and Myth,* 198.

14. Ellsworth Collings, *The Old Home Ranch: The Will Rogers Range in the Indian Territory,* 33.

15. Betty Rogers, *Will Rogers: His Wife's Story,* 108.

16. Harold Keith, *Boy's Life of Will Rogers,* 30.

17. The letter is quoted in Gilbert Fite, *George N. Peek and the Fight for Farm Parity,* 4. Other facts given here on farm income are from the same source.

18. John D. Hicks, *Republican Ascendancy: 1921-1933,* 77.

19. Robert E. Spiller, *The Cycle of American Literature: An Essay in Historical Criticism,* 245.

20. *NYT,* 1 December 1927, p. 29.

21. Gamaliel Bradford, *The Quick and the Dead,* 252.

22. John Ward, "The Meaning of Lindbergh's Flight," *Studies in American Culture: Dominant Ideas and Images,* Joseph J. Kwiat and Mary C. Turpie, eds., 35-36.

23. *NYT,* 12 March 1932, p. 17.

24. See, respectively, Daniel G. Hoffman's *Paul Bunyan: Last of the Frontier Demigods* and Carpenter's *American Literature and the Dream.*

25. Jerome Beatty, "Betty Holds the Reins," *The American Magazine,* 110 (October, 1930), 62.

26. Charles W. Dwyer, quoted in *Folks Say of Will Rogers: A Memorial Anecdotage,* William Howard Payne and Jake G. Lyons, eds., 74.

27. Robert W. Ruhl, quoted *ibid.,* 188.

28. Rebroadcast on Part Two of "Biography in Sound: Will Rogers," produced by NBC News, May 22, 1955. For other testimony to the natural quality of Will Rogers' public image, see Irvin Cobb, quoted in *Folks Say of Will Rogers,* Payne and Lyons, eds., 79. See also Otis Ferguson, "Two Show Figures," *New Republic,* 84 (September 4, 1935), 104.

29. Quoted from *The Daily Herald* in "Will Rogers in London," *The Literary Digest,* 90 (August 28, 1926), 22; the passage quoted by Day is found in *Will Rogers: A Biography,* 191; see, finally, Ferguson, *New Republic,* 84 (September 4, 1935), 104.

30. Quoted in Day, *Will Rogers,* 159.

31. Miscellaneous Scrapbook # 1, Will Rogers Memorial.

32. Quoted in *Folks Say of Will Rogers,* Payne and Lyons, eds., 150.

33. Burns Mantle, quoted in Day, *Will Rogers,* 242.

34. Carl Stearns Clancy, "Aviation's Patron Saint," *Scientific American,* 141 (October, 1929), 283.

35. Quoted in *Folks Say of Will Rogers,* Payne and Lyons, eds., 192.

36. The concepts of material and formal identification are drawn from Kenneth Burke, *A Rhetoric of Motives.*

37. *NYT,* 13 August 1928, p. 19; 7 November 1931, p. 19.

38. *TDW,* 22 February 1925, V, p. 4. Much of this implies also an ideal of absence of prejudice and as such is appropriate also to the dream of freedom.

39. *TDW,* 17 June 1928, V, p. 4.

40. *TDW,* 9 May 1926, V, p. 3; *NYT,* 17 April 1930, p. 29.

41. To John D. Hicks, *Republican Ascendancy,* I am indebted for the metaphor.

42. *NYT,* 18 May 1934, p. 23; 16 September 1933, p. 15; 25 December 1933, p. 25.

43. *TDW,* 22 February 1925, V, p. 4.

44. *TDW,* 20 January 1925, IV, p. 6.

45. *TDW,* 12 July 1931, IV, p. 7.

46. *NYT,* 24 February 1930, p. 23.

47. "Unemployment," October 18, 1931, Radio Speeches, binder .005, Will Rogers Memorial, 31.

48. *NYT,* 1 March 1928, p. 27.

49. *NYT,* 13 February 1929, p. 23.

50. "Letters of a Self-Made Diplomat to His President," *The Saturday Evening Post,* 199 (August 21, 1926), 10 and 11.

51. *TDW,* 2 June 1929, V, p. 1.

52. *The Saturday Evening Post,* 199 (August 21, 1926), 170.

53. *TDW,* 9 May 1926, V, p. 3; "Plan Day," May 5, 1935, CBS text from sound recordings in Will Rogers Memorial.

54. *TDW,* 5 July 1931, IV, p. 9.

55. "Planning in Nutshells," April 21, 1935, CBS text from sound recording, Will Rogers Memorial; *TDW,* 29 October 1933, IV, p. 4.

56. *TDW,* 1 January 1933, IV, p. 4.

57. *TDW,* 3 May 1925, V, p. 6.

Will Rogers

58. "Letters of a Self-Made Diplomat to His President," *The Saturday Evening Post*, 199 (July 10, 1926), 53-54.
59. *NYT,* 7 February 1927, p. 21.
60. *TDW,* 17 March 1935, IV, p. 6; 15 July 1934, IV, p. 4.
61. *NYT,* 25 March 1931, p. 27; *TDW,* 16 December 1934, IV, p. 6.
62. *TDW,* 2 August 1931, IV, p. 7; *NYT,* 18 April 1934, p. 21; 9 August 1932, p. 19; 5 November 1934, p. 21.
63. *NYT,* 23 November 1934, p. 21.
64. *TDW,* 8 January 1933, IV, p. 4.
65. *Ibid.; NYT,* 11 March 1923, IX, p. 2.
66. Dixon Wecter, *The Hero in America: A Chronicle of Hero Worship,* 482, 485, 486.

Notes to Will Rogers, American Democrat

1. Walter Lippmann, *Public Opinion,* 311.
2. Quoted in James Truslow Adams, *The Epic of America,* 102.
3. Henry Bamford Parkes, *The American Experience: An Interpretation of the History and Civilization of the American People,* 193.
4. Ralph Waldo Emerson, "Politics," in *The Complete Essays and Other Writings of Ralph Waldo Emerson,* Brooks Atkinson, ed., 431-32.
5. Walt Whitman, "Democratic Vistas," *Leaves of Grass and Selected Prose,* John Kouwenhoven, ed., 471.
6. Henry Seidel Canby, *Walt Whitman: An American,* 265.
7. See Henry Alonzo Myers, "Whitman's Conception of the Spiritual Democracy," *American Literature,* 6 (June, 1934), 239-53.
8. Russel B. Nye, *This Almost Chosen People: Essays in the History of American Ideas,* 322.
9. Quoted in Francis Graham Wilson, *The American Political Mind: A Textbook in Political Theory,* 181-82.
10. See *ibid.,* 179-85 for a fuller account of these issues.
11. Quoted in Herbert Croly, *The Promise of American Life,* 15-16.
12. Walt Whitman, "Democratic Vistas," *Leaves of Grass,* 491, 492, 490.
13. *Ibid.,* 490.
14. Constance Rourke, *American Humor: A Study of the National Character,* 221.
15. Marshall W. Fishwick, *American Heroes: Myth and Reality,* 203.
16. William Albig, *Modern Public Opinion,* 145.
17. For further elaboration of ideas in this paragraph, see Wilson's *The American Political Mind* and Raymond G. Gettell's *History of American Political Thought.*
18. Betty Rogers, *Will Rogers: His Wife's Story,* 43.
19. Ellsworth Collings, *The Old Home Ranch: The Will Rogers Range in the Indian Territory,* 33.
20. Quoted in Homer Croy, *Our Will Rogers,* 5-6.
21. Donald Day, *Will Rogers: A Biography,* 11.
22. Quoted in David Milsten, *An Appreciation of Will Rogers,* 71.
23. Quoted in *Folks Say of Will Rogers: A Memorial Anecdotage,* William Howard Payne and Jake G. Lyons, eds., 116.

24. Details of the show from Harold Keith, *Boy's Life of Will Rogers,* 68.
25. Woodrow Wilson, *The New Freedom: A Call for the Emancipation of the Generous Energies of a People,* 284, 282-83.
26. John D. Hicks, *Republican Ascendancy: 1921-1933,* 23.
27. Quoted in *The Talkative President: The Off-the-Record Press Conferences of Calvin Coolidge,* Howard H. Quint and Robert H. Ferrell, eds., 113. The editors say this is Coolidge's "most famous remark" (page 113); William Allen White, in *A Puritan in Babylon: The Story of Calvin Coolidge,* 282, refers to the statement as Coolidge's "American ideal."
28. *NYT,* 28 August 1928, p. 25.
29. John Morton Blum, *The Promise of America: An Historical Inquiry,* 111.
30. Gilbert C. Fite, *George N. Peek and the Fight for Farm Parity,* 122.
31. Quoted *ibid.,* 124.
32. *NYT,* 14 April 1927, p. 29.
33. *NYT,* 16 April 1930, p. 31; 5 September 1928, p. 29; the study of 1928 election results is from Ruth C. Silva, *Rum, Religion, and Votes,* 50.
34. *NYT,* 16 January 1931, p. 3; 6 March 1933, p. 15.
35. Dixon Wecter, *The Age of the Great Depression, 1929-1941,* 150, has the estimate; Rogers' comment appeared in *NYT,* 14 September 1934, p. 29.
36. H. L. Mencken, *The Philosophy of Friedrich Nietzsche,* 102-3.
37. "Will Rogers meant more in Morrow's winning Mexican regard than has been appraised," believes Josephus Daniels, *Shirt-Sleeve Diplomat,* 273.
38. *NYT,* 4 September 1932, IX, p. 4.
39. *NYT,* 1 July 1917, VIII, p. 6.
40. *NYT,* 3 October 1915, VI, p. 6; *Shawnee* (Okla.) *Morning News,* quoted in *Folks Say of Will Rogers,* Payne and Lyons, eds., 20.
41. Quoted *ibid.,* 202.
42. Monroney's story is told in Part Two of "Biography in Sound: Will Rogers," produced by NBC News, May 22, 1955.
43. Brougher is quoted in *Folks Say of Will Rogers,* Payne and Lyons, eds., 205-6. Monroney spoke in Part Two of "Biography in Sound."
44. *NYT,* 1 October 1934, p. 19.
45. *TDW,* 13 November 1927, VII, p. 4.
46. *Ibid.*
47. *NYT,* 11 May 1924, IX, p. 2; CBS broadcast, April 21, 1935; *TDW,* 18 January 1931, VI, p. 7.
48. *TDW,* 23 November 1924, IV, p. 4; 30 July 1933, IV, p. 4.
49. *NYT,* 18 April 1933, p. 17; *TDW,* 6 November 1927, VII, p. 4.
50. *TDW,* 12 May 1929, V, p. 1; 13 September 1932, p. 1; *NYT,* 18 April 1933, p. 17.
51. *TDW,* 22 February 1925, V, p. 4; *NYT,* 8 March 1930, p. 19; 26 November 1930, p. 21; CBS broadcast, October 14, 1934.
52. *NYT,* 19 April 1934, p. 27; 29 December 1934, p. 17.
53. *TDW,* 8 January 1933, IV, p. 4; "Letters of a Self-Made Diplomat to His President," *The Saturday Evening Post,* 199 (December 4, 1926), 230; *TDW,* 19 July 1925, V, p. 3.
54. *NYT,* 19 February 1927, p. 17.
55. *NYT,* 7 February 1929, p. 27; 25 January 1928, p. 25; 19 April 1927, p. 29.
56. *NYT,* 9 November 1928, p. 27; 18 December 1926, p. 19; 22 May 1933, p. 17; quoted in *Folks Say of Will Rogers,* Payne and Lyons, eds., 112.
57. *NYT,* 16 April 1932, p. 17.

Will Rogers

58. *TDW,* 8 May 1927, V, p. 5.

59. *NYT,* 27 February 1931, p. 21; 9 March 1927, p. 27; *TDW,* 30 June 1929, V, p. 1.

60. *TDW,* 24 May 1925, V, p. 4.

61. *NYT,* 8 November 1927, p. 29; *TDW,* 16 March 1930, V, p. 1.

62. *NYT,* 31 March 1931, p. 29; 11 July 1933, p. 19; 25 May 1935, p. 17.

63. *NYT,* 13 March 1933, p. 15; *TDW,* 10 August 1930, V, p. 1; *NYT,* 9 February 1935, p. 17.

64. *TDW,* 28 February 1926, V, p. 3.

65. NBC and CBS broadcast, August 27, 1933.

66. NBC and CBS broadcast, October 18, 1931; *NYT,* 5 October 1932, p. 23.

67. *TDW,* 8 January 1933, IV, p. 4.

68. *NYT,* 19 March 1927, p. 19; *The Saturday Evening Post,* 201 (March 30, 1929), 161.

69. *NYT,* 5 November 1928, p. 25; Dorothy Van Doren, "Will Rogers," *The Nation,* 127 (October 3, 1928), 314.

70. *TDW,* 9 November 1924, IV, p. 4; 30 October 1932, IV, p. 8.

71. Text of broadcast from *NYT,* 15 November 1932, p. 2; *TDW,* 21 April 1935, IV, p. 6.

72. *NYT,* 19 July 1934, p. 19.

73. *TDW,* 14 December 1927, IV, p. 2; *NYT,* 10 January 1927, p. 25; 9 February 1928, p. 27.

74. *NYT,* 23 January 1934, p. 21; *The Saturday Evening Post,* 204 (March 12, 1932), 97, 100; *NYT,* 10 October 1934, p. 25; *TDW,* 6 May 1930, p. 1.

75. Text from file of speeches collected by Donald Day, Will Rogers Memorial.

76. *The Saturday Evening Post,* 199 (January 8, 1927), 6-7; (July 24, 1926), 129-30; *TDW,* 18 February 1934, IV, p. 4; quoted in *Scientific American,* 141 (October, 1929), 285-86. See also *TDW,* 17 June 1928, V, p. 4.

77. *The Saturday Evening Post,* 199 (January 8, 1927), 230; *NYT,* 9 September 1923, VIII, p. 2.

78. *The Saturday Evening Post,* 199 (August 21, 1926), 10.

79. *NYT,* 26 October 1929, p. 31; 21 October 1932, p. 23.

80. *TDW,* 29 July 1934, IV, p. 4.

81. *TDW,* 14 November 1926, V, p. 4.

82. Quoted in Rogers, *His Wife's Story,* 135.

83. Jerome Beatty, "Betty Holds the Reins," *The American Magazine,* 110 (October, 1930), 61.

Notes to Will Rogers, Self-Made Man

1. *TDW,* 30 December 1934, IV, p. 6. For full-length treatments of the literary and subliterary materials on the success dream, see Kenneth S. Lynn's *The Dream of Success: A Study of the Modern American Imagination* and Irvin G. Wyllie's *The Self-Made Man in America: The Myth of Rags to Riches.*

2. Henry Ward Beecher, *Addresses to Young Men,* 26-28.

3. Quoted in Wyllie, p. 36.

4. Albert Beveridge. *The Young Man and the World,* 56, 54.

284

5. Russell Conwell, "Acres of Diamonds," in Agnes Rush Burr, *Russell H. Conwell and His Work*, 414-15; Ralph Waldo Emerson, "Wealth," in *The Complete Essays and Other Writings of Ralph Waldo Emerson*, Brooks Atkinson, ed., 700.

6. Daniel Boorstin, *The Americans: The National Experience*, 29, 31-33.

7. Quoted by Walt Whitman, "Democratic Vistas," *Walt Whitman: Complete Poetry and Selected Prose*, James E. Miller, Jr., ed., 457.

8. Russel B. Nye, *This Almost Chosen People: Essays in the History of American Ideas*, 105.

9. Kingsley Davis, Harry C. Bredemeier, and Marion J. Levy, *Modern American Society: Readings in the Problems of Order and Change*, 41.

10. Beecher, *Addresses to Young Men*, 21-22.

11. Marshall W. Fishwick, *American Heroes: Myth and Reality*, 157.

12. Matthew H. Smith, "Elements of Success in Business," *Hunt's Merchant's Magazine*, 31 (July, 1854), 56.

13. John Morton Blum, *The Promise of America: An Historical Inquiry*, 39.

14. "Wealth," *Complete Essays and Other Writings*, Atkinson, ed., 702, 715.

15. Betty Rogers, *Will Rogers: His Wife's Story*, 34.

16. Quoted *ibid.*, 64, 68-69.

17. Homer Croy, *Our Will Rogers*, 82.

18. Quoted in Rogers, *His Wife's Story*, 79; Rogers' comments on Texas Jack are quoted on p. 78.

19. See Lynn, *The Dream of Success*, 122-23.

20. James Truslow Adams, *The Epic of America*, 398.

21. John D. Hicks, *Republican Ascendancy: 1921-1933*, 118.

22. *NYT*, 5 January 1929, p. 21; "Talks to Bankers" from sound recording in Will Rogers Memorial; the original talk was probably made in the 1920's.

23. Gamaliel Bradford, *The Quick and the Dead*, 252-53.

24. Daniel G. Hoffman, *Paul Bunyan: Last of the Frontier Demigods*, 103-5.

25. Robert E. Spiller, *The Cycle of American Literature: An Essay in Historical Criticism*, 223.

26. *NYT*, 26 December 1929, p. 17.

27. See Dixon Wecter, *The Age of the Great Depression, 1929-1941*, 33; Wyllie, *The Self-Made Man in America*, 173, quotes Babson.

28. *NYT*, 28 September 1926, p. 29.

29. *NYT*, 2 June 1927, p. 11.

30. *NYT*, 2 June 1927, p. 11; 28 June 1927, p. 12.

31. *NYT*, 9 April 1931, p. 18.

32. Jerome Beatty, "Betty Holds the Reins," *The American Magazine*, 110 (October, 1930), 61.

33. *NYT*, 1 July 1917, VIII, p. 6; 14 October 1934, X, p. 5.

34. Quoted in *Folks Say of Will Rogers*, Payne and Lyons, eds., 194.

35. *NYT*, 2 July 1931, p. 27; "The Hoofing Kid from Claremore," *The American Magazine*, 107 (April, 1929), 34.

36. *Ibid.*, 175.

37. "Coolidge," *The American Magazine*, 107 (June, 1929), 88; *NYT*, 17 April 1930, p. 29.

38. "The World's Best Loser," *The American Magazine*, 110 (September, 1930), 30, 131-32, 133.

39. "The Grand Champion," *The American Magazine*, 108 (December,

1929), 34-35; "Henry Ford," broadcast of June 1, 1930, in *Wit and Philosophy from the Radio Talks of America's Humorist, Will Rogers*, 35.

40. *NYT*, 28 March 1928, p. 29; *TDW*, 25 October 1925, V, p. 5.

41. *The American Magazine*, 108 (December, 1929), 34; *TDW*, 4 January 1925, II, p. 12.

42. *NYT*, 29 December 1927, p. 25; 12 June 1929, p. 31; *TDW*, 20 July 1930, V, p. 1.

43. *NYT*, 31 August 1924, VIII, p. 2; *TDW*, 7 March 1926, V, p. 3.

44. *TDW*, 29 July 1934, IV, p. 4; 24 March 1934, IV, p. 6.

45. *TDW*, 15 November 1925, V, p. 5.

46. *TDW*, 29 July 1928, V, p. 4.

47. *NYT*, 28 May 1927, p. 19; *TDW*, 8 May 1927, V, p. 5.

48. *NYT*, 7 January 1931, p. 27; 23 January 1931, p. 25; broadcast text from *NYT*, 23 January 1931, p. 17.

49. *NYT*, 31 January 1931, p. 19; 1 February 1931, p. 23.

50. NBC and CBS broadcast, October 18, 1931; *NYT*, 23 March 1932, p. 23.

51. *TDW*, 21 January 1934, IV, p. 4.

52. Paula McSpadden Love, *The Will Rogers Book*, 137.

53. *NYT*, 9 April 1931, p. 18.

54. *TDW*, 31 December 1933, IV, p. 4.

Notes to Will Rogers, American Prometheus

1. *The Essays, Humor, and Poems of Nathaniel Ames*, Sam Briggs, ed., 285-86.

2. Francis Graham Wilson, *The American Political Mind: A Textbook in Political Theory*, 175.

3. "Culture," *The Complete Essays and Other Writings of Ralph Waldo Emerson*, Brooks Atkinson, ed., 736.

4. "Emerson and the Idea of Progress," *American Literature*, 12 (March, 1940-June, 1941), 19.

5. Whitman's comment is in *Leaves of Grass and Selected Prose*, John Kouwenhoven, ed., 479.

6. Russel Nye, *This Almost Chosen People: Essays in the History of American Ideas*, 230.

7. James Truslow Adams, *The Epic of America*, 216-17.

8. "The American Heritage of Hope, 1865-1940," *The Mississippi Valley Historical Review*, 37 (June, 1950-March, 1951), 442.

9. Henry George, *Progress and Poverty*, 405-6.

10. V. L. Parrington, Jr., *American Dreams: A Study of American Utopias*, 69-70.

11. See *ibid.*, 74-87, 180-81, and 189-91.

12. *Ibid.*, 28-34, 46-47, 167-70.

13. Quoted in R. W. B. Lewis, *The American Adam: Innocence, Tragedy, and Tradition in the Nineteenth Century*, 34.

14. Charles L. Sanford, *The Quest for Paradise: Europe and the American Moral Imagination*, 11.

15. Henry Bamford Parkes, *The American Experience: An Interpretation of the History and Civilization of the American People*, 78.

16. Quoted in Herbert Croly, *The Promise of American Life*, 18.

17. Daniel J. Boorstin, *The Americans: The National Experience*, 222.

18. Marshall Fishwick, *American Heroes: Myth and Reality*, 123.

19. Matthew Josephson, *Edison: A Biography*, 434, 479.

20. Dixon Wecter, *The Age of the Great Depression, 1929-1941*, 418.

21. Betty Rogers, *Will Rogers: His Wife's Story*, 82.

22. Frederic I. Carpenter, "The American Myth: Paradise (to be) Regained," *PMLA*, 74 (December, 1959), 601.

23. John W. Ward, "The Meaning of Lindbergh's Flight," *Studies in American Culture: Dominant Ideas and Images*, Joseph J. Kwiat and Mary C. Turpie, eds., 36.

24. R. G. Collingwood, "Oswald Spengler and the Theory of Historical Cycles," *Antiquity*, 1 (September, 1927), 311-25; John R. Willingham, "The Whitman Tradition in Recent American Literature," 165, 167-68.

25. John D. Hicks, *Republican Ascendancy: 1921-1933*, 167.

26. Quoted in Wecter, *The Age of the Great Depression*, 35.

27. See Hicks, *Republican Ascendancy*, 265, 271-74, 218-39, 224, 264-65, 270; Rogers' comment is in *NYT*, 27 November 1930, p. 25.

28. Commentators are quoted in A. M. Schlesinger, Jr., *The Age of Roosevelt*, Vol. I, *The Crisis of the Old Order: 1919-1933*, 459; Rogers is in *NYT*, 23 December 1932, p. 19.

29. *Toward Civilization*, Charles Beard, ed., 304-5, copyrighted by Longmans, Green & Co., Inc., New York, 1930.

30. *NYT*, 23 December 1932, p. 19.

31. See Schlesinger, *The Crisis of the Old Order*, 461-64.

32. C. C. Furnas, *The Next Hundred Years: The Unfinished Business of Science*, 2.

33. Carl Stearns Clancy, "Aviation's Patron Saint," *Scientific American*, 141 (October, 1929), 284.

34. *TDW*, 20 January 1935, IV, p. 6; 5 July 1931, IV, p. 9; 6 September 1931, V, p. 5.

35. *NYT*, 19 April 1933, p. 19.

36. NBC and CBS broadcast, October 18, 1931; *TDW*, 18 January 1931, IV, p. 7.

37. *TDW*, 17 June 1934, IV, p. 4; *NYT*, 27 December 1932, p. 15.

38. *NYT*, 8 April 1931, p. 25; NBC broadcast, July 8, 1934; *NYT*, 24 February 1930, p. 23.

39. *NYT*, 29 June 1934, p. 21; 15 April 1927, p. 23; *TDW*, 11 December 1927, I, p. 12.

40. *NYT*, 29 May 1930, p. 25.

41. *NYT*, 30 June 1931, p. 27; 16 February 1935, p. 15.

42. *NYT*, 29 April 1933, p. 15; *TDW*, 1 March 1931, IV, p. 5; *NYT*, 23 October 1933, p. 17.

43. *TDW*, 13 January 1929, V, p. 2; "Letters of a Self-Made Diplomat to Senator Borah," *The Saturday Evening Post*, 204 (April 2, 1932), 21, 52.

44. *NYT*, 24 June 1930, p. 27.

45. *NYT*, 1 January 1934, p. 25; *TDW*, 14 July 1935, IV, p. 4; *NYT*, 6 August 1935, p. 19.

46. *NYT*, 22 July 1923, VII, p. 2.

47. *The Saturday Evening Post*, 204 (April 2, 1932), 82; *NYT*, 30 March 1928, p. 27; 30 November 1926, p. 31; 7 March 1927, p. 21; 17 February 1930, p. 23; 29 May 1933, p. 15.

48. *NYT*, 26 November 1929, p. 31; 24 January 1935, p. 21; 19 September 1929, p. 33.

Will Rogers

49. *TDW,* 17 April 1927, V, p. 5.

50. *NYT,* 19 October 1927, p. 29; 20 October 1927, p. 31.

51. "Flying and Eating My Way from Coast to Coast," *The Saturday Evening Post,* 200 (January 28, 1928), 38, 40.

52. *TDW,* 3 November 1929, V, p. 1.

53. *NYT,* 14 December 1927, p. 31; 17 April 1931, p. 25.

54. *NYT,* 28 July 1934, p. 15; 30 July 1934, p. 15; 24 August 1934, p. 17; "Letters of a Self-Made Diplomat to His President," *The Saturday Evening Post,* 199 (October 23, 1926), 164.

55. *NYT,* 18 January 1932, p. 17; *TDW,* 24 March 1935, IV, p. 6.

56. "Florida Versus California," *The Saturday Evening Post,* 198 (May 29, 1926), 72.

57. NBC broadcast, July 8, 1934.

58. *TDW,* 18 September 1932, IV, p. 6.

59. Homer Croy, *Our Will Rogers,* 293; Cox is quoted in *Folks Say of Will Rogers: A Memorial Anecdotage,* William Howard Payne and Jake G. Lyons, eds., 159.

60. *NYT,* 8 August 1935, p. 19; 9 August 1935, p. 19; 12 August 1935, p. 17; 15 August 1935, p. 21.

Notes to Perspectives

1. Roy P. Basler, *The Lincoln Legend: A Study in Changing Conceptions,* 131.

2. Remarks of Leon C. Phillips, in U. S. Congress, House, Joint Committee on Printing. *Acceptance of the Statue of Will Rogers: Presented by the State of Oklahoma.* House Doc. 471. 76th Cong., 1st sess., 1939, pp. 23-24, 26.

3. *Ibid.,* 36.

4. *Ibid.,* 30.

5. *Ibid.,* 48-49.

6. *Ibid.,* 30-31.

7. "Letters of a Self-Made Diplomat to His President," *The Saturday Evening Post,* 199 (July 31, 1926), 82.

8. Muzafer Sherif and Carolyn W. Sherif, *An Outline of Social Psychology,* 53.

9. *NYT,* 18 July 1928, p. 23.

10. Roger Butterfield, "The Legend of Will Rogers," *Life,* 27 (July 18, 1949), 78.

11. Alistair Cooke, *One Man's America,* 173-74.

12. Part Two of "Biography in Sound," produced by NBC News, May 22, 1955.

Bibliography

PRIMARY SOURCES

Published Materials by Will Rogers

"Bucking a Head Wind." *The Saturday Evening Post*, 200 (January 28, 1928), 6-7, 36, 38, 40.

"Coolidge." *The American Magazine*, 107 (June, 1929), 20-21, 88, 90, 92, 94.

Daily column for the McNaught Syndicate from 15 October 1926 to 15 August 1935, carried by *The New York Times*.

"Florida Versus California." *The Saturday Evening Post*, 198 (May 29, 1926), 10-11, 70-72.

"Flying and Eating My Way from Coast to Coast." *The Saturday Evening Post*, 200 (January 21, 1928), 3-4, 110, 113-14, 117.

"The Grand Champion." *The American Magazine*, 108 (December, 1929), 34-37.

"The Hoofing Kid from Claremore." *The American Magazine*, 107 (April, 1929), 34-35, 175.

"A Letter from a Self-Made Diplomat to His Constituents." *The Saturday Evening Post*, 199 (January 8, 1927), 6-7, 230, 233-34, 238.

"Letters of a Self-Made Diplomat to His President." *The Saturday Evening Post*, 199 (June 10, 1926), 3-4; (July 10, 1926), 53-54; (July 17, 1926), 6-7, 157-58, 161-62; (July 24, 1926), 10-11, 126, 129-30; (August 21, 1926), 10-11, 169-70; (October 23, 1926), 6-7, 158, 161-62, 164; (December 4, 1926), 6-7, 222, 225-26, 230.

"Letters of a Self-Made Diplomat to His President." *The Saturday Evening Post*, 200 (May 12, 1928), 3-4, 192; (June 9, 1928), 18-19, 40-42, 44.

"Letters of a Self-made Diplomat to Senator Borah." *The Saturday Evening Post*, 204 (March 5, 1932), 8-9, 86, 88, 90; (March 12, 1932), 8-9, 96-97, 100; (March 19, 1932), 6-7, 79-82; (April 2, 1932), 21, 51-52.

"Mr. Toastmaster and Democrats." *The Saturday Evening Post*, 201 (March 30, 1929), 3-5, 161.

Sunday column for the McNaught Syndicate from 24 December 1922 to 28 September 1924. Carried by *The New York Times*.

Sunday column for the McNaught Syndicate from 5 October 1924 to 25 August 1935. Carried by *The Tulsa Daily World*.

Texts or reports of thirty-seven speeches from 1922 to 1935 (including banquet speeches, lectures, and a few radio talks) published by *The New York Times.*

Wit and Philosophy from the Radio Talks of America's Humorist, Will Rogers. New York: E. R. Squibb & Sons, 1930.

"The World's Best Loser." *The American Magazine,* 110 (September, 1930), 30, 131-33.

Unpublished Materials by Will Rogers

Miscellaneous speech texts, available in file gathered by Donald Day, Will Rogers Memorial, Claremore, Oklahoma.

Radio Speeches, Binder .005, Will Rogers Memorial, Claremore, Oklahoma.

Seventeen radio talks, mostly between 1934 and 1935, available in phonographic recordings, Will Rogers Memorial, Claremore, Oklahoma.

SECONDARY SOURCES

Books

Adams, James Truslow, *The Epic of America.* Boston, Little, Brown and Company, 1941.

Albig, William, *Modern Public Opinion.* New York, McGraw-Hill Book Co., 1956.

American Poetry and Prose, Norman Foerster, ed. 4th ed. rev. Boston, Houghton Mifflin Co., 1957.

The Autobiography of Will Rogers, Donald Day, ed. Boston, Houghton Mifflin Co., 1949.

Bailyn, Bernard, *The Ideological Origins of the American Revolution.* Cambridge, The Belknap Press of Harvard University Press, 1967.

Baldwin, Leland Dewitt, *The Meaning of America: Essays toward an Understanding of the American Spirit.* Pittsburgh, University of Pittsburgh Press, 1955.

Basler, Roy P., *The Lincoln Legend: A Study in Changing Conceptions.* Boston, Houghton Mifflin Co., 1935.

Beecher, Henry Ward, *Addresses to Young Men.* Philadelphia, Henry Altemus, n.d.

——, *Life Thoughts.* Boston, Phillips, Sampson and Co., 1858.

Beveridge, Albert, *The Young Man and the World.* New York, D. Appleton & Co., 1923.

Blair, Walter, *Native American Humor: 1800-1900.* New York, American Book Co., 1937.

Bibliography

Blum, John Morton, *The Promise of America: An Historical Inquiry.* Boston, Houghton Mifflin Co., 1966.

Boorstin, Daniel J., *The Americans: The National Experience.* New York, Random House, 1965.

Bradford, Gamaliel, *The Quick and the Dead.* Boston, Houghton Mifflin Co., 1931.

Burke, Kenneth, *A Rhetoric of Motives.* New York, Prentice-Hall, Inc., 1950.

Burr, Agnes Rush, *Russell H. Conwell and His Work.* Philadelphia, John C. Winston Co., 1917.

Bury, J. G., *The Idea of Progress.* Introduction by Charles A. Beard. New York, Dover Publications, 1955.

Canby, Henry Seidel, *Walt Whitman: An American.* Boston, Houghton Mifflin Co., 1943.

Carpenter, Frederic I., *American Literature and the Dream.* New York, Philosophical Library, Inc., 1955.

Collings, Ellsworth, *The Old Home Ranch: The Will Rogers Range in the Indian Territory.* Stillwater, Okla., Redlands Press, 1964.

The Complete Essays and Other Writings of Ralph Waldo Emerson, Brooks Atkinson, ed. Foreword by Tremaine McDowell. New York, Modern Library, 1950.

Cooke, Alistair, *One Man's America.* New York, Alfred A. Knopf, Inc., 1952.

Craven, Wesley Frank, *The Colonies in Transition: 1660-1713.* New York, Harper & Row, 1968.

————, *The Legend of the Founding Fathers.* New York, New York University Press, 1956.

Croly, Herbert, *The Promise of American Life.* New York, The Macmillan Co., 1911.

Croy, Homer, *Our Will Rogers.* New York, Duell, Sloan & Pearce, Inc., 1953.

Daniels, Josephus, *Shirt-Sleeve Diplomat.* Chapel Hill, The University of North Carolina Press, 1947.

Davis, Kingsley, Harry C. Bredemeier, and Marion J. Levy, *Modern American Society: Readings in the Problems of Order and Change.* New York, Rinehart & Co., 1949.

Day, Donald, *Will Rogers: A Biography.* New York, David McKay & Co., Inc., 1962.

Emerson, Ralph Waldo, *The Complete Essays and Other Writings of Ralph Waldo Emerson,* Brooks Atkinson, ed. New York, Random House, Inc., 1950.

The Essays, Humor, and Poems of Nathaniel Ames, Sam Briggs, ed. Cleveland, privately printed, 1891.

Fiedler, Leslie A., *An End to Innocence: Essays on Culture and Politics*. Boston, the Beacon Press, Inc., 1955.

Fifty Years of Popular Mechanics: 1902-1952, Edward L. Throm, ed. New York, Simon & Schuster, Inc., 1952.

Fishwick, Marshall William, *American Heroes: Myth and Reality*. Washington, D. C., Public Affairs Press, 1954.

Fite, Gilbert C., *George N. Peek and the Fight for Farm Parity*. Norman, University of Oklahoma Press, 1954.

Folks Say of Will Rogers: A Memorial Anecdotage, William Howard Payne, and Jake G. Lyons, eds. New York, G. P. Putnam's Sons, 1936.

Furnas, C. C., *The Next Hundred Years: The Unfinished Business of Science*. New York, Reynal & Hitchcock, 1936.

George, Henry, *Progress and Poverty*. New York, Robert Schalkenbach Foundation, 1955.

Gettell, Raymond G., *History of American Political Thought*. New York, Century Co., 1928.

Hart, William S., *My Life East and West*. Boston, Houghton Mifflin Co., 1929.

Hicks, John D., *Republican Ascendancy: 1921-1933*. The New American Nation Series, Henry Steele Commager, and Richard B. Morris, eds. New York, Harper & Row, Publishers, Inc., 1960.

Hitch, Arthur Martin, *Will Rogers, Cadet: A Record of His Two Years as a Cadet at the Kemper Military School*. Boonville, Mo., privately printed, 1935.

Hoffman, Daniel G., *Paul Bunyan: Last of the Frontier Demigods*. Philadelphia, University of Pennyslvania Press for Temple University Publications, 1952.

Holbrook, Stewart H., *Dreamers of the American Dream*. New York, Doubleday & Co., Inc., 1957.

Howard, Leon, *Literature and the American Tradition*. Garden City, Doubleday & Co., Inc., 1960.

Jackson, Hollbrook, *Dreamers of Dreams: The Rise and Fall of Nineteenth Century Idealism*. New York, Farrar, Straus & Co., 1949.

Josephson, Matthew, *Edison: A Biography*. New York, McGraw-Hill Book Co., Inc., 1959.

Journals of Ralph Waldo Emerson, Edward Waldo Emerson, and Waldo Emerson Forbes, eds. Vols. III, V, VIII. Boston, Houghton Mifflin Co., 1909-1914. 10 vols.

Keith, Harold, *Boy's Life of Will Rogers*. New York, Thomas Y. Crowell, Co., 1937.

Bibliography

Langer, Susanne K., *Philosophy in a New Key: A Study in the Symbolism of Reason, Rite, and Art.* New York, Mentor Books, 1960.

Lerner, Max, *America as a Civilization.* New York, Simon & Schuster, Inc., 1957.

Lewis, R. W. B., *The American Adam: Innocence, Tragedy and Tradition in the Nineteenth Century.* Chicago, University of Chicago Press, 1955.

Lippmann, Walter, *Public Opinion.* New York, The Macmillan Co., 1922.

Love, Paula McSpadden, *The Will Rogers Book.* Indianapolis, Bobbs-Merrill Co., 1961.

Lynn, Kenneth S., *The Dream of Success: A Study of the Modern American Imagination.* Boston, Little, Brown & Co., 1955.

Lyons, Eugene, *The Red Decade: The Stalinist Penetration of America.* Indianapolis, Bobbs-Merrill Co., 1941.

Macdougall, Curtis D., *Understanding Public Opinion: A Guide for Newspapermen and Newspaper Readers.* New York, The Macmillan Co., 1952.

Marx, Leo, *The Machine in the Garden: Technology and the Pastoral Ideal in America.* New York, Oxford University Press, 1964.

Mencken, H. L., *The Philosophy of Friedrich Nietzsche.* Boston, John W. Luce, Co., 1913.

Milsten, David, *An Appreciation of Will Rogers.* San Antonio, Naylor Co., 1935.

Noble, David W., *The Eternal Adam and the New World Garden: The Central Myth in the American Novel Since 1830.* New York, George Braziller, Inc., 1968.

Nye, Russel B., *This Almost Chosen People: Essays in the History of American Ideas.* East Lansing, Michigan State University Press, 1966.

Paine, Thomas, "Common Sense," *Life and Writings of Thomas Paine,* Daniel Edwin Wheeler, ed. Vol. II. New York, Vincent Parke and Company, 1908. 10 vols.

Parkes, Henry Bamford, *The American Experience: An Interpretation of the History and Civilization of the American people.* 2d ed. rev. New York, Alfred A. Knopf, Inc., 1955.

Parrington, Vernon L., Jr., *American Dreams: A Study of American Utopias.* Providence, Brown University Press, 1947.

Pasley, Fred D., *Al Capone: The Biography of a Self-Made Man.* Garden City, Garden City Publishing Co., 1930.

Phillips, Leon C., remarks in U. S. Congress, House, Joint Committee on Printing. *Acceptance of the Statue of Will Rogers: Presented by the State of Oklahoma.* House Doc. 471. 76th Cong., 1st sess., 1939.

Rocker, Rudolf, *Pioneers of American Freedom: Origin of Liberal and Radical Thought in America,* trans. by Arthur E. Briggs. Los Angeles, Rocker Publications Committee, 1949.

Rogers, Betty, *Will Rogers: His Wife's Story.* New York, Bobbs-Merrill, 1941; Garden City, Garden City Publishing Co., 1943.

Rourke, Constance, *American Humor: A Study of the National Character.* New York, Harcourt, Brace & Co., 1931.

Sanford, Charles L., *The Quest for Paradise: Europe and the American Moral Imagination.* Urbana, University of Illinois Press, 1961.

Schlesinger, A. M., Jr., *The Age of Jackson,* Donald P. Geddes, ed. New York, Mentor Books, 1949.

———, *The Age of Roosevelt,* Vol. I, *The Crisis of the Old Order: 1919-1933.* Boston, Houghton Mifflin, 1957. 3 vols.

Sherif, Muzafer, and Carolyn W. Sherif, *An Outline of Social Psychology,* 2d ed. rev. New York, Harper & Brothers, 1956.

Silva, Ruth C., *Rum, Religion, and Votes.* University Park, Pennsylvania State University Press, 1962.

Smith, Henry Nash, *Virgin Land: The American West as Symbol and Myth.* New York, Vintage Books, 1957.

Spiller, Robert E., *The Cycle of American Literature: An Essay in Historical Criticism.* New York, The Macmillan Co., 1955.

The Talkative President: The Off-the-Record Press Conferences of Calvin Coolidge, Howard H. Quint, and Robert H. Ferrell, eds. Amherst, University of Massachusetts Press, 1964.

Taylor, Deems, Marcelene Peterson, and Hale Bryant, *A Pictorial History of the Movies.* New York, Simon & Schuster, Inc., 1943.

Thoreau, Henry D., *The Portable Thoreau,* Carl Bode, ed. New York, The Viking Press, 1947.

———, *The Works of Henry D. Thoreau.* New York, Thomas Y. Crowell Company, 1940.

Thoreau: People, Principles, and Politics, Milton Meltzer, ed. American Century Series, New York, Hill & Wang, Inc., 1963.

Toward Civilization, Charles Beard, ed. New York, Longmans, Green & Co., Inc., 1930.

Turner, Frederick Jackson, *The Frontier in American History.* New York, Henry Holt and Co., 1920, 1948.

Walt Whitman: Complete Poetry and Selected Prose, James E. Miller, Jr., ed. Boston, Houghton Mifflin, 1959.

Bibliography

Ward, John J., "The Meaning of Lindbergh's Flight," in *Studies in American Culture: Dominant Ideas and Images,* Joseph J. Kwiat, and Mary C. Turpie, eds., Minneapolis, University of Minnesota Press, 1960.

Wecter, Dixon, *The Age of the Great Depression, 1929-1941.* Vol. XIII, in A History of American Life Series, Arthur M. Schlesinger, and Dixon Ryan Fox, eds. New York, The Macmillan Co., 1929-1948. 13 vols.

——, *The Hero in America: A Chronicle of Hero Worship.* New York, Charles Scribner's Sons, 1941.

White, William Allen, *A Puritan in Babylon: The Story of Calvin Coolidge.* New York, The Macmillan Company, 1938.

Whitman, Walt, *Leaves of Grass and Selected Prose,* John Kouwenhoven, ed. New York, Random House, Inc., 1950.

——, *Leaves of Grass: Comprehensive Reader's Edition,* Harold W. Blodgett, and Sculley Bradley, eds. New York, New York University Press, 1965.

Wilson, Edmund, *The American Earthquake.* New York, Doubleday & Co., Inc., 1958.

Wilson, Francis Graham, *The American Political Mind: A Textbook in Political Theory.* New York, McGraw-Hill Book Co., Inc., 1949.

Wilson, Woodrow, *The New Freedom: A Call for the Emancipation of the Generous Energies of a People.* New York, Doubleday, Page & Co., 1913.

Wyllie, Irvin G., *The Self-Made Man in America: The Myth of Rags to Riches.* New Brunswick, Rutgers University Press, 1954.

Articles and Periodicals

Atkinson, Will, Letter to the Editor. *The New York Times,* 11 February 1928.

Beatty, Jerome, "Betty Holds the Reins." *The American Magazine,* 110 (October, 1930), 60-62, 113-14, 116.

Butterfield, Roger, "The Legend of Will Rogers." *Life,* 27 (July 18, 1949), 78-82, 84, 86, 89-90, 92, 94.

Carpenter, Frederic I., "The American Myth: Paradise (to be) Regained." *PMLA,* 74 (December, 1959), 599-606.

Clancy, Carl Stearns, "Aviation's Patron Saint." *Scientific American,* 141 (October, 1929), 283-86.

Collingwood, R. G., "Oswald Spengler and the Theory of Historical Cycles." *Antiquity,* 1 (September, 1927), 311-25.

Cowley, Malcolm, "American Myths, Old and New." *The Saturday Review,* 45 (September 1, 1962), 6-8, 47.

Delmage, Rutherford E., "The American Idea of Progress, 1750-1800." *Proceedings of the American Philosophical Society,* 91 (December, 1947), 307-14.

Ferguson, Otis, "Two Show Figures." *New Republic,* 84 (September 4, 1935), 104.

Fishwick, Marshall William, "Diagnosing the American Dream." *The Saturday Review,* 46 (December 21, 1963), 8-11.

"It's a Less Colorful America Now." *The Daily Oklahoman.* 17 August 1935, p. 10.

Klapp, Orrin E., "The Clever Hero." *Journal of American Folklore,* 67 (January-March, 1954), 21-34.

———, "The Creation of Popular Heroes." *American Journal of Psychology,* 54 (September, 1948), 135-41.

———, "The Folk Hero." *Journal of American Folklore,* 62 (January-March, 1949), 17-25.

———, "Hero Worship in America." *American Sociological Review,* 14 (February, 1949), 53-62.

Miller, Perry, "The Shaping of the American Character." *New England Quarterly,* 28 (December, 1955), 435-54.

Myers, Henry Alonzo, "Whitman's Conception of the Spiritual Democracy." *American Literature,* 6 (June, 1934), 239-53.

Riddell, John, "An Open Letter to Will Rogers." *Vanity Fair,* 32 (October, 1929), 90.

Robbins, L. H., "Portrait of an American Philosopher." *The New York Times,* 3 November 1935.

"Rogers and Post." *Commonweal,* 22 (August 30, 1935), 416.

Shafer, Boyd C., "The American Heritage of Hope, 1865-1940." *The Mississippi Valley Historical Review,* 37 (June, 1950-March, 1951), 427-50.

Silver, Mildred, "Emerson and the Idea of Progress." *American Literature,* 12 (March, 1940-June, 1941), 1-19.

Smith, Matthew H., "Elements of Success in Business," *Hunt's Merchant's Magazine,* 31 (July, 1854), 56.

Van Doren, Dorothy, "Will Rogers." *The Nation,* 127 (October 3, 1928), 314-15.

"Will Rogers in London." *Literary Digest,* 90 (August 28, 1926), 22-23.

Unpublished Materials

Alworth, E. P., "The Humor of Will Rogers." Ph.D. diss., Department of English, University of Missouri, 1957.

"Biography in Sound: Will Rogers." NBC News, May 22, 1955.

Bibliography

"Evening with Will Rogers." WKY-TV News, November 28, 1961.

Love, Paula McSpadden, Curator, Will Rogers Memorial, Claremore, Oklahoma, Interviews. August 13, 1961; July 19, 1963; July 22, 1963; January 3, 1964.

Miscellaneous Scrapbook #1 and Scrapbook #16, Will Rogers Memorial, Claremore, Oklahoma.

"Will Rogers." NBC Special Events Department, Project 20, September 12, 1961.

Willingham, John Robert, "The Whitman Tradition in Recent American Literature." Ph. D. diss., Department of English, University of Oklahoma, 1953.

Index

Adams, Samuel, 30
Agrarianism, 108, 110-12, 117-18
"Ah, Wilderness," 189
Air Transport Association plaque, 276
Akron, Ohio: Rogers on, 243
Alabama: Rogers on, 135-36, 252
Alaska: Rogers on, 39, 254-55
Alger, Horatio: hero of, 171-72; Rogers' publicity as, 188-90
Allen, Fred, 20
American Adam: nature of, 24-25, 39, 42, 43-44, 46, 47, 48-52; influences on Rogers toward, 54-57; during 1920's and 1930's, 61, 62; Rogers' publicity as, 62-66; and other values, 167, 172-73, 210-12, 217-18
American Credo, The, 121
American democrat: influences on Rogers as, 108-13; publicity as, 122-26 *passim,* 156-57
American dream: major categories of, 24, 32-33; and revolutionary thought, 29-31; appropriateness of Rogers' identifications to, 262-73
American Jewish Congress, 137
American language: Rogers on, 76, 77; Rogers' slang, 86-87; Rogers' sentence structure and, 204-5, 251; Rogers' practice of simplification in, 205-6; Rogers and form of, 252-53. *See also* Analogy, Catachresis, Hyperbole
American Liberty League: Rogers on, 127
American Mercury, 121
American Prometheus, and American Adam: discussed, 218-20; Rogers' publicity as, 232-35
American Revolution: Rogers on, 148
Americanism: Rogers as symbol of, 23; Rogers on, 69, 70, 119, 128, 131-32, 141; continuum of, 76, 92, 120-21, 123-24, 283*n*27
"Amos 'n Andy," 121
Analogy: Rogers' use of, 268
"Anti-Bunk" party: Rogers on, 145-46
Appropriateness: of Rogers' identifications with American dream, 261-73
Arkansas: Rogers on, 78, 186-87, 200-201

Arthur, Timothy S., 164
Asia: Rogers on, 148, 241
Aviation: Rogers' publicity on, 186-87, 232-34; Rogers' first experience in, 224-25; Rogers on, 237-40, 241, 245-47, 249-50, 251-53, 254-55

Babbitt, 183
Babson, Roger, 184
Baltimore Sun, 17
Bancroft, George, 91
Bankers: Rogers on, 147, 149, 180-81, 196-97, 230
Barkley, Alben, 261
Barrie, James M., 21
Bellamy, Edward, 214-15
Benny, Jack, 273
Beverly Hills: Rogers on, 243
"Big Normal Majority": Rogers on, 69, 70
"Bigger and Better": Rogers on, 75-76, 237, 244; as slogan, 213; and Rogers, 223
Billy Budd, 50
Birth of a Nation, 137
Boone, Daniel, 51, 221
Boosting, and progress, 219, 271-72; Rogers on, 242-47
Borah, William E.: Rogers on, 145
Boy Scouts: Rogers on, 142
Brougher, J. Whitcomb, 127
Bryan, William Jennings: Rogers on, 134-35
Buffalo Bill (William F. Cody): as freedom symbol, 105, 113
Business: Rogers on, 130-31, 143, 192-93
Buttram, Pat, 273
Byrns, Joseph W., 17

California: Rogers on, 78, 80, 244
Capone, Al: Rogers on, 61; as success anti-hero, 182
Carillo, Leo, 252
Carnegie, Andrew, 212
Catachresis: Rogers' use of, 84-85
Cherokee Kid: Rogers as, 177, 178
Chicago: Rogers on, 37, 243, 244; fairs, 112, 224, 231-32

Index

Christian Commonwealth, 26
Civil disobedience, 92, 93, 101-2
Civilization: Rogers on, 37, 72, 235-36
Claremore, Okla.: Rogers on, 243
Clarke, Edward Y., 118
Clemens, Samuel. *See* Mark Twain
Cobb, Irvin S., 252
Cohan, George M., 64
Colorado: Rogers on, 78
Common man: Rogers as symbol of, 19-23; Rogers on, 22, 37, 38, 68-74, 149-50, 266; empire dream of, 24-25, 26; powers of, 40-42, 48-49, 53, 70, 97, 162, 171-72; Emerson as spokesman of, 41; goodness of, 42-44, 52-53; self-fulfillment of, 44-45; Rogers' stance toward, 56-57, 67, 262; hopes of, 95, 100, 106, 213-16; and view of history, 227-28
Communism: Rogers on, 20-21, 132-33, 147, 154-55; and free speech, 116
Community Chest: Rogers on, 202
Competition: Rogers on, 38; Beveridge on, 163; and success, 167-68
Conferences: Rogers on, 141, 148
Conformity: Rogers on, 38, 69, 145; American rejection of, 45; Rogers' publicity and, 63-64
Constitution: Sandburg on Rogers and, 18-19; and modification of European political thought, 31-32; Rogers on, 128, 135
Conwell, Russell, 163, 165, 179
Coolidge, Calvin: mentioned, 60, 181-82; quoted, 115, 283 *n*27; Rogers on, 149, 192; and 1927 flood, 185, 186-87
Cooper, James Fenimore, 48-49
Cooweescoowee, Okla. (district), 54
Coughlin, Father James E., 120
Cowboy: as hero of freedom and equality, 105-6; Clem Vann Rogers as, 108, 113; as Rogers' hero, 111-12, 152-53; Rogers as, 112-13, 123-24, 151-52, 198, 263; in movies, 122; as success icon, 169
Cox, James M., 253
Coxe, Tench, 217
Crackerbox philosopher: appeal for Americans, 22, 254; Rogers' publicity as, 63, 65, 190; Rogers on, 69
Crane, Hart, 227
Crèvecoeur, St. John de, 25, 52
Crime: Rogers on, 37, 61, 73, 152
Crises: Rogers on, 81
Crozier, J. B., 101
Curtis, Charles: Rogers on, 85

Darrow, Clarence, 269

Darwinism, 166, 173, 183, 212
Davidson, Jo, 15
Dawes, Charles G., 86
Dearborn, Mich.: Rogers on, 247
Declaration of Independence: mentioned, 19, 30, 31-32; Rogers on, 128
Decline of the West, 227
Democracy. *See* Freedom
Democrats: Rogers on, 75, 145, 146, 202
Denver Rocky Mountain News, 17
Depew, Chauncey, 154
Dignity and Worth of Individual: description of, 39-45; action corollaries of, 45-47; heroes symbolizing, 48-51; influences on Rogers toward, 54-57; status of in 1920's and 1930's, 57-62; Rogers' publicity on, 62-68; Rogers' identification with, 67-87; relationship with freedom and equality, 91
Disaster relief: Rogers on, 199-202, 205-6
Downing, Major, Rogers' ancestor, 53
Dramatic irony: Rogers' use of, 247
Dreiser, Theodore, 114, 183
Durant, Will, 72, 227, 235
Dwyer, Charles, 63

Easterners: Rogers on, 246
Eating: Rogers on, 38, 82, 150
Edison, Thomas A., 221-22, 247, 269
Education: Rogers on, 77, 107-8, 198
Eliot, John, 26
Eliot, T. S., 49, 59
Equality, and frontier: mentioned, 24-25; Rogers on, 38, 141, 142-44, 149-50, 155-56; of opportunity, 96-97, 100-101; spiritual, 97, 165; and individuality, 97-98; social, 97-98, 103-5, 108-9; political, 98-99; achievement of, 101, 165-66; economic, 100, 142, 166; and success, 164-66; Utopian novels and debate on, 215
Equality dream: description of, 95-102, 104; and relation to success, 100; action corollaries of, 104; heroes of, 105-6; influences on Rogers toward, 108-11; status in 1920's and 1930's, 113-14, 115-17, 121-22; Rogers' publicity on, 124-27, 184-85, 186-87, 197, 261; Rogers' identification with, 135-44, 146-51, 153-57
Europe, and Americans: mentioned, 18, 42, 51, 102; Rogers on, 75-76, 85-

Index

86, 148, 150-51, 180

Evans, Lewis, 25, 52

Evolution: Rogers on, 37, 134-35

Experience: mentioned, 45; Rogers on, 77-78; and Rogers' slang, 86-87

Fairbanks, Douglas, 60

Fair play: mentioned, 104; and code of the West, 106; Rogers on, 147-49; and success, 168

Farm problem: Rogers on, 57-58, 117-18, 146, 229

Florida: Rogers on, 80, 250; real estate, 180, 185, 250-51

Ford, Henry: discussed, 115, 118, 169-71, 181, 221-22; Rogers on, 136, 142, 194-96, 238, 247, 250

Foreign policy: Rogers on, 20, 85-86, 118, 147-49, 267; role in, 284*n*37

Forest, Lee de, 230

Four-H: Rogers on, 142

Franklin, Benjamin, 25, 169-70

Freedom: Rogers on free speech, 21, 132-34, 155; civilization and, 72; political and social, 127-28; religious, 127-28, 134-37; from want, 129-30; from special interests, 130-31; of press 131-32; in other lands, 147-49; from domination, 24-25, 92; and libertarianism, 29-30, 92-96; and *laissez faire,* 40, 92, 163-64; and democracy, 91, 93-95, 101, 106-8, 165-66; relation to other values, 91, 93-94, 96, 173, 210; basic ideas and rights of, 92; from prejudice, 92-93; and free will, 114-15, 164-65

Freedom dream: description of, 91-96; action corollaries of, 101-4; heroes of, 104-8; influences on Rogers toward, 111-13; status of in 1920's and 1930's, 113-15, 118-22; Rogers' publicity on, 122-24; Rogers' identification with, 127-36, 144-52

Friendship: Rogers on, 37, 38, 83; publicity on, 65-66; among Cherokee families, 108-9

Fundamentalism, 118-19

Future: Rogers on, 70-71, 206, 237-41, 250-51; Americans' optimism toward, 209-10, 218-20, 225-26

Future Farmers of America: Rogers on, 142

Garden myth: discussed, 25, 51-53, 99, 106-7, 162-63, 228-29; Rogers ranch and, 55-56

Gandhi, Mohandas: Rogers on, 148-49

Garland, Hamlin, 52, 182-83

Gestures: Rogers' use of, 84-85, 153-54, 203, 272

Gibbons, James, Cardinal, 216-17

Gilbreth, Lillian, 230

Gladden, Washington, 216-17

Godfrey, Arthur, 274

Goodnight, Charles, 275

Government: relation of, to individual and business, 81, 92-95 *passim,* 107-8, 113-18 *passim,* 178-79, 213-16, 235; Rogers on, 119, 129-30, 142-44, 206, 229, 236-37

Grady, Henry W., 222

Grapes of Wrath, 62

Great Depression: Rogers on, 19-20, 69-70, 129-30, 143-44, 147, 183-84, 200-202, 206, 228-32, 235-36, 241-42; effects of, on American dream, 61-62, 119-20, 183-85, 228-32

Gunter, Elizabeth, 33, 53

Gunter, John, 28, 33

Hadassah, 137

Hamilton, Andrew, 213

Happiness: Rogers on, 37, 72

Harrison, Luther, 261

Hawaii: Rogers on, 248-49

Hawks, Captain Frank, 186-87, 201, 240

Heflin, Thomas: Rogers on, 135-36

Henry VIII: Rogers on, 85

Hero worship: symbolism in America, 9-10; of Rogers, 15-20 *passim,* 23, 124, 261, 274-76; of Adam, 48, 52-53, 87; of Coolidge, 60, 181-82; of cowboy, 105-6, 112, 124; of self-made man, 168-72 *passim,* 181-83, 191-96 *passim;* of progress heroes, 220-22, 225-26; of Abraham Lincoln, 259-60; Rogers on, 273

History: Rogers on, 38, 85, 140, 201, 241

Hitler, Adolph: Rogers on, 136-37

Hoffer, Eric, 9

Holmes, Dr. Oliver Wendell, 217

Hoover, Herbert C.: on Rogers, 18; Rogers on, 22, 85-86, 146, 147, 155; administration of, 119, 229

Hoover, Mrs. Lou Henry: Rogers on, 138-39

Hope, Bob, 273-74

House, Edward M., 215

Hughes, Charles Evans, 185

Human Comedy, The, 121

Humor: mentioned, 18, 22; Rogers' theory of, 79, 80, 81, 264

Hyperbole: Rogers' use of, 154-56, 250-51

Identification: as concept, 67
Individualism: mentioned, 46; and freedom and equality, 94, 100, 104; chief aim of, 161; and success, 163; and progress, 211
In His Steps, 216
Ironic masks: Rogers' use of, 266-67

Jackson, Andrew, 98, 106, 111, 168-69
James, Henry, 50-51, 74
James, Will, 124
Jazz Singer, The, 226
Jefferson, Thomas, 31, 106-8
Johnson, Edward, 26
Johnson, Lyndon B., 9
Jolson, Al, 226
"Judge Priest," 189
Jungle, The, 215

Kaye, Danny, 273
Kelland, Clarence Budington, 23
Keller, Helen, 199
Kemper Military Academy, 110-12 *passim,* 198
Kennedy, John F., 9
Kent, James, 99

Labor: Rogers on, 81, 147, 195, 235
Lane, Maude Rogers, 55, 139, 174
Lanman, James, 52
Last of the Mohicans, The, 48
Lathrop, John, 27
Latin America: Rogers on, 86, 148, 152, 205, 248
Lecture tours, Rogers', 65, 69, 124, 125*, 234, 245
Lee, Josh, 261
Lewis, Sinclair, 183
Lincoln, Abraham, 259-60, 274
Lindbergh, Charles A.: mentioned, 60, 225; Rogers on, 241
Lipton, Sir Thomas: Rogers on, 148, 192-93
Literary Digest, The, 64
Locke, John, 29, 30, 31
London, Jack, 182-83
Long, Huey: Rogers on, 78-79, 120
Looking Backward, 214
Lorimer, George Horace, 198
Los Angeles: Rogers on, 244
Louisiana: Rogers on, 78-79

McAdoo, William Gibbs, 146
McCormack, John, 185
McGuffey, William Holmes, 162
MacNeil, Ben Dixon, 111
McSpadden, Sallie Rogers, 82, 174, 224
Malone, Ted, 189
Manners: Rogers' publicity on, 64, 65; Rogers on, 71, 138, 141-42, 149-51, 268-69; befitting Americans, 95, 103-4, 161-62, 167, 219-20
Mather, Cotton, 27
Mellon, Andrew, 135, 267
Melville, Herman, 50-51, 54
Mencken, Henry L., 121, 205
Merriam, Frank F., 67
Military preparedness: Rogers on, 20-21, 70
Millennial dream, 26-28
Minority Groups: Cherokee Indians, 24, 26, 28, 33, 53, 54, 109, 174, 276; Rogers on Negroes, 83-84, 136-39 *passim;* Rogers and Negroes, 109-10, 126; Rogers on Indians, 110-11, 139-41, 248; Rogers' publicity and, 110-11, 124, 126, 127, 188; Jews as, 118; Rogers on Catholics, 135-36; Rogers on Jews, 136-37
Mix, Tom, 110
Moby Dick, 50
Monroney, A. S. Mike, 16, 125-26, 127, 275
Montana: Rogers on, 245
Morgan, J. P.: Rogers on, 155-56
Morrow, Dwight, 122, 192
Motion pictures: and Rogers, 79-80, 188-89, 252
Muirhead, James, 220
Mussolini, Benito, 19
Mysterious Stranger, The, 61

Nathan, George Jean, 121
National Cowboy Hall of Fame, 275
National Press Club, 17
Natural aristocracy, 96, 108, 109, 116, 165-66
Natural Rights, 29-31, 98, 99-100
Nature: mentioned, 42-43, 46-47, 48-49, 162, 217-18; Rogers on, 77
Nevada: Rogers on, 78, 252-53
New England: Rogers on, 78, 85
"New Freedom," 114-15
New Humanism, 116
New Orleans: Rogers and, 186, 244
New Orleans Times-Picayune, 17
New York: Rogers on, 78
Newspaper: Rogers on, 59, 60, 80, 81, 131-32, 133-34, 145

Index

Niebuhr, Reinhold, 17
Nietzsche, Friedrich, 121, 183
Norris, George W., 115
Northwest: Rogers on, 78
Notes on Democracy, 121
Noyes, John Humphrey, 119

Oklahoma: Rogers on, 38, 75, 87, 155, 244, 251
Oklahoma City, Okla.: Rogers on, 78
Oologah, Okla., 82
Opportunity: Rogers on, 191-92, 199
Oratory: Rogers on, 149-50; Rogers and, 153-55
Oropeza, Vincente, 113
Otis, James, 30

Paradise: mentioned, 217, 219-20; Rogers on, 248-50
Parker, Theodore, 162
Payne, John Barton, 186
Peek, George N., 117
People Yes, The, 62
Pets: Rogers on, 82
Philanthropy: discussed, 166, 168; Rogers' publicity on, 185-86; Rogers on, 196-97
Phillips, Leon C., 260
Pickett, Bill: Rogers on, 137
Pilgrim's Progress, 267
Politics: and Rogers, 16; Rogers on, 37, 38, 78, 85-86, 119, 138-39, 144-46, 147-48, 149-50, 155-56, 238, 267-68; and garden myth, 53, 102, 107
Populists, 92, 108
Post, Emily: Rogers on, 150-51
Post, Wiley: Rogers on, 239, 254-55
Prejudice: mentioned, 92-93, 103-4, 118; Rogers on, 119, 128-29, 135-37, 138, 141
Progress: Rogers on, 37, 71-72, 134, 206, 235; concepts of, 209-18, 221-22, 227-28, 230; Rogers and, 222-25, 236-37, 263
Progress dream: mentioned, 32; described, 209-18; action corollaries of, 218-20; heroes of, 220-22; influences on Rogers toward, 222-25; status of, 1920's and 1930's, 225-32; Rogers' identification with, 234-53
Prohibition: mentioned, 17, 119; Rogers on, 37, 115, 145-46, 155, 239
Publicity: Rogers as American Adam, 61-68; as American democrat, 122-27; as benefactor, 185-88; as American Prometheus, 232-35
Public opinion: Rogers on, 22, 115, 222, 230, 252-54
Pupin, Michael, 230

Radio broadcasts: on Rogers, 16, 18, 19, 20-21, 64, 189-90; Rogers', 21, 72-73, 76, 77, 133-34, 141, 143, 144, 146-47, 186-87, 194, 202, 236-37, 238, 251
Rags-to-riches myth: mentioned, 165; and Rogers, 188-90, 199; and Lincoln, 259
Ranching: Rogers on, 39, 151-52, 152-53, 155, 249
Randolph, John, 99
Rauschenbusch, Walter, 216
Rayburn, Sam, 18
Red Cross: Rogers and, 185-86; Rogers on, 200, 205, 229
Reduction to absurdity: Rogers' use of, 266-67
Reed, James A., 267
Religion: Rogers on, 38, 83-84, 119, 127, 128-29, 134-36, 146
Republicans: Rogers on, 78, 85-86, 130-31, 145, 184
Revere, Paul, 201
Rhetorical study: briefly described, 10
Rickard, Tex: Rogers on, 252-53
Rockefeller, John D., Sr.: Rogers on, 196-97
Rodgers, John, 28
Rogers, Clement Vann, father of Will Rogers, 52, 108, 109, 112-13, 173-77 *passim*
Rogers, Clement Vann, playmate of Will Rogers, 109-10
Rogers, Mary America Schrimsher, mother of Will Rogers, 53, 108, 109, 174-75 *passim,* 224
Rogers, May, 174, 224
Rogers, Robert, 174-75
Rogers, Robert, II, 33, 53
Rolph, James, 133
Roosevelt, Franklin Delano: on Rogers, 18; Rogers on, 20, 119-20, 143, 147, 149-50, 254
Roosevelt, Theodore, 16, 275
Roping: Rogers and, 62-63, 113, 124
Rousseau, Jean Jacques, 29-30, 42, 43, 71, 74, 105
Runyon, Damon, 33

St. Louis, 223
Sandburg, Carl, 18, 22, 62
San Francisco: Rogers on, 242
Santa Monica, Calif., 56, 252
Saroyan, William, 121

302

Schrimsher, Martin Matthew, 33, 53
Scopes trial: Rogers on, 134-35
Scott, Howard, 231
Selfishness: Rogers on, 15
Self-made man: and Rogers, 178, 184-85, 276
Self-reliance, 42, 46-50 *passim*
Shaw, George Bernard, 21
Sheldon, Charles M., 216
Sherwood, Robert, 146
Shriner, Herb, 273
Sinclair, Upton, 120, 215
Single tax, 214
Skelton, Red, 273
Smith, Al: Rogers on, 146, 186-87
Social gospel, 216-17
Social Register: Rogers on, 141-42
Socratic irony: Rogers' use of, 266-67
Sokolosky, George, 230
South: Rogers on, 78-79, 139
South Bend, Ind.: Rogers on, 243
Southwest: Rogers on, 78
Special interests: Rogers on, 130-31, 143
Speech delivery: Rogers', 153-54. *See also* Gestures
Spengler, Oswald, 227
Sperry, Elmer, 230
Spoils system, 100
Sports: Rogers on, 38, 75, 82-83, 148, 191-92, 252
Statuary Hall, 15, 260-62, 274
Steinbeck, John, 62
Stereotypes, 107, 137-38, 249
Stewardship: mentioned, 164; Rogers' practice of, 199-202
Stock Market: Rogers on, 19-20, 58, 131, 138, 194
Stone, Fred, 65, 252
Stoughton, William, 26
Strategy: Rogers' identification of, with American dream, 265-69
Success: Rogers on, 73; relating individualism and, 189-90; relating equality and, 190-91; rules for, 191-96 *passim*, 199, 202
Success dream: relation to other values, 161-67, 168, 172-73, 211-12; rules of, 161-69 *passim*, 172-73, 179, 180-81; and opportunities, 164, 165, 179, 181, 183, 184-85; heroes of, 167, 168-72, 182, 183, 191-93, 197-98; influences on Rogers toward, 173-78; status of during 1920's and 1930's, 178-85; Rogers' identification with, 189-206
Suffrage, 99-100
Symbols: iconic, conventionalized, 85

Tahlequah, Okla. (district), 54
Tahlonteeskee, Okla. (district), 54
"Technocracy": mentioned, 230; Rogers on, 231
Technology: discussion of, 212, 214; Rogers on, 237-40
Texas: Rogers on, 78, 86, 151-52, 201, 244
Texas Jack, 177-78
Thayer, William M., 259
Thompson, William: mentioned, 118; Rogers on, 131-32
Three Cheers, 65, 125*
Tocqueville, Alexis de, 107, 161
Tools and the Man, 216-17
Transcendentalism, 45-46, 97-98
Travel: Rogers on, 39, 251-52, 254-55; Rogers', 176-77, 248-49
Tugwell, Rexford, 133, 236-37
Tulsa: Rogers on, 78, 201-2, 242-43
Twain, Mark, 61, 114, 274

Union for Social Justice, 120
U.S.S.R.: Rogers on, 133, 154-55, 249, 251
Universities: Rogers on, 76, 243-44
U.S. Congress: Rogers on, 133-34, 181, 201
U.S. Senate: Rogers on, 85-86, 145, 155, 238
Utah: Rogers on, 78, 246
Utopianism, 26, 213-16

Vann, Sallie, 33, 53
Variety Clubs International, 276
Vaudeville, 66, 178, 198, 223, 276
Versatility: mentioned, 46; and Rogers, 65-67
Virtue: work as, 26, 165; and natural rights, 30; Emerson on, 42-43, 163, 165-66, 173; gift of West to, 52; rural, 107, 162-63; of cowboy, 112, 124, 152-53; and *laissez faire,* 162; and success, 161-64, 165-66, 167-68, 177, 184-85, 263; images of, 169, 170, 171; Americans' distaste for during 1920's, 182; Rogers' publicized, 188-90; in Utopia, 215; and Edenic quest, 217-18

Walker, "Babe," 110
Walker, Dan, 110, 111-12
Walker, Timothy, 217
War: Rogers on, 81, 86-87, 128

Index

Ward, Artemus, 104
Washington, George, 33
Wasteland, The, 59
Wealth: Rogers on, 39, 142-44, 155-56, 202, 236-37; and American dream, 116-17, 120-21, 163, 165-66, 179-80, 211-12, 229
Wild West shows, 105, 112-13, 123, 176-77, 198-99
Will Rogers Memorial, 15, 275-76
Wilson, Edmund, 131, 184

Wilson, James, 32
Windsor, Edward Windsor, Duke of: mentioned, 63-64, 122, 264-65, 275; Rogers on, 149-50
Winthrop, John, 26
Winthrop, Robert, 169
Wise, Stephen S.: and Rogers, 137
Wolfe, Thomas, 121
"Work and Win": and Rogers, 263

Ziegfeld Follies, 139, 198, 276